To My Friend Ted.

Marilyn Stargell

Sometimes we have No Choice

Marilyn Starzer

WESTBOW PRESS®
A DIVISION OF THOMAS NELSON & ZONDERVAN

WestBow Press books may be ordered through booksellers or by contacting:

WestBow Press
A Division of Thomas Nelson & Zondervan
1663 Liberty Drive
Bloomington, IN 47403
www.westbowpress.com
1 (866) 928-1240

ISBN: 978-1-5127-0504-1 (sc)
ISBN: 978-1-5127-0505-8 (hc)
ISBN: 978-1-5127-0503-4 (e)

Library of Congress Control Number: 2015911814

Print information available on the last page.

WestBow Press rev. date: 08/26/2015

Praise For the Father

In memory of Richard Starzer,
who showed how to die with dignity

For stroke victims and their caregivers

Thanks to my son, Mike, whose help made this possible, my daughter, Stephanie and granddaughter, Nicole who went through the grieving and writing with me.

To all the family and friends who supported me

Contents

Prologue

Alaskan summers were often warm with bright sunrises and sunsets and many blooming wildflowers. Leah Kerry loved roaming the woods looking for wild berries and fiddlehead ferns to make jams and veggie omelets, colorful mushrooms to paint, and scenic areas to photograph. This summer promised to be an exceptionally nice one with long days to picnic, roam and entertain Roger. He'd had his second open-heart surgery and had many plans for his pending retirement.

They planned to spend the summer days of his recuperation driving around to see all the places they hadn't had time for while working. Roger would probably be off from work for a couple months. He then planned to retire in another year and begin the cruises and travel both he and Leah had looked forward to.

Leah loved cruises and wanted to take several. Roger had always wanted to visit Australia and New Zealand and spend at least a month there seeing all the areas they had read about. Leah had collected brochures and travel magazines, and they had spent many long hours in the hospital scanning them and making plans.

The first order of business when she could stay home would be to manicure the lawn and garden since little had been done spending all her days at the hospital with Roger.

She would get it all done while Roger recuperated. She had no idea how many struggles they would face or the length of time it would encompass. She would soon learn the surgery had been only the beginning and she would spend many more days and nights in hospitals.

Chapter 1

The warm sun's rays peeked around the sides of the room darkening shades and cast themselves across the silver gray carpet and walls. They warmed and brightened the room, resting on the satin-covered body in the bed. Leah slowly stirred and then sank deeper into the sea-foam green comforter.

Suddenly the alarm went off, and she yawned herself into semi-consciousness, opening her eyes slightly. She rose up on her elbows and looked lazily into the mirrored closet doors at the other end of the long room she and Roger had completed remodeling just months before. They had removed the wall separating two bedrooms and made them into one large room with the bath across the hall, making the downstairs a comfortable master suite.

It had saddened her at first as the other bedroom had belonged to their only son, and it was difficult to part with the mementos he left behind for college and then marriage. She had retrieved the piece of wallboard on which he had marked his growth, ever fearful he would get his height from his five-foot tall mother rather than his five-foot-eleven father. His sisters' growth rate was pretty close to his as they entered their teens, making him very anxious until his spurt came.

She gazed at the mauve-pink Ethan Allen chairs, just as pleased with them now as when she first saw them in the showroom priced at nine hundred dollars each. She had convinced herself they were perfect but too expensive, and Roger had readily agreed on the expensive part. She couldn't believe it when she read the newspaper ad that said they had been marked to half price, and she anxiously drove to the store, certain they would be gone. But here they were in their beautiful room! And they were perfect. She indulged herself an unspoken compliment, reveling in the beauty they had created with the limed oak paneling and white trim. It all fit beautifully and was reflected in the mirrors so she could enjoy the entire room.

With another yawn and a stretch, she was fully awake and remembered what day it was. She felt a surge of joy as she recalled that Roger was coming home from the hospital today. She jumped out of bed, pulling off the comforter and tossing it aside as she pulled off the sheets. She would wash them and get everything ready before going to the hospital to retrieve her spouse. She had arrived home after nine the night before and worked for two hours getting the rest of the house dusted and all put in place for the homecoming.

She was so glad the room was finished, as he would have his TV, comfortable chairs and bed so he could get all the rest he needed with no need to navigate the stairs for the first few days. She gathered the sheets and pillowcases in her arms, quickly surveying her surroundings to make sure everything was arranged within easy access for Roger. She had purchased brass-and-glass tables that fit under and over the bed so he wouldn't have to reach for anything. His chest had been so sore for such a long time after the first surgery that reaching had been very difficult. She contemplated placing a bell on one of the tables.

"Nah!" she spoke out loud and laughed at herself, thinking she was spoiling him enough and would be traversing the stairs plenty without being summoned by a bell. Roger had always been fond of being waited on and, now that he had an excuse, was sure to take advantage of it. He was her big baby when sick, and the surgery justified his being treated like one. He had been through so much, and she had been so unprepared. He had appeared the picture of health when she met then married him, but seven years and three children later, he had experienced his first heart attack—a mild one but a strong warning to change his way of life. He did for a while, but it was soon forgotten when his health returned and their life became busier.

Still stretching, Cory, their poodle, began to wag his tail at the sound of her voice, sure she must be talking to him as no one else was in the house. Smiling, she patted his head and quickly headed for the laundry room, feeling rather giddy with excitement. Stepping into the hall, she was hit by the difference in the light of the dark oak paneled hallway and the lighter oak paneled bedroom and decided she must put a stronger light bulb in the hall fixture. She had tried to make every change before it became necessary, attempting to anticipate each problem before it occurred. Cory followed her gaze with his big brown eyes then blinked and followed her to the washer. He continued to stay at her side, hoping she would stay at home with him; he was tired of the loneliness.

As the washer filled, she ran upstairs to make coffee, her main means of waking up each morning—a rich brew of steaming French roast. As she finished pouring in the water and turned the pot on, the phone rang. She was tempted to let the recorder answer it but decided it could be Roger, just as anxious as she was.

"Hello."

"Have I interrupted anything?"

"Not really. I was just making coffee. I don't make much sense before I've had my first cup."

"I remember! I just called to check on you and Roger. How's he doing?" Angela had called almost every day to inquire or offer help or a shoulder if needed.

"He's doing great! He doesn't seem to be in as much pain as the first time. Of course, he's very sore, and his color was a little ashen last night, but he wasn't complaining nearly as much as he did just after surgery."

"Terrific! I know you feel better when he does."

"I think he knew what to expect the second time around, and while he keeps saying it was very different, I think he's just anxious to get home now."

"Do you have any idea when that will be?"

"Today!!! He's coming home today! I'm putting the finishing touches on the room, changing the sheets, and putting everything in easy reach for him." Leah's excitement was evident in her voice. "I'm so glad we decided to remodel the downstairs. It's going to be so nice for him and lots easier for me than the last time."

"I love what you did with the downstairs; it's so bright and cheery. It's a perfect place to make anyone feel better. The garden and backyard look so lovely from the windows, and everything is green and in bloom now. I'm sure glad to hear he's coming home. I know you're both very tired of the hospital."

"You can say that again! I've read all my books and almost finished all my letter writing," Leah said, laughing. "I'm even weeks ahead on our Bible class."

"I'll keep you in my prayers as you've been through so much. Is there anything you need me to do for you? Could I cook something?"

"We do appreciate your offer, but Roger's diet is so strict. I'm not even sure what I'll cook for more than two or three days. It's going to be a real challenge."

"I'm sure."

"Oh, well, I like to cook, and now I'll try revising all our favorites to make them low fat and low calorie. Do keep praying as we still have a long way to go to get him well and on his own again. I'm confident we're going to be fine with God's help and all our wonderful friends. Your offer is appreciated: I may be calling in the future to help me revise."

"You bet. Anytime!"

"Thanks so much for your concern and keeping in touch. Please tell everyone at the office hello for me."

"I sure hope your ordeal is over, and he'll mend quickly. I also hope you'll take care of yourself and get some much needed rest once he's home."

Angela's tone became more serious.

"Spending so much time at the hospital is a real drag and exhausting. I'm concerned about your health too. You do your best to hide it, but I can hear the fatigue in your voice. You must take care of yourself in order to take care of him."

Angela and Leah had worked in the same office, both just starting in the insurance business. They had become close friends during that time and shared many common bonds. Angela had dark, curly hair and an olive complexion that Leah envied. The unruly curls were kept short in an attempt to keep them in place, and she could go in the sun all she cared to and get beautiful tans; both her hair and skin oily.

Leah was quite the opposite with her straight, dry, heavy locks and fair complexion that was prone to burning. She had to constantly condition and use both sunscreen and moisturizers. Angela had informed her that she was just as envious of Leah's ability to change hairstyles with permanents. They both loved to cook and spent numerous weekends making tamales, lasagna, and other dishes. Angela had lived in New Mexico and learned to cook all the Mexican dishes like a pro. Leah had been in close contact with neighbors from Greece, Portugal, and Norway and had learned several of their recipes while living in Fairbanks. They shared experiences and created new dishes together, much to the delight of their office mates. They had instituted regular potlucks, and Leah felt sad as she reminisced missing the camaraderie.

"Everyone here asks about you frequently. Sure would like to have you back on our team. Joan was saying just last week how much fun we used to have at lunch."

Joan was married to an agent and had worked side by side with him over the many years they had been married and raised a family. They were retirement age and, in spite of their financial independence, couldn't seem to give up their business. Both were a delight to work and play with, the years having been very kind with few extra pounds, gray hairs, or wrinkles. They were both delighted to share their experiences and wisdom with the younger agents and assistants. Leah and Angela lunched with them many days, attempting to pick their brains about business and other things. Leah smiled as she recalled the time they had been crossing an icy street as Joan hesitated, reached down, and continued on, hardly missing a step. Her half-slip elastic had broken and fallen off, but no one would have guessed as it was in her purse before the street was crossed!

"I really don't have any idea, but I hope it will just be a few months."

With that, Leah thanked Angela again and begged to get off the phone as she had much left to do to get ready. She took time to give Cory some loving as she poured herself a cup of coffee. He wasn't sure why he had been left alone so much lately and didn't care for it at all, but he was always available for petting and loving of any type. He was so skinny but when you constantly wag from the neck down, it requires more calories than can be consumed. He had adjusted to many changes in the household in recent years as the children left home and Leah went back to work. Now that he was fifteen, he needed more rest and took lots. Leah noticed his charcoal hair was getting lighter, with gray hairs becoming prominent, especially in his beard and mustache. He was definitely a member of this family!

Leah leisurely sipped her coffee, gazing around the small kitchen that had been too small while housing three hungry teenagers but was now just right for her alone and Roger occasionally. She noticed the cafe-valance above the window she had made with matching shade was fading and needed replacing. The appliances were an outdated turquoise so she had used that with several lighter colors in the print to offset and put focus on the accessories. She filled a pitcher and gave Cory fresh water, then the telephone rang again. She swallowed a large steamy sip and answered it. This time, it was their minister asking about Roger, and she repeated the good news that he was being released from the hospital today. She said he should come by and see him in a few days. Roger had been very tired the night before when she left but all vital signs were good, so a few days of rest should have him ready for company.

"I'll relay the news to everyone at church and make sure they know to call before dropping by."

He was a tall, slender, handsome man with an equally lovely wife, who was rather shy until she got up to a microphone to belt out a song. Leah had been very surprised several years before to learn she was part of the entertainment at a fundraiser and genuinely shocked when she heard her lovely voice without the slightest hint of stage fright. The two couples had been good friends for many years when he took over the job of education minister. Leah had worked several years under his supervision, finding him extremely supportive of her efforts with the teenagers. His son had been their son Dave's closest friend since they met as youngsters and had spent lots of time at the Kerry home as they grew up. They still kept in touch, and the parents often got news from each other.

She went downstairs, put the clothes in the dryer, and began to dress. As she put on her makeup, she recalled the first heart by-pass surgery and how difficult the first few weeks had been when Roger could only raise up on the sofa by locking his arms around her neck, letting her pull him up. She had pulled her back out of place and had required several chiropractic treatments. Their bedroom had been upstairs with no TV, and the bathroom had been at the end of the hall, not just a few steps across it. The twelve stairs had exhausted Roger, but he had refused to be exiled to the loneliness of the bedroom, so he spent much of his time lying on the living room sofa. Now they had everything within a few steps, and Leah could spend most of her time with him watching TV, reading, and working on her hobbies when he slept.

The laundry room at the far end of the downstairs area was also the hobby room where Leah painted and sewed, keeping all the clutter hidden away from the family areas. She had left several unfinished projects awaiting completion. She had found no time for painting, sewing, knitting, or crocheting since Roger's heart attack. Somehow she didn't feel much like doing any crafts, wanting to spend as much time as possible with him. Two by-pass surgeries had made her feel like he was on his third chance at life, and they had to make the most of it.

This time, they were ready, with an answer for each trial they would face and a solution they had tried and proven. This time was going to be much easier even though Roger repeated over and over that it was different from the first surgery and not for the better. She wasn't sure what he meant, but he had been doing so well that she felt great relief that life would finally get back to normal. She would soon learn that their life would never be normal again.

She returned her attention to the task at hand and noticed the color had faded from her light brown hair, showing gray roots. Leah thought she must have it colored again as soon as she could take the time away from Roger. She had found her first gray hair just before her eighteenth birthday and had been horrified. Only a few more joined it until after her thirtieth, when they seemed to multiply daily. They were thickest around her face, where they seemed to scream for attention each time she looked in the mirror. The color always faded there first.

She also needed a haircut, she decided. She kept her thick hair short now as it was becoming drier, and she could keep it in better condition by letting it dry naturally without the use of dryers or curling irons. Color and an occasional permanent were about all it could stand. Constant conditioning kept it fairly healthy until she began her gardening chores each summer, loving to dig in the dirt and watch the plants grow. She knew she should wear a hat in the sun and meant to but almost always forgot.

The buzzer sounded on the dryer. She removed the sheets, made the bed, dusted the room again, and checked one last time to make sure everything was ready. The phone rang again, and this time it was John from Roger's office. He was a great friend, just a little younger than Roger and still very handsome with his dark black hair, fair complexion, and smiling eyes.

"I'm going to get him shortly. The doctor should release him this morning, so he should be home by noon."

"What a relief that will be for both of you. I'll pass the word around the office so the phone won't be ringing off the wall."

"I would appreciate that, at least for the first week."

The crew Roger worked with had been very concerned, calling daily to check on his progress. Most of the men in his office were fairly close in age and felt vulnerable when someone in their group had a serious health problem, slapping them with the realization that time was marching on. She could hear the relief in John's voice as he told her they were all available for any help they needed and would be around to visit and keep Roger company while she got out for a bit. They referred to themselves as the "Over the Hill Gang" since they were all close to retirement. Paul was tall, lively, always cheerful, and kept the gang in good spirits. His sparkling, deep-blue eyes made everyone around him feel good, so he would be great company for Roger. He had told her numerous times that he would be available. Ray was the carpenter in the bunch, always working on something at his home, needing a steady supply of projects to keep him busy. Leah couldn't understand how he kept that rotund body with all his activity, but she knew those smiling hazel eyes and capable hands would be around to do any repair work they needed. They were very lucky to have such good friends. Gene had even called to ask if she needed any money; he probably had plenty as he always held onto it so tightly. She smiled at the thought of Gene's reaction if she actually asked for any.

Everyone had been so kind in offering to do anything she wanted, and she was very grateful but certain she and Roger could handle things together. She was thankful for so many good friends and probably would need to take them up on the offers to stay with Roger while she shopped for groceries and other necessities. They had a long recuperation period ahead; the second time would probably take longer than the first.

"I really appreciate you guys and know Roger would love to see you. He needs male company."

"We'll wait for your go-ahead to be sure he's up to company."

"Great! Thanks."

As she returned the telephone to its cradle, she glanced at the clock beside it and realized it was half past nine. Roger always called her by eight o'clock to be sure she was awake and getting ready to come to the hospital to keep him company. He hated hospitals, but why wouldn't he? He had spent a month there in March after the heart attack. Six weeks later, he had the treadmill test and then the angiogram that determined the original by-passes had clogged again, requiring another surgery.

It had been devastating, but they took it in stride, living a day at a time and trying not to think about it until their lawyer had called, asking Leah if their wills were in order or needed to be reviewed to conform with statutes of the State of Alaska. That had really put Leah down and raised all her fears and anxieties to the surface. But they had worked through that also.

Oh, well, he was coming home and getting away from hospitals, and she would be at home with him to keep him entertained and help him recover. She was glad she had quit her job; even though her boss had said they would keep her position open, she knew they would have to fill it soon. She would probably need to stay home for the next few months at least. She did love her work and the associations at the office, but Roger came first.

She decided she had better call him as the phone had probably been busy when he tried to call her. She dialed directly to his room and let it ring for twelve times before she decided he must be in the bathroom.

She put all his pajamas in to wash and then went to her closet and chose the new denim pantsuit with the poodle on the pocket that Roger had picked out for her. He hated shopping, but they had been looking for a dress for the office party so she had been able to drag him along. He had spotted the pantsuit and, though it was not what they were shopping for, had insisted she buy it. Now she approved her image in the full-length mirror and proceeded upstairs, where she checked to make sure she had everything needed for his diet. Twelve hundred calories per day weren't many; it would require lots of fresh fruit, vegetables, and planning. He did enjoy eating!

She dialed his room again and again, let the phone ring twelve times. She was just about to hang up, feeling concerned and anxious, when a female voice answered.

"Mr. Kerry's room."

"Oh," Leah replied cheerily, "this is Mrs. Kerry. I was just calling to see if the doctor has been in to sign his release form and when he would be ready to come home."

"Oh, my dear….." answered the voice on the phone, the tone softening. "Mr. Kerry has had a stroke!"

Chapter 2

Leah felt the life flow out of her. Feeling faint, she almost dropped the phone while attempting to steady herself as the room began to spin. The dog jumped up on her leg, apparently sensing something was wrong, but she hardly felt it. Shaking her head to regain her composure, she whispered into the phone, "I'll be.... right...there."

She arrived in his room without knowing how she got there, her mind struggling to fathom what she had been told.

His eyes immediately told her he knew her and was very glad to see her. They also showed fear and frustration, and he struggled trying to tell her something seemingly important. His skin was very gray and filled her with fear and panic, but she was determined not to show it. Finally, after agonizing over several difficult tries, he managed to get out the word "okay" audibly.

Immediately Leah thought of Tom and his stroke a year before that had left him paralyzed and unable to communicate or move. She knew Roger was trying to convey that he was not in the condition Tom had been, and she silently prayed he was right.

He and Tom had worked together and shared a number of remote assignments. They had become good friends, and Tom's stroke had been devastating to Roger. Tom was a rather small man with a huge personality and temper to match. His brown eyes turned black and shot lightning bolts when someone fired up his anger, though it took a serious injustice to fuel it. Leah had wondered if that anger had caused the stroke. After a visit with Tom, Roger had told Leah he did not want to live like a vegetable and had asked her to promise she would not try to keep him alive by artificial means. It had upset her so much that she had burst into tears and refused to discuss it further.

Tom had improved, in a year's time, to communicating with a pencil carefully placed in his mouth so he could punch out words on a computer-like machine. He had moved one foot the last time they had visited him in the hospital. It was such a slight movement that Leah hadn't been sure about it until she saw the proud smile in his eyes that brought tears to hers. Roger had left so depressed that he had been unable to return before Tom was moved to a VA hospital in Kansas.

"I could see him relax when you came into the room. He definitely recognized you, and that is a good sign."

The nurse interrupted Leah's mental pictures. She was an attractive and sweet lady with very expressive hazel eyes. They filled with empathy as she looked at Leah, so she quickly looked away brushing back her long brown hair. Recovering her composure, she studied Leah carefully to ascertain that the small lady was capable of absorbing the shock without falling apart.

She had taken care of Roger since he came from ICU and had grown attached to his grateful attitude toward everything she did. He rarely complained about any of the rigors of recovery from surgery. Some patients really moved you, and Roger Kerry was one such patient. She had felt like crying when she discovered that he had suffered a stroke during the night. He had been very strong through all the pain, refusing many meds and willing himself to get well. His wife appeared to have the same strength, and she was sure that they would be okay.

Roger's face became more ashen as he struggled to try to communicate, and he looked very tired. He motioned to a pad of paper and a pencil on the nightstand beside his bed. Leah handed it to him, and he held the pencil in several positions before it felt right to him. He then attempted to write his name, handing the pad back to Leah. The R was a capital, but it was turned backward, and the rest was misspelled, with one letter left out completely.

Leah felt fear wash over her again as she gazed at his furrowed brow, trying to maintain a calm façade for him. She managed to give him a smile and patted his hand, afraid to speak. The nurse checked Roger's vital signs, tried to reassure Leah that all were normal, and then turned to leave the room as Roger fell asleep.

"I'll check him again in an hour. Is there anything I can do for you in the meantime?"

"Not unless you can make him well," Leah answered, gazing at Roger.

The nurse patted her shoulder as she left. Waiting long enough to be sure he would sleep for a while, Leah hurried down to the waiting room to call their children, not wanting to discuss anything in Roger's room. She wasn't sure how long she could maintain control over the emotions welling up within her. She reached their son at his office, grateful he had not left for the meeting he had scheduled for that day.

"Dave,...Dad...had a...stroke...last night. He can't...speak or swallow." With that, she burst into tears and could say no more.

"Oh, no," he mumbled to himself and then spoke into the phone. "Where are you now?"

"I'm...in the...waiting...room."

"I'll be right there, Mom. Try to calm yourself; you sound pretty stressed out. Stay in the waiting room for a few minutes and try to relax before you go back to Dad's room. I'll call Cindy and the girls and then meet you there."

Dave stood in his office, shaken but hoping he had been able to conceal it from his mother. She sounded near the breaking point and must be scared to death. He called his wife, Cindy, with the awful news, asking her to call his sisters for him, and then walked into his boss's office as he put on his coat.

"My dad's had a stroke, and I've got to get to the hospital. I'll call as soon as I know something and let you know if I can make the meeting. My mom sounded very upset so I may need to stay with her."

"Geez, Dave....I'm sorry to hear that. Take as much time as you need and don't worry about the meeting. We can postpone if necessary. Let us know if there's anything we can do."

Leah hung up the phone in the hospital waiting room and closed her eyes. She was becoming overwhelmed with feelings of fear and anxiety. Why did this have to happen after he was doing so well? What had gone wrong? Had someone done something or not done something to cause it?

She remembered his complaints in intensive care that the nurses had ignored his call light and were playing cards at the desk. Leah was sure he was hallucinating due to the morphine. He had been out from under the anesthesia within three hours this time when it had been nearly twelve after the first surgery, so she really didn't think he'd had the same drugs. He had continually repeated that this time was not like the first time; it was much worse. What had he meant? No one had offered an answer for her among his doctors and nurses. No one had much information for her at all.

Her eyes filled with tears, just as they had numerous times this day, but she refused to let them flow and wiped them away as she had also done numerous times this day. She felt as though she had to keep the dam from breaking or she would lose control altogether. The waiting room had been empty when she came in, but now she heard the television switch on and realized someone else was in the room. She looked up to see another couple seated across from her was watching the set. They nodded to her, and she attempted a smile in return. She wondered how long they had been there and then leaned back and closed her eyes, trying to shut out all the frightening events of the day. A short time later, she roused and shook her head to clear away the negative thoughts.

She returned to the room just as his cardiologist arrived. He put his arm around her shoulders and asked if she believed in premonition. She knew he was referring to the mix-up prior to surgery. They had checked Roger into the hospital a week before, as scheduled, only to have his surgeon arrive that evening to ask what they were doing there. The doctor explained that he had to leave town due to an emergency and would not be able to operate the next day. The admissions office had been informed not to admit Roger, but someone must have goofed. He offered to have his assistant go ahead the next day, but Roger was already out of bed and dressing before the doctor had a chance to finish.

"I'll go home and wait for you, Doc. I want you to do my surgery!" had been his emphatic retort.

The doctor had been brought to town by the surgeon who had done Roger's first surgery. The surgeon had to have by-passes done on himself and had picked this man, so he was a pretty good recommendation. He was from India with the dark complexion, hair and eyes native to his country; also a bright, reassuring smile.

They had returned the following week after the surgeon's phone call, telling them he was ready only to find all Roger's paperwork, ID bracelets, and other materials with the assistant's name listed as attending physician. Roger had called his cardiologist and was entering the elevator to leave when the cardiologist met him. He had taken care of the mistakes in the admissions office and had ordered the changes made, and Roger had checked in. However, Leah had been in tears, feeling that all was not going right, and this was a bad omen.

She had wanted to cancel and go to a heart specialty clinic; she had recently read about the state-of-the-art facilities there, but Roger had just laughed at her, and the doctors had assured her he would have just as good care here. So the surgery had gone on as scheduled.

"I sure do," Leah replied.

"Squeeze my hand," said the doctor to Roger. "Good! Couldn't bear to leave this pleasant resort and the gourmet food, huh?"

The doctor had been watching Roger's responses very closely. Roger laughed—a strange, unfamiliar, husky laugh.

"How do you like that sexy voice, Leah?" Dr. Roberson asked, turning to Leah.

He was a tall, slender man with salt-and-pepper hair and a smile that was contagious. He had been Roger's cardiologist since the first attack, and the empathy he felt for the couple in the room was evident. Leah liked him and felt Roger was in good hands but, just now, she was hardly ready for small talk.

"I'm partial to my husband's deep voice. I find it even sexier," Leah replied sadly.

The doctor squeezed her shoulder, realizing it was taking all her strength to maintain composure.

"Have patience. I know it's tough."

He explained that Roger's laugh indicated he understood what was said to him and had responded correctly to all questions. There seemed to be a loose connection between the brain and mouth that made speech difficult. The simplified explanation made Roger smile, and Leah forced one in return.

"How long will it take for him to regain his speech? What about his difficulty swallowing?"

"We will just have to wait and see. There is no way to judge as each case is different, and each patient responds on his or her own time schedule. His inability to swallow is due to the paralysis and is usually temporary; normal reflexes should return quickly. The stroke was on the right side, much better than the left. It will take therapy and work on Roger's part to regain his speech, and his attitude and effort will make the difference," the doctor replied.

Leah would hear those words "wait and see" so many times in the coming years, she would learn to despise them and think of them all as four letter words.

In his office building, Dave hit the 'down' elevator button, and the doors opened almost immediately. Riding down the four floors, he felt sick to his stomach, hardly believing what his mother had told him. His dad had looked pale and fatigued the previous night, but he had just had surgery five days before.

That was to be expected, but a stroke? His strong, capable, determined dad...?

The elevator reached the lobby, and Dave walked into the parking lot and got into the Jimmy, squinting in the bright sunlight. It was almost eleven, and the meeting was scheduled for one o'clock. His presentation was ready and, he felt, well done so his boss could give it if necessary. He was noted for his expertise at research and developing presentations, so he would prefer to give it himself, but his family came first.

So much was going through his mind as he drove methodically to the hospital, giving little thought to anything but his parents. He arrived, parked, and reached his dad's floor, still deep in thought. His parents were so close to retirement and doing the traveling they had always looked forward to. This was certainly not in the plans!

He arrived at the room, and the doctor again explained what had happened and that they had to wait and see how Roger improved as there was no way of knowing just how long the recovery would take. The right side was showing signs of paralysis and meant that the stroke had been on the left side of the brain, which affects speech and memory, so relearning some things would be required. He emphasized that the right side would have been much worse and the chances of recovery less. He told them of another patient the same age who had also had a stroke, and it had also occurred five days after his second heart by-pass surgery.

The words were new and the terms unfamiliar to Leah, but she was sure she could help him relearn whatever was necessary. In reality, she would be learning definitions for many years to come and had not an inkling of what was in store for them.

Dave seemed to make Roger relax more, and he drifted off to sleep again. Dave informed Leah that he had reached his wife, and she was calling his two sisters to inform them of what had happened. He had suggested they wait until after work to come up as there was nothing their parents needed or anything they could do at this time and both parents needed rest. He took his mother down to the waiting room and got her a cup of coffee.

"Cindy didn't like Dad's color last night and felt he seemed more tired than usual. She didn't know what to make of it but was concerned."

"I felt uneasy about it also but tried to ignore it as all vitals were normal, and the doctors were encouraging. He was so eager to come home, and I was so eager to have him home. I never... even...considered...the possibility...of...something like...this, not...in...my worst nightmare."

She began to cry again, and her son put his arms around her. He had always been a source of strength, and she had leaned on him more than she felt she should. But right now, she felt so alone with Roger unable to talk to her or even swallow. She was so afraid of what lie ahead. After a short time lost in thought, she began to regain her composure; she wiped her eyes, blew her nose, and looked up at her son, forcing a sort of smile.

"I'm okay....son. There's nothing to be done here, and you need to get back to your office. I appreciate you so much. You have no idea how much you've helped me by coming and sharing the shock with me. Dad is going to sleep a lot, I'm sure. It's a real struggle for him to try to communicate, and it seems to exhaust him. You can come by tonight after work with Cindy. Dad loves to have you here and seems to brighten when he sees you."

"I can stay if you want me to. The meeting can be postponed if necessary. All I have to do is make a phone call. Ted can even make the presentation."

"It isn't necessary. You've put in lots of time on that report, so you should give it and be sure all the facts are correct. I'll be fine. You go on, and I'll see you tonight. I'm sure Dad will sleep for a while as he seems so tired. You've been a great comfort, but I'm fine now, and I want to check with the nurses on the progress of the other stroke victim. He had his three days ago, so maybe I can learn something."

"Promise you'll eat something? I'm sure you've had only coffee, and you will need your strength. You must take care of yourself too."

"I promise."

"And remember, Mother, the other man may be very different from Dad. Don't let his prognosis upset you because we both know how strong Dad is."

Dave kissed his mother on the cheek as he left. Leah watched him go down the long hallway, thinking what a handsome and self-sufficient man her firstborn had become. He had her fair coloring and thick, straight hair that bleached in the summer sun and darkened each winter. She felt very proud of his numerous accomplishments, and it brought a joy to a very bleak day. He had been a cross-country runner during high school and had done very well. An accident his senior year had caused him to lose a great deal of weight and started his weight training. He was now very muscular and in great shape.

So was Roger at his age. The thought startled Leah and she determined to speak to Dave about having a stress test very soon, hoping she wasn't becoming paranoid...but he was his father's son.

Leah went back to Roger's room to check on him, found him still sleeping, and then went to the nurse's station. She inquired about the other stroke victim and was told he was coming along as well as could be expected. The nurse stated that he appeared to be regaining his speech but couldn't seem to put thoughts together to get much meaning from them. That seemed to be the area of permanent damage.

"Oh?" Leah questioned, shocked to hear the word permanent. "Don't you think he will regain all his abilities with time?"

"There's always some permanent damage after a stroke. It just takes time to determine what it is and the extent."

Leah felt faint and queasy as the nurse spoke and excused herself after thanking her for the information and stating that she would check back again. She was not ready to accept the possibility of Roger having any permanent disability and was convinced that with her help, he would be himself again very soon.

She felt so ignorant of the problems of a stroke and how to cope with it. She didn't know where to turn for information. She wandered around the halls for a few minutes to regain her composure, noticing all the people coming in. It must be lunch time.

She hurried back to Roger's room as his lunch tray came. He had tomato soup, juice, milk, and coffee. The nurse placed a straw in the juice and a soup spoon in Roger's hand. Roger just looked at the spoon, so the nurse took it and fed him some of the soup. He made a face, indicating it was not to his liking. Then the nurse handed the spoon to Leah. She fed Roger more of the soup and then some of the juice, coaxing him along.

"I'd like you to finish this. I know it isn't your favorite, but you need to build up your strength."

She laid the spoon down to give him the juice and Roger picked it up. He looked at it, turning it over several times then put it in his milk. He had difficulty getting his hand to his mouth as his right side was not working properly. The doctor had tested the strength on that side; Roger had been able to give only a slight squeeze.

Leah wanted to cry as she watched his struggle but smiled her cheeriest while praising and encouraging him. He ate very little more, showing with his eyes that he found it tasteless. He had always talked with those big brown eyes, and they had always invoked many feelings in Leah. Now she wished she could turn back the clock and remove the fear and frustration from them. She managed to get Roger to take a few more sips of juice and milk before he was tired and closed his eyes again.

She pushed the tray to one side and looked out the window. The sun was still shining bright, and she noticed the bright-red geraniums, snow-white alyssum, and royal-blue lobelia blooming profusely in the neatly manicured beds around the parking lot. She didn't remember seeing the flowers as she came in. She had to have passed them, but she hadn't been aware of anything she had seen before now.

She looked around the room, taking account of the carpet; it was medium blue, tightly woven, and not very soft. Undoubtedly, it was functional and not chosen for aesthetics. Most hospital rooms she had been in had no carpet, only vinyl tile that was easy to mop and keep clean. She wondered why she hadn't noticed the carpet before. Anyway, carpet was nice.

This wing was known as Progressive Care and was much cheerier than Intensive Care. She had been so happy when he was moved out of there and could have visitors. It was also much more comfortable for her and gave them some privacy.

Leah picked up a magazine and thumbed through it, hardly seeing what was on the pages. She wondered if she had put the dog in the garage or turned off the coffee pot. She thought of all the phone calls she would have to make to the family, informing them of Roger's condition. She wished she could avoid that but knew it must be done.

Roger's dad was a heart patient and his mother was hard of hearing, so she decided it would be best to call his aunt and have her tell them in person. She could keep a watch on Pop to see if he was getting too upset and get a doctor if necessary. She was always very calm and could take charge quickly, having taught school many years and dealing with all sorts of problems.

The nurse arrived with Roger's evening meal, which was almost the same as his lunch, and it was received with about the same reaction. Leah asked if she could prepare some of his favorite soups at home or maybe some pudding, but the nurse said only clear liquids. Leah managed to get Roger to eat about the same amount as before, and he fell asleep again.

Leah turned on the television set and watched the news and several shows, trying to divert her mind with little success. She was aware of activity outside in the hall as the door opened and Suzan and Melanie walked into the room. They each kissed her and whispered their love and concern. Roger awoke, and they kissed him and put big smiles on their faces, trying to be cheerful and reassuring, but Leah could see the fear concealed in their eyes.

Suzan had been so helpful during Roger's first surgery and recuperation six years ago. Melanie had a very hard time dealing with her father's fallibility as she still needed to feel protected by him. She had the most trouble dealing with his personality change and had told a friend, "My dad went to the hospital for a heart operation and a stranger came home."

She had been only fourteen at the time and Suzan only sixteen, but they had helped her so much. She had felt they responded as much older than their years and couldn't have imagined dealing with the loneliness without them.

Roger tried to speak but could only manage a word occasionally, after a great struggle. His eyes showed the fatigue he felt, still he was able to communicate a lot with his eyes. He was visibly happy to see his girls, and they began to relax.

Dave and Cindy arrived less than thirty minutes later, and Roger tried to talk with them also but couldn't. He motioned for his paper and pencil and tried to write, but he couldn't accomplish that either. He struggled for some time to achieve a few letters, some backward and looking like a kindergartner's.

"Don't even try to talk, Dad. Save all your energy for healing, and we'll do the talking for you. Your speech will come very soon but just rest for now. Mom," Dave turned to Leah, "are you going to spend the night?"

"Yes. I want to be sure he gets what he needs when he needs it. He can't use the urinal, so he needs help to get up. I'll be fine, and I'll call the parents tomorrow."

"Mother, what have you eaten today?"

"I haven't felt hungry."

"I figured as much." Suzan turned to Melanie and Cindy.

The girls insisted Leah should have something to eat, so they took her to the cafeteria, leaving Dave to keep his father company. They were all full of questions: How did it happen? What had caused it? How long would he be like this? Leah had no answers and fought tears as she tried to give them all the information she had.

"I want you to eat this soup. It's cream of vegetable and looks pretty good."

Melanie set a bowl of steaming soup in front of her mother and placed several packets of crackers beside it. It had no flavor at all, so she only took a few bites.

"I'm sorry but I really don't feel much like eating. I'm just so glad to have you all here. I've felt so helpless all day."

She had no desire for food, only to make Roger well, but she knew that was an impossible desire. Was this a bad dream? Would she wake up and find that none of it had happened? Suzan took her hand and squeezed it, jolting Leah back into focus on the present.

"Mother, I love you, and I want you to take care of yourself. Daddy is going to be okay"

"I know." Leah tried to sound confident.

Chapter 3

The hospital had a large remodeling project underway; the cafeteria had just been finished and was very bright and open. The roof was a number of large skylights, allowing sun and sky to shine through and giving the towering tropical plants the light they thrived on. The carpet was medium blue with borders of mauve, both colors repeated in the new molded chairs; it was not picked for comfort but for ease of cleaning. The wallpaper was a thin blue stripe amidst satiny white stripes on which vines of tiny multicolored flowers swirled. One wall was all windows looking out onto a courtyard full of brightly colored flowers and lush green trees surrounded by white wrought-iron tables and chairs. It was all very appealing, but Leah took little notice of her surroundings as she was lost in her own thoughts.

"You looked as if you were far away," Suzan said lovingly to her mother, "and I'm getting worried about you. Please try to take care of yourself. We all need you. You've always been so strong." Leah smiled at her and nodded. She knew how much her family depended on her to handle anything that life threw at them, but she sure didn't feel strong right now.

The oldest of six children, Leah had always been the one called for any health problem or family crisis with her parents.

Her brothers and sisters also depended on her for help and advice with their problems, and she had always been happy to do anything she could. Right now, she wished she could call someone to do something about her crisis but knew her only help would have to come from God.

"This place has sure improved since Dad's last stay."

Melanie was looking around the room. She worked for an interior decorating shop and was always surveying her surroundings.

"You should spend time down here during Dad's naps and soak up some sun. You're too pale, and the plants seem to be thriving on it." They all laughed at her observation.

Back in the room, Roger appeared so tired that the children decided they should leave after Dave assured his mother they were all only a phone call away and would be keeping in touch.

"I would be glad to call the family for you, Mom."

"Thank you, Cindy, but I need to do it myself. There's no real hurry, and maybe I'll know more by tomorrow morning. I'll go home for a shower sometime." Leah's voice faltered as she felt so unsure of anything.

She loved Cindy like her own daughter, and many thought she was. She was fair with blue eyes and long blonde hair; she was as sweet as she was pretty. She reminded Roger of Princess Diana, and he had called her Diane when he meant Cindy a couple of times.

"I can stay," Suzan volunteered. She was now twenty-two, and Leah thought how much she looked like Roger's sister, Dorothy. She had died just before Melanie was born, and it had been a great loss. Dorothy was a very beautiful and very talented woman, and her family had felt a great emptiness. Suzan had the same olive complexion as Roger, but she had blue eyes like Leah's instead of Roger's brown. She had inherited her high-strung nerves as well as her physical beauty from her aunt and could talk with her eyes as well as her dad did with his. Dorothy's had appeared to be black and sparkled with emotion.

"So can I," Melanie added.

She was fair skinned with light brown hair and blue eyed as was Dave. They had taken their coloring from their mother. Both girls were very pretty, and many teachers as well as peers had thought they were twins, though Leah couldn't understand why. They looked very different to her. As they became teenagers, many thought Melanie was the oldest, much to Suzan's chagrin.

"She even acts juvenile if you ask me. It's insulting!" was always her retort when she heard anyone mention their ages.

Roger's eyes opened and rolled at Leah, letting her know he did not want either of his daughters to take care of him just now. They all had to laugh at the apparent discord clearly visible in his eyes. He looked puzzled at their laughter and then smiled at Leah.

"Don't worry, darling. I don't intend to leave you for a moment. Thanks, girls, but I think your father would be more comfortable with me as he feels rather indisposed just now. I'll manage just fine, and I'll call if we need anything. You all go on home and get some rest; we'll need you in the future, I'm sure. Could one of you to go by the house and check on Cory? He's very lonely and confused about all the going and coming. He could use more food and water, I'm sure."

Melanie volunteered. The last child at home, she had felt Cory was all hers and loved him very much, and he definitely loved her. He was quick to show his joy when any of the children came by.

The nurse came in to check Roger's vital signs, and the children left. All were fine, and Roger drifted off to sleep again. Leah attempted to stretch out on two chairs, but sleep was impossible. She switched the TV on again but saw nothing as the tears began their escape down her cheeks. She prayed once more that God would take this horrible situation away. She felt somewhat betrayed to think that all their many plans and dreams of retirement had been in vain. Just let Roger live and be able to enjoy the travels he had looked forward to, she thought. She really wanted God to back up time as if the events of today had never happened but knew she was being unrealistic and selfish. They had dealt with many heavy problems in their twenty-six years of marriage and would deal with this too. She prayed God would forgive her weakness and give her renewed faith and strength.

The door opened, and Roger's internist, Dr. Stevens, entered the room. Leah sat up and looked at her watch.

"My goodness! It's twenty minutes after midnight. What are you doing here at this hour?"

"I always make my rounds late at night. That's when things seem to happen."

"That's for sure," Leah agreed. "Last night was certainly no exception." She felt tears trying to escape and choked them back again.

"Don't try to hold your feelings inside, Leah. Go ahead and cry and let them out. This is a terrible ordeal, and Roger is going to need you like never before. You'll have plenty of time to be strong in the future but keep yourself healthy physically and emotionally. He seems to be doing as well as can be expected, so I'll see him again tomorrow. I'll be keeping up on his progress with his cardiologist. Is there anything I can do for you? Do you need something to keep you calm......an antidepressant? It would also help you sleep."

"No, thanks. I'll keep it in mind if I feel I need it, but I want to keep alert right now."

Roger's nurse passed the room just as Dr. Stevens left and came in to see if they needed anything.

"You poor dear! That chair must be terribly uncomfortable. I'll bring in a recliner, a blanket, and a pillow so maybe you can get a little sleep. You need your rest too. I'll just be a few minutes."

Leah waited, hoping she would get something more comfortable and be able to sleep a little. She heard commotion and lots of footsteps out in the hall, but no one came into the room, so she decided something must have happened. She rolled her jacket up for a pillow and stretched out on the carpet between Roger's bed and the bathroom so she would know if he attempted to get up. The floor would never have been considered at all soft, so Leah decided it would be good just to rest her eyes even if she couldn't fall asleep. She figured someone would be coming in anyway. She stretched out and asked God to forgive her for her anger and to help her get herself and Roger through this.

"I must have fallen asleep." Leah told the nurse as she stretched and rose to clear the way for her to get to the bed. She looked at her watch and was surprised to learn it was after four a.m. She had slept, in spite of the hard floor, for almost three hours.

"I'm so sorry I woke you, but it's time to check his vitals. I apologize for not getting back with the recliner, but as I passed the room next door, I saw the man was covered with blood. We had hardly taken care of him when the lady in 204 went into cardiac arrest. It's been quite a night!"

"Are they alright?" Leah asked. "I heard noises and figured something was happening.

"I believe they will be. Everything's quiet now."

"I wonder if Roger will sleep awhile longer. I need to go home to check on the dog, take a shower, and call our families."

"Go ahead, honey. I know you're going on nerves, and you need some rest too. He will sleep a lot for the next few days, and things have settled down, so I will keep a close watch on him. Try to sleep for a while before you come back to the hospital."

Leah gathered her purse and left for home. It was now nearly 5:00 a.m. and there was no traffic. All seemed very quiet and peaceful. The sun was rising after having just gone down, and the air was cool, so Leah lowered the window and took several long breaths. Could it have been less than twenty-four hours since she was so happily preparing for a homecoming?

She passed a newspaper carrier bicycling with his load of morning papers to deliver, and then a garbage truck stopped to scoop up its load of castaways. Trees were beginning to leaf out, and perennials were making their presence known in the spring landscape. Everything appeared to be quite normal and peaceful in the early morning. How Leah wanted her life to be the way it had been just hours before when she had been happy and full of plans!

Cory was so excited to see her and more excited when she let him out to potty and filled his food and water bowls. He followed her around, wagging constantly as if begging her to stay awhile. She said a silent prayer for strength and the ability to relay the sad news to their parents without falling apart and causing more distress than need be.

"Aunt Constance, this is Leah. I need your help."

"Leah, what a surprise! Is anything wrong?"

"Yes....Roger has had a stroke."

"Oh, no! How is he?"

Leah explained as best she could, trying not to cry.

"I would appreciate it if you would go down and tell Mom and Pop. I'm very concerned about Pop's reaction and his heart."

After Leah filled in a few more details, Constance agreed to leave immediately and expressed her concern. She made Leah promise to keep her informed and to let them know how they might help now or in the future. Leah knew she meant it and would be available for anything anytime. Constance was well aware of her brother's heart problems and also had diabetes so would be especially cautious.

"Mother," Leah began to cry as her mother answered the phone.

"Leah? What's happened?"

"Roger had a stroke yesterday—the day he was to come home."

Leah felt near exhaustion as she explained everything as she knew it to her mother and assured her she was okay, just bone tired, and would keep her informed and let her know if anything she could do. She was not fond of flying, and there was nothing to be done here anyway. Her mother would call Leah's brothers and sisters and let the family know the sad news. Leah was just glad to have her to talk to.

With the phone calls finished, she went down and took a shower, intending to go right back to the hospital. As she dried herself, she was overcome with fatigue and decided to sleep for just an hour; it was still only 6:00 a.m. She set the alarm and collapsed under the soft satin comforter.

"Hello, darling! I had a shower and a short nap and I feel great. Do I look great?"

It was now 9:50 a.m. as she entered Roger's room; Leah had managed to sleep nearly three hours and really did feel better. Thank goodness their home was just a mile from the hospital. She could go back and forth in just minutes. She was finding many things to be thankful for, even in the wake of yesterday's awful events, and was developing a more positive attitude.

Nevertheless, a nagging feeling of foreboding kept jumping back into her thoughts. She really wished she could pinpoint what was haunting her but couldn't take time to pursue it. What else could happen? It was probably just a reaction to shock.

Roger's eyes sparkled, and he made it clear he was very happy to see her.

"Have you had breakfast?"

He moved his head slightly up and down and made a face indicating it wasn't very good. Then the door opened, and the nurse came in holding a clean pair of pajamas.

"Time to get cleaned up, Mr. Kerry."

Leah saw that the pajama top had long sleeves. Roger had a heart monitor with a wire going down his left arm and an IV on his right arm. How were they going to get the pajama top off and a clean one on with all that?

"Don't you have any button-front pajamas? Or short-sleeved ones? Those look terribly difficult and uncomfortable."

"No. These really are a nuisance to get in and out of; we really do need something better."

Roger had several pairs of button-front pajamas but all had long sleeves and they would still be difficult. She decided to go shopping that afternoon while he slept and find new ones with short sleeves and button fronts.

She and the nurse managed to get him washed up and dressed, and he settled down to sleep. It had been an exhausting ordeal for him, and Leah knew he would be sleeping for a while and decided to go shopping for the pajamas.

Driving directly to the nearest shopping center, she went into the two department stores and two men's specialty shops. This was Alaska, and short-sleeved pajamas weren't in much demand. She finally found two pairs at the last shop, but they also had short legs. She made her purchase and headed back to the car, grateful she hadn't run into anyone they knew. She just didn't have time to chat, and she wasn't sure she could talk about Roger without crying.

"These were the only short-sleeved button front pajamas I could find anywhere."

Leah held up the new summer pajamas with the short sleeves and pants for Roger and the nurse to see. Roger rolled his eyes and gestured with his mouth, causing both Leah and the nurse to burst out laughing.

"Well, I guess I'll return these and exchange for long pants. They will also have long sleeves, but I'll cut them off and hem them for you. I can do that while you take a nap."

Roger looked dismayed.

"Not now. I'll stay until you get tired and then go while you sleep. You won't even know I left. I told you I'll always be here whenever you need me."

The nurse smiled and told Leah it was obvious how relaxed he became when she entered the room.

"We've been married so long, I can almost read his thoughts, and I can read his eyes. He doesn't need words to convey his likes or dislikes."

The nurse agreed, laughing as she left the room.

Leah read the newspaper she had brought to Roger, not sure if he understood any of it, but he seemed to enjoy it. She kept up a light chatter, trying to lift his spirits and letting him know she knew he was fine. She was careful not to let any of her doubts or concerns slip through. She was about to turn on the TV when Roger touched her arm and motioned to the drawer in the bedside table. She opened it and took out his glasses. He shook his head no. She took out his toothbrush and floss. He again shook his head no. She picked up his electric razor and held it up. He smiled, nodded yes, and touched his chin. Leah's fingers froze around the razor as she realized he wanted her to shave him. She had never shaved anyone in her life and knew nothing about electric razors. She had nicked herself many times with the 'safety' razor she used and didn't know if she could injure Roger with his. She contemplated what she should do, praying God would give her an out when the door opened and Max Bolin came into the room. He was their neighbor and had talked with Dave and learned of Roger's stroke, sparing Leah the necessity of discussing it.

"I'm so very glad to see you. Roger wants to shave, and I haven't the slightest idea where to begin. I'm afraid I'll nick him or something. I don't think he's too crazy about my doing it either."

"Go get a cup of coffee and relax. Let me take care of it," Max laughed.

He was a big man with a big heart and had been a wonderful neighbor for so long that he seemed like family. His dark-auburn hair was also getting much lighter as gray crept in, and he had put on a little too much weight since retiring from the oil pipeline. He took the razor from Leah's hand and gave her a hug as he turned her toward the door.

"Hi, Sport. So you want a shave. How about a haircut while I'm at it? The price is right."

Roger smiled his crooked smile with the right side not responding. Max hurt to see his good friend in this condition. He and Roger had spent many afternoons talking and working in their yards, with more talk than work. He turned on the razor and soon had the job done, producing another big smile from Roger. It was obvious the shave made him feel better. Max kept up a light, one-sided conversation until he could see Roger needed to rest.

"I'll be back before you need another shave. If you think of anything else, I'll take care of that too."

Leah headed down the hall toward the waiting room. Roger's nurse passed her and told her to go into the conference room where fresh coffee waited as it would be more comfortable and private.

Leah poured herself a cup of coffee, added a half teaspoon of sugar, and stirred methodically. She set the cup on the end table and leaned back as she sat down on the comfy sofa. As she slowly sipped the hot coffee, she realized she was actually feeling very angry. Angry at the rotten luck! A stroke just as they were about to begin realizing all their dreams for retirement. Angry that Roger couldn't hold her and take care of everything for her as he had always done before. Angry that she had always let him take care of everything, leaving her stupid about finances, cars, repairs, etc. What would she do? How would she manage it all? Then she felt guilty for feeling so angry. So many emotions were fighting inside her that she felt exhausted and frustrated as she sat staring into space for a long time.

Max walked into the room and poured himself a cup of coffee. Leah realized she had been lost in her thoughts for half an hour.

"Roger is clean shaven and resting now. So how are you?"

"I'm fine..." she answered. She sat looking at Max, feeling a little dishonest. "No, I'm not...I'm very, very angry! This is not fair! We've worked hard, and saved, and made plans, and done the best we knew how, and now that we are ready to begin enjoying our reward, this has to happen. He's already been through so much! It just isn't fair!"

Leah raved furiously, and the tears began to fall, silencing her outpouring of feelings and emotions. Suddenly, she began to shiver as if freezing. Her nerves were getting the better of her.

"Your anger is very understandable and normal, and there is nothing wrong with being angry. Anyone would be under the circumstances; it's a perfectly natural emotion. Give yourself some time to come to grips with everything, and take it one day at a time. I imagine Roger's feeling a little angry too. I certainly would."

Max reached over and put his arm around her shoulders like a big brother. Leah leaned on him and felt somewhat protected for just a minute and then leaned back and regained her composure.

"Thanks for all your understanding, Max. I need to be strong for Roger, and it's a new reverse role for me. I've always let him be the strong one."

"You know Lorene and I are always here to talk to or help in any way...even shaving. And you don't have to be a pillar of strength. You will be when needed! I know you and know you can adjust to whatever fate has in store."

He grinned, and Leah felt really dumb. She wasn't reacting like she wanted to at all. Max and Lorene were such a sweet couple and always made you feel good just by being around them. Lorene had a wonderfully sweet smile that warmed those around her but could be as strong and tough as nails when needed.

"I know. I just need to get some of my feelings out. I'm very tired and not coping very well just now."

"Try to remember that you can't do anything for Roger if you let yourself get down. Do try to relax. Lorene and I will be up later on, and you know you can call us anytime."

Max and Lorene had lived next door several years before Roger and Leah had moved there and had introduced them to the area and neighbors, advising them on everything from caring for the yard to babysitters. They had made them feel at home and had helped with more than Leah could recount. Their home was beautiful, and the yard matched as they both spent many hours inside and out. Alaskan summers were so short that one had to make the most of the time available. Lorene was among a very few who tried to raise roses, requiring setting them out in summer and taking them in for the winter. But they were beautiful, and her rose garden made visitors stop their cars to observe it. Leah didn't want to go to such lengths herself but always looked forward to enjoying Lorene's roses all summer.

Chapter 4

Leah sat for a while after Max left until her anger, fear, and frustration subsided. She just felt numb and wanted to curl up on the sofa and blot out all the events of the past two days. Had it only been two days? Two days since her world had been turned upside down? She had to gather strength and had to help Roger.

She poured herself another cup of coffee and let the hot, black liquid revive her. She gazed around the room, seeing for the first time the beautiful painting hanging across from her. It was a typical Alaskan scene with mountains, streams, and lots of snow. The beauty was in the way the color had been used, pink to indicate the time of day and light source, greens and browns peaking through the snow to indicate spring was approaching and new life beginning. It was really lovely and relaxing, which struck Leah as an excellent choice for a hospital conference room. How many families had received bad news about loved ones in this room? How many had come here to cry about the fate of their loved ones?

The sofa was soft and comfortable and would also be a comfy bed if needed for that use. Leah would file that information for use in the future. Her mind seemed to drift in and out of reality and the world around her to thoughts and questions about the future. She seemed to have trouble keeping it on one track. Back in the room, Roger was still resting, so she switched on the TV to find a talk show on. The subject today seemed to be troubled teens, and she changed channels. She had enough troubles and didn't need anyone else's. Finally she found the shopping channel and lost herself for a while, watching the parade of items of clothing and jewelry featured.

Roger awoke and gave her a knowing look as he saw the program she had on, so she switched it off and gave him a hug and kiss. That seemed to please him, so they just sat smiling and holding hands for a long while.

The children came after work and visited for a short time, relaying good wishes from work, neighbors, and friends. They again took her to the cafeteria, which proved to be a pleasant diversion, if only to break the monotony of the hospital. They assured her they would check the house and dog, so she needn't worry about anything but their dad.

That night, she had a foam "egg crate" from Roger's previous hospital stay and her own pillow, plus a blanket she had brought from home. She made quite a nice bed on the floor and slept soundly, amazed that no one interrupted for almost four hours straight. Most of the time, a nurse or doctor was in every hour.

She helped with all Roger's care and listened intently to all reports and questioned every doctor and nurse who came in, trying to understand and verify the information they gave her. It was of little use, but it made her feel better and a part of his team. He wanted her to hold his hand most of the time he was awake, so she spent most of the next two days in his room, leaving only for a cup of coffee or a sandwich.

Friday night arrived, and Dave insisted on staying with Roger so Leah could get away for a while. She had left for no more than two or three hours at a time since the first night and had been sleeping on the floor and eating at the hospital for four days, which left a lot to be desired. She felt guilty for leaving but knew Roger would love having Dave there.

She spent most of Saturday morning with Cory watching her cooking soup and pudding for Roger and making some pasta salad to keep her going the next few days. He knew he would get at least a taste in his bowl and kept a close watch on Leah's movements. He also knew he would get lots of petting if he stayed underfoot. It felt really good to Leah to stay at home for a morning as the hospital was very depressing and there was little to watch on TV during the day on weekends. Roger could now have small soft bits of food in his soups, so she put it through the blender, being careful nothing would cause him to choke.

She found a couple of Roger's old button-front pajamas, cut the sleeves off, and hemmed them quickly before she left. He now had four pairs, which should be plenty. She was relieved that the phone had stayed quiet, allowing her to get a good night's uninterrupted sleep and then get several tasks accomplished. She had pulled out the tablecloth she was crocheting for Suzan, thinking she would work on it a little more as she kept Roger company. It had been put away since Roger's return from the hospital after the heart attack that had necessitated the angiogram, which found the first by-passes were almost blocked. It was almost done, needing only a few more rows to fit a large table. She was on her way to the closet for a sweater when the phone rang for the first time this day.

"Hello."

"Sis, it's Jenna."

"My goodness, I didn't expect to hear from you. How are you doing?"

"I'm doing fine. The question is how are you doing? And how is Roger doing? Mother called me right after she heard from you but suggested I wait and get word from her since you were spending most of your time at the hospital."

"Well, it's a nightmare, but I'm adjusting, and Roger is so helpless. He can swallow a little better, and he can let us know he understands us and knows us, but that's about it."

"My, goodness, Sis. You all have been through the mill. I don't know how you've coped with it all. I could never get through all you've had to deal with."

"Sure you could. Nobody ever asked me; I wasn't given a choice. You just do the best you can with what you get. I had no preparation; it's just life. Certainly not what Roger expected, but we are both doing the best we know how and we're making it okay."

"I'm sure you are, but I do feel for you and wish I knew how to help. I think of you all the time."

"That's what we need—prayers and moral support! The doctors keep saying 'wait and see'...that's the hard part...waiting and not knowing what's to come."

"Well, hang in there and tell Roger to do the same. I'll check back before long, and keep you in my prayers, and put you both on our prayer chain. Love you all."

Leah hung up the phone, put on her sweater, and headed for the garage with Cory at her heels. She didn't hear from Jenna often as she never wrote and led too busy a life to even call very often. It had been a delight to hear from her, and Leah left in high spirits.

As she drove down the street, she saw several neighbors who waved as they worked in their yards, but she didn't stop as she knew Lorene had kept them informed. It was a very nice neighborhood with pride of ownership showing everywhere around the area. Lush, green lawns and brightly colored flower beds adorned the block. They were lucky to live among such very nice people; it was like one big family. When Roger and Leah's front yard had to be dug up to replace a broken pipe, some of them actually cried with Leah to see her carefully cultivated lawn destroyed. No one would know it had ever happened now.

Dave was glad to see her. She was sure he was bored and hungry. He told her he had breakfast in the cafeteria and had been fine, but she knew the food too well and was sure he was anxious to get home, shower, and have lunch with Cindy. She had brought soup and pudding for Roger with pasta salad and breadsticks for herself. They would be fine, and she sent Dave home with a big hug and a thank you.

"I can stay tonight again, Mom."

"Thanks, Son, but you have a class to teach tomorrow morning and then work the next day. Sleep in your own bed and relax. Last night was great and plenty. We're doing fine. The egg crate is really not too bad. Did you use it?"

"I did but found the recliner more to my liking and slept a few hours at a time. I'm okay."

Reluctantly, Dave followed his mother's dismissal with the usual offers of help and reassurance; they were only a phone call away. She gave Roger a big hug after Dave closed the door behind him.

"Did you sleep well? Did you enjoy Dave?"

Roger nodded yes to both questions and motioned to the paper she had brought. He took it from her, put on his glasses, and spent almost an hour reading it. Leah wasn't sure he understood what he read, but she was pleased for any show of normalcy. She really felt he had progressed quite a bit as it had only been five days, and he was swallowing better and trying to speak more. He just couldn't get much to come out and when it did, it was obvious it wasn't what he wanted to say most of the time.

The doctors came in each day and assured her he was improving and progressing well. She wasn't at all sure what 'well' meant. Pressing for more information yielded little, so she had ceased questioning. Her impatience wasn't getting her anywhere, and she didn't want to irritate any of them. 'Just waiting to see' had never been easy for her as she felt she must be able to do something. She just wasn't sure what! Always one to keep busy, the inactivity of the hospital room and sitting around were very difficult for her, and the time seemed to drag.

She usually took on more than time would allow and hated to waste any so she felt useless, and her muscles grew stiff just sitting. She would be so glad to get him home, whenever that would be. The club and church work would have to be given to someone else, but she knew that wouldn't be a problem. She was supposed to teach a class on Proverbs but didn't want to leave Roger alone and knew he would hate being 'sat with.'

She began to look forward to slowing her busy schedule and getting some projects finished while staying at home. Work had always kept her too busy, and she had many things she planned to do sometime. Maybe 'sometime' was now!

The following week, Roger was moved to a regular care unit. The rooms were not as attractive and the nurses more scarce than in progressive care. The view of colorful flowers in bloom was replaced with a view of brick buildings and the side parking lot for doctors only. The floor had no carpet, and the cream walls, beige and cream linoleum, and beige blankets were rather drab. Leah was not so happy with the change, but his ability to swallow had returned somewhat over the past week as had the strength on his right side. He was now on a soft diet and had relearned how to feed himself. He could get around by himself in the room and could walk the halls with help. His speech was slowly returning with daily therapy and much effort on his part. He could manage one or two words at a time, but it was difficult, and he had to think for some time about what he wanted to say.

All the nurses and doctors continually praised the speed with which he was improving, but Leah was not very impressed. She was truly grateful for each little step forward, but it was such a far cry from the intelligent, capable man she had lived with for twenty-six years. She longed to have him back the way he was. She had really expected the speech and physical therapy to go faster.

He seemed to know everyone, although he frequently called the family members by the wrong names. Leah wasn't sure he knew his relationship to anyone and was concerned if he remembered their relationship. Sometimes he treated her as his mother and other times more like a sister. Finally, she decided to ask.

"Roger, do you remember how we are related? Am I your mother? Wife? Sister?"

Roger looked at her and thought for some time. From his eyes, Leah could tell he was searching his memory for the right word. Finally, with great effort, he managed to get out the word "lover." Leah was very relieved and laughed excitedly.

"That's close enough, darling! I can accept that."

Roger grinned and rolled those brown eyes, leaving Leah unsure if he was serious or being playful. He loved to tease.

The next few days were somewhat routine and all seemed to be going well. Leah was at the hospital with Roger from about 8:00 a.m. to 9:00 p.m. reading, crocheting, watching TV, and trying to act as normal as possible while attempting to motivate Roger to try talking. His speech was improving steadily with the help of the therapist, but the progress was still very slow. He couldn't seem to get words or ideas from his brain to his mouth, and his struggles were visible and heartbreaking. He seemed to spend most of the time in his own world but would try to appear involved in some conversations. He spent a great deal of time sleeping.

Several of the nurses spent time in his room, watching the soaps and trying to talk with him. The conversations were very one-sided, and Leah would chuckle to herself as she knew he hated soaps. He was very tolerant and never let on that he wanted the channel changed. One nurse was from the Philippines and a delight, with a bubbly personality and laughing black eyes that sparkled. She had dark hair and complexion and was a little taller than Leah's five feet. Roger lit up when she came in, and she always made him laugh—his new husky laugh.

A former coworker of his, Ray, was admitted with heart problems, and Roger seemed to improve with his visits. His speech seemed to come quicker when he talked about the jobs they had both worked on. They had worked together nearly ten years before, and Leah was surprised Roger seemed to remember details so well. Less than a week after he was admitted, Ray came into the room looking rather grim and asked Leah to walk down the hall with him. He needed to give her the sad news that Tom had passed away. Leah was very upset but decided not to give Roger the news until he was much better and at home, so she expressed her appreciation for informing her and for not telling Roger. He kept his promise and continued to visit, continually finding more memories to remind Roger of. He always kept him trying to converse, and Leah was disappointed for Roger when he was released but happy for him. She was sure that what Roger needed was a different motivation to improve. The speech therapy seemed to be a chore for him, and Leah had to constantly encourage him to continue.

Two weeks after he was released from the hospital, she found a message on the recorder at home that Ray had passed away; he had dropped dead as he returned home from work. Speculation was that he had gone back too soon, but no one really knew. It put such a fear in Leah that she could hardly breathe. Two of Roger's coworkers were gone within such a short time, and all of them were near the same age! It was too much to cope with. She couldn't tell Roger but hated keeping secrets from him. She just didn't want to chance the damage depression could do to his psychological ability to heal.

Finally, two weeks after he had been moved, he was able to return home. Leah was happy and frightened at the same time. She was so tired of the hospital and knew he was too, but she wasn't a nurse. How would she occupy his time and help him? He could still only get one or two words out at a time.

She had everything ready and tried to appear enthusiastic as she arrived to drive him home. He was obviously ready to go but agreed to stay until after lunch, not that he was interested in the 1200 calorie, low-fat menu he was on, but he did it to please Leah. This was another concern. Roger enjoyed eating and ate large portions. Keeping him full and happy on 1200 calories was not going to be easy. She had felt prepared before, but now he had difficulty swallowing and was still on soft foods and ground meats.

He had been in the hospital for six weeks prior to the surgery due to the heart attack. At that time, he had complained that no one paid any attention to what he ordered for his meals. He never got what he checked on the menus, and he let the nurses know about it. One morning after expressing his displeasure with his breakfast, the door opened, and a dietician entered. She quickly ascertained it was indeed Roger Kerry and then gave him a very stern look.

"Your eating habits are atrocious! You are digging your grave a bite at a time, and I refuse to send you what you order. No wonder you have heart disease!" She made several further comments about his diet before she instructed him to forget the menus; she would send him what he should have. Roger was thoroughly reprimanded. Confident she would hear no more complaints, the dietician left. He had looked like a scolded puppy and didn't mention food further except to let Leah know he didn't care to cross the dietician again, though the food was most unappetizing.

That had been two months before the surgery. He enjoyed his food, especially rich desserts and bar-b-q ribs. Traveling to remote sites, with great chefs employed to keep workers happy, he had all the foods Leah tried to get him to avoid, contributing to extra pounds, a rise in his triglycerides and heart problems .

Chapter 5

They left the hospital with prescriptions in hand, along with numerous instruction papers and a speech therapy appointment for the following Monday. He had frowned when he saw that appointment but was glad to be going home. He seemed very tired just getting dressed and moving from his room to the car. He was quiet all the way home.

Cory's eyes widened and filled with excitement when he saw Roger. He wagged so hard Leah was sure he would break in two. He ran to the door, saw Roger, ran back to pick up the paper and then to the door in such quick motions Roger couldn't get inside until he picked the rapidly moving dog up.

Cory had learned early on that none of the family liked to be licked, so he always held something in his mouth to prevent irritating anyone while he got his petting. Roger was visibly pleased with the enthusiastic reception, but Leah took the dog from him quickly, afraid he would hit Roger's incision.

Roger surveyed the room resting his eyes on the long overstuffed sofa. He turned back to Leah, smiling.

"...house...gr...eat...glad...I......so...fa!"

The sofa was seven feet long, and Roger had insisted it had to be long enough for him to lie on comfortably. She could pick color and style but not the size!

Shortly after arriving home, Leah had Roger settled on the sofa watching TV, Cory at his feet. Suddenly she realized she had not seen him given his noon medication, which always came just before lunch. She called the hospital and learned that indeed he had not been given that dose. He needed it right away as it was his heart medication plus a blood thinner. She was beginning to feel panic when the doorbell rang.

Leah opened the door to her neighbor from across the street. She had come to see if they needed anything, and Leah welcomed her in excitedly.

"I'm so grateful you came just when you did. I need someone to stay with Roger while I go get his prescriptions filled. The hospital failed to give him his noon meds and here it is mid-afternoon, so I need them right away. He will probably just take a nap while I'm gone. Could you stay? I shouldn't be more than thirty minutes."

"Certainly I'll stay and don't hurry. I'll just sit here and read while Roger naps, so do whatever you need to. My children won't be home from school for two more hours."

Leah was so grateful for such good neighbors and knew she meant what she said. She and her family had moved from North Dakota into the only all-brick house in the neighborhood. Sue was a sturdily built blonde with deep-set eyes, and her husband was a very large muscular man with a heart as big as his size. Sue had helped Leah learn to make scented silk flowers and decorate cakes, although the flowers turned out much better than the cakes.

She hurried out to the car and suddenly felt very angry with the nursing staff, which had forgotten to give him his noon medication before releasing him. Wasn't her life difficult enough without this? What if no one had been home in the neighborhood to stay with him? The more she thought about it, the more alone she felt as if she was solely responsible for Roger's recovery, and that thought chilled her.

Boy, are you feeling sorry for yourself! Better cut it out! Leah's inner self gave her a through reprimand, and she smiled. She took time to thank God for sending someone in their time of need and asked him again to forgive her anger. She also prayed for more patience!

She backed out of the driveway and turned onto the street, noticing the sun had burned off all the morning fog, allowing a beautiful day to burst forth into the afternoon. It made her aware of her surroundings—the colorful peonies, daisies, and irises in the lawn ahead. The azure sky was tinted with lavender, and puffs of billowy clouds began to appear moving lazily into view. It cooled her anger and made her anxious for Roger to improve so she could enjoy the rest of this fantastic Alaskan summer with him.

She parked near the grocery store and hurried to the pharmacy. It would take about thirty minutes for the prescriptions, and she seized the opportunity to browse through the produce section, looking for anything new to put into Roger's salads and soups. She saw some fresh herbs and radishes, picked out the best bunch, and walked back to the pharmacy. She had already shopped before bringing Roger home, so little room remained in the refrigerator. She could use the veggies he loved for garnish until he was able to start eating more solids. She had been instructed to slowly introduce new things.

The prescriptions were ready. Leah listened to all the instructions, folded the information sheets, and headed for the checkout counter.

"Leah! Wait a minute. How's Roger?"

It was Lorene Bolin, so Leah stopped and chatted a minute while waiting in line. She told Lorene that Roger was home and about the medications. She insisted Leah call her and Max if she needed anything else. They would be over to see Roger the next day. Leah checked out and checked the time; almost an hour had gone by so she headed home.

"Thank you so much, Sue. I appreciate you very much."

"You know I'm glad to help any way I can. Roger has been asleep since you left and just opened his eyes when you came in. I'll go now but call anytime. I'm sure glad he's home."

"Me too! Thanks again." Leah called as she went out the door.

Roger sleepily opened his eyes and took the pills Leah offered him. She handed him the TV remote control and then waited for him to turn it on. He handed it back to her, so she punched the power button and turned the channel to CNN, making sure Roger could see everything she did. He rose up on the pillows and began to watch. Leah kissed his forehead and told him she was going to begin preparing dinner as she retreated to the kitchen.

It was so hard to watch his confusion over such small things as operating the TV, but his memory of many learned functions was impaired. She wondered how long it would take to get it back. Tears filled her eyes and spilled down her cheeks as she opened the refrigerator and cabinets, busying herself with their dinner preparation to maintain control.

She made a salad, cottage cheese, and fruit for herself and mashed potatoes, asparagus, ground chicken, and tapioca pudding for Roger.

Dinner was well received and Roger seemed to be happy with what she had prepared and consumed most of it. There was not much variety, but he didn't complain as she tried to vary it for the following week. He was able to swallow better, and she added more solid food gradually.

A couple weeks later, she made him a real treat with some of his favorites—lemon dill salmon with rice pilaf (more of the mushrooms, onions, and parsley than rice), Jell-O salad, and green beans. It sure took longer to make all the little extras that made the diet more palatable, but it was worth it to see his delight at the tomatoes and radishes cut into flowers. He ate hungrily, so Leah felt justified spending extra time and effort. Thank goodness he was very fond of fish as he was supposed to have it twice a week at least. Leah wasn't a fish lover but could tolerate mild-flavored white fish while Roger's favorite was salmon. They had eaten so much of it all these years in Alaska that she didn't even care to cook it but would, of course. He seemed to do fine with the rice and even the small pieces of the radish. Leah was delighted!

After dinner, he seemed tired and laid on the sofa only a short time before indicating he was ready for bed. Leah helped him down the few stairs, waited for him to wash up and brush his teeth, and then tucked him into bed. It was still quite early, so Leah read over the reports from the hospital and then went through some of the mail. She picked up the information packet on strokes, reading only a few sentences before tears flooded her eyes and flowed down her face as if a dam had just broken. It felt like it too as she could now let go without upsetting Roger.

She put all the papers aside and climbed the stairs to the upstairs bathroom, not wanting to wake him. She turned on the hot water then poured some bubble bath into the tub, letting it foam almost to the top. When she stepped into the warm bubbles, she could feel herself drifting back to happier times and sat for a long time, daydreaming about previous vacations in Hawaii. Her mind wandered through the islands, wondering if they would ever return. They had enjoyed such fun times there with the children.

In her mind's eye, she watched them throwing coconuts they found beneath the palms along the shore, attempting in vain to crack them open. She watched as Suzan jumped into the hotel pool, went under, and started to scream. Roger, knowing she had just panicked, threw her a towel, which she pulled into the pool with her. Recovering, she swam to the side and gave her father a rather disgusted look, stating, "Some help you are! A towel?"

The entire family had a good laugh, and Suzan decided to join in the gaiety, her anger short-lived. It was such a beautiful area filled with many shades of greenery and multicolored flowers swaying slowly in the soft breezes.

Thoroughly warmed and relaxed, Leah dried off, pulled on her nightgown, and went down to the bedroom. As she started into the room, Roger moaned loudly, a heart-wrenching moan. She slowly turned and climbed the stairs to the upstairs bedroom, too tired to stay awake. She remembered the same sounds after his first heart surgery, which the doctor had said was due to subconscious memories and not from any discomfort. She slept soundly but awoke as tired as when she went to bed.

She dressed, made coffee, and read the paper before she heard Roger stirring. He had wanted to know where she had slept and why she had gone upstairs. She told him he was sleeping so soundly that she didn't want to chance waking him.

"What would you like for breakfast today?" Leah asked cheerily as Roger finished his coffee.

She had taken the coffee pot down to the bedroom, and they had enjoyed their morning coffee, basking in the bright sunshine pouring in on the light gray driftwood paneling that framed the flowering strawberry plants outside the window. His big, brown eyes stared at her a long time before he answered.

"Fr...uit...ca...ke."

"Fruitcake?" Leah repeated puzzled.

She climbed the few stairs to the main level and entered the kitchen. Then she smiled. Roger had never cared for fruitcake, but he did like cereal with bananas, so she deduced he must mean that. As he entered the dining room, she pulled three of his favorite cereals out of the cupboard and held them out to him. He smiled and pointed to the rice cereal, and she knew she had made the correct deduction. She took in a pitcher of milk, bananas, toast, and the cereal. He ate a good breakfast as she munched on her toast and coffee.

Several days passed, each one bringing more challenges determining what he wanted or was talking about with only one or two words to go on. Friends came to visit and tried to talk with Roger, but it was obvious he understood little of what was being discussed. Even coworkers' tales of mischief and antics at the office just invoked a half-hearted smile when they had always kept Roger in stitches before. Leah wanted to cry every time she saw the bewildered, frustrated, or faraway looks in his eyes. She wanted so badly to help him, but all she could do was put her arms around him and squeeze him, hoping he understood how much she loved him and was willing to do to help if she only knew how.

On one of their visits, someone mentioned Tom and Ray. Roger had looked up questioningly. Leah had told them to go ahead and tell him the truth, and his reaction had been shock followed by unfathomable sadness. It had put him in a gloom for two days, and his color had become gray again, but he didn't want to discuss it. Leah let him work it out in his own way. They had been his close friends.

Showering was a very traumatic experience. Roger had shook his head 'no' when she offered to sit in the bathroom, insistent he could do fine alone, but Leah had waited outside the door fearful he would slip getting out of the tub. It was exhausting, keeping poised to burst in if needed and straining her ears to hear his every move. She seriously considered having a walk-in shower installed or at least a peephole.

Dave and Cindy came, Suzan and Melanie came, and neighbors came. Roger just sat trying to look attentive but only attempted to talk one-on-one. If several were around talking, he just sat staring into space. Numerous times, Leah found him sitting alone, head in his hands, as if trying to figure something out. He seemed so lost, and the pain of seeing him like that crushed her. At times, she felt as if she couldn't breathe, choked by the tears she couldn't release.

"Leah, this is Donna. Have I called at a bad time? No? Good! How's Roger?" It was a lady they had done business with in the past. She had called several times during the past two weeks since he was home keeping tabs on his progress.

"He's doing well physically, but it's so hard to tell about his mental and emotional state. He says so little and never complains, but I don't see any great strides in progress. He can manage phrases and is better able to communicate his needs and wants, but it's so slow. He seems very tired and sleeps a lot. I'm never sure what to do to help him improve."

"It must be very hard for you; I wouldn't begin to know what to do. He is such a sweetheart; it must be agony for him too."

"I'm sure it is. He looks so lost sometimes."

"I think of you all so often and was talking to a friend about Roger. I don't know how you feel about holistic medicine, but my friend is really into it. She told me to tell you that the scent, flavor, and color of orange are very helpful to stroke victims."

"I know nothing about holistic medicine, but I don't know how using orange could hurt him. I'll try anything that won't do harm."

They talked a bit longer, and then Leah thanked her for calling and for the information as she hung up and thought about what Donna had said.

Leah got out the orange place mats she had intended to put in a garage sale. She found orange-scented and colored candles and placed them around the living room and bedrooms. A few days later, she went shopping and found an orange-striped sheet for the bed along with an orange apron. She also found an orange blouse but decided against it as the color made her look really bad, and she didn't think it would help Roger if she looked awful.

She stocked up on orange juice, mandarin oranges, navel oranges, orange Jell-O, orange room freshener, and orange-scented oil; everything she could find. Roger had always liked oranges, so incorporating lots into his diet was no problem. Max had come to stay with Roger while she made each shopping trip. They had a lot in common, and Roger enjoyed his company. He seemed to talk more easily to him.

If Roger wondered about all the orange, he didn't complain. The house constantly smelled of orange. Leah figured it must not be too much as no one who came to see them mentioned it. Max certainly would have, if no one else, as he was almost family and gave them lots of advice about many things.

Life seemed to be going along rather smoothly, and Leah was constantly sending up her 'arrow prayers,' thanking God for all his help, requesting strength, and covering for any problems she didn't know about. There were so many of those as there had never been any strokes in their family or circle of friends until Tom, and she chose not to consider that one. Everyone seemed to be understanding of Roger's inability to hold up his end of a conversation, but then the visits dropped off, and she was trying to find more ways to entertain and challenge him to talk. TV had been a comfort in past years as he watched CNN for news and stock information, but now he didn't seem to understand what he watched. She tried reading to him and working on words and names, but he got frustrated quickly and wouldn't continue. Monday would be his first speech therapy. Leah had high hopes.

Chapter 6

Leah drove a melancholy Roger to the hospital for his speech therapy session on Monday. The therapist was friendly, but Roger did not seem happy to be there. When he came out of the session, he was frowning. As they drove home, he was silent, lost in his own thoughts. Leah felt something was wrong.

After dinner, she sat beside him and asked about the session, wondering if he felt he was improving and if he felt the therapy was helping.

"No…not…help…ing! No…good!" Roger managed to get out.

"Is it because the material doesn't interest you?" Roger shook his head yes.

"Surely we can find some material that will. Perhaps she could get something related to your work."

That seemed to perk him up, and Leah told him she would call the therapist. The next day, she called only to learn the therapist knew nothing about Roger's interests or work and could only use the material she had as she had to work within the hospital guidelines. Leah felt very frustrated and went about the next few days thinking of little else.

The next session at the hospital brought forth several words of displeasure at having to return to "this place." Leah realized

Roger was put in a depressed state just by entering the building. Why wouldn't he be? It certainly didn't conjure up any pleasant memories for her either, and he had been forced to spend too much time there already.

That afternoon, she searched the phone book and found only two independent speech therapists listed. She called both. The first one was very anxious to work with Roger after Leah explained the situation. However, during the course of the conversation, she stated she usually worked with children, so Leah knew it wouldn't work. The second one said she understood the problem and would be happy to work out the material to spark his interest. Leah made an appointment for the following week and said a little prayer that it was the right thing to do. She then called the hospital to inform them they were changing because the hospital depressed Roger. They were very understanding and said it would not be a problem.

Roger seemed enthused when she told him about the change and went down to his file cabinet. He came back up with some papers related to his job and handed them to Leah. She filled with excitement when she saw them. It was the first time Roger had taken the initiative to help himself, and it indicated real thought and memory processes.

Men called from the office to inquire if Roger felt like company, and Leah was delighted. Three came, and Roger just sat smiling and looking from one to the other. Leah could tell he couldn't understand much of the conversation, if any of it. He went to the bathroom, and Leah quietly explained he could only understand one at a time and only if they spoke slowly. They did their best and told Leah they would try to visit one at a time in the future. She explained how much they appreciated their concern and how much he needed the visits, even if he didn't respond much.

The children quickly realized their father couldn't keep up with multiple conversations, so they began to visit separately and tried to converse one-on-one. Dave especially seemed to incite attempts at communication from Roger. They had always been very close, and Roger had missed him terribly when he left for college. He had been overjoyed when Dave and Cindy moved back, both finding jobs in Alaska. They lived just twenty miles away, so they could visit often.

The following week, Leah and Roger visited the new speech therapist, and Roger seemed entirely different when the session was finished. The building looked like any office building and had an atrium filled with healthy exotic plants. It had a completely different atmosphere from the hospital, and Roger's response was much better.

The therapist encouraged Roger to try to tell her about his work. She tested both Leah and Roger. Roger's comprehension was only approximately eighty words per minute, and Leah's normal speech was one hundred and fifty. She gave Leah some pamphlets on strokes and aphasia, or speechlessness. They were both enlightening and encouraging; there were several types of aphasia.

Leah determined that Roger fit more the description of Broca's aphasia as he seemed to know what he wanted to say and write but couldn't quite manage it. He also had difficulty producing the names of people or objects, frequently getting them wrong, which was called anomic aphasia. His inability to read and write was called alexia and agraphia. The pamphlets explained the condition and the treatment. They gave his problems a name but little else except that most patients improved greatly with therapy and counseling; Leah learned the best approach for patients is to let them struggle and finish the sentence as best they can, regardless of how long or hard it was.

This was extremely difficult for Leah; watching Roger struggle tore at her heart, and she caught herself many times trying to anticipate what he wanted to communicate and finish it for him. She would have to work on that. She would have to try to slow down when she talked to him.

On the drive home, Roger showed Leah some exercises he had done. His writing was still labored and most words were misspelled, but he seemed pleased with what he had accomplished, so Leah praised his efforts and prayed he would make it all the way back and soon. It hurt so much to see her husband in this condition.

It was a beautiful sunny day, so Leah suggested they go for a drive after lunch. Roger had been at home for almost a month and was showing signs of boredom and a need for entertainment. TV was about the most he had, and Leah still wasn't sure he understood much of that. Roger was enthused and directed her as she drove the car to the outskirts of the city.

They had two mountain ranges and the ocean surrounding the town; one mountain range could be seen from their picture window, which displayed a beautiful knoll as if painted on their living room wall. The swamp spruce trees were spindly and few stood straight, but many types of birch intermingled, giving the landscape color and a more elegant appearance. Wild irises sprinkled purple around, and Roger seemed to want to see it all.

He began to attempt to tell her about various landmarks. Leah looked at him closely and asked if he had been there before as it was a new area to her. He nodded and laboriously managed to convey to her that he had surveyed it for materials for a job. Leah was really excited now as the area seemed to spark memories and get him talking about past experiences. He seemed more relaxed and talked better when telling her about his work, though it took a long time to get it out.

They drove around for almost two hours before Roger got tired and wanted to go home for a nap. He had talked more during those two hours than any time since the stroke, and Leah was sure she had hit on a way to encourage him to try harder to communicate.

They drove home, and Roger lay down on the sofa while Leah started dinner. Tonight was veggie fajitas with Mexican rice and beans. He seemed to like most meals, although she was never sure he liked anything very much. His tastes seemed to have changed, but Leah continued to work at making his former favorites low fat and low calorie.

She finished the relish dish of radishes, pickled peppers, and green onions and placed it on the table. She called to Roger and took the fajitas in. Roger ambled to the table, sat down, and took a survey of what was set before him.

"Hungry?" Leah inquired. "I hope you like this Mexican dinner. It's pretty spicy."

"Can't ... taste," Roger replied as he took a bite of his fajita.

He had always loved hot sauce and very spicy foods. Leah was surprised to hear he couldn't taste all the cilantro she had used.

"You can't taste all the spices—garlic, cilantro, chili powder—I used? I was afraid it might be too much."

"Can't ... taste ... anything!"

"You can't taste anything?"

Roger nodded yes.

"You haven't been able to taste anything since your stroke?" Leah asked, quite shocked at this revelation. Roger nodded yes again.

Leah sat back in her chair and nearly choked as she thought of all the time she had spent preparing meals, trying to make them tasty and appealing to the eye as well. She had spent lots of time reading and experimenting with spices and felt exasperated to learn it had all been useless. Oh, well, she thought, at least I learned a lot. A lesson in futility; another 'wait and see.'

Leah had to chuckle to herself. At least she could laugh about it, and the laughs had been few the past weeks. Roger gave her smiling face a questioning look.

"I've learned a lot about spices and revising your favorite recipes. Good thing you didn't tell me sooner you couldn't taste anything. I could have given you bread and water...and oranges!"

Roger looked at her for a moment letting the words sink in. Then he laughed; it was the husky laugh he'd had since the stroke, not the deep hearty laugh he'd had before, but it made Leah feel happy just the same. She longed for the sound of the voice of the man she had married, longed for him to hold her tight and tell her all their problems were over, and he would take over again. She longed to crawl into bed beside his warm body and have him hold and caress her as he had done so many times before. She wondered if they would ever regain the intimacy they had enjoyed before. However, each day he showed more signs of his old personality. They were okay!

The next day dawned bright and beautiful, and Leah noticed the yard was in need of cutting. She called the boys who usually took care of it for them only to learn they were out of town on vacation for two more weeks. She remembered they had told her several weeks ago but so much had happened. She decided she would cut it herself before they took a drive. She had the mower going and the front yard finished when Roger came out and sat on the patio. He looked sad and frustrated, so Leah shut off the mower and went to sit with him.

"Time for a break! How about a glass of iced tea?"

Roger nodded yes. As Leah handed him the cold drink, he looked up at her and muttered, "Feel bad."

"What? Where do you feel bad?" Icy fear gripped Leah!

"My job ... grass. No use."

Leah understood immediately; it wasn't where but why. Roger had always taken great pride in his lovely lawn. She felt the warmth return to her body. Recovering her voice, she gave her best effort to sound encouraging.

"You've done your share of yard work. I'm enjoying the exercise," Leah lied.

Roger smiled knowingly as Leah had always hated starting the lawn mower and emptying the grass clippings. That was Roger's job or that of the neighbor boys while Leah cultivated her flowers and vegetables and house plants. They had certainly been neglected this summer but still managed to survive and color the yard with the many perennials Leah had collected over the years. The rhubarb was in seed as she had no time to fool with cutting and freezing it. She and Roger ate very little as it took too much sugar, but Dave had loved it and the many cakes and pies she had made with it when he was at home.

She recalled once when she had made rhubarb sauce with the strawberry rhubarb, and Dave had made a real pig of himself. He must have eaten at least two cups of it and later screamed from the bathroom, "Mom! Come quick! Something's wrong!" She had run downstairs to find the toilet bowl full of red and Dave sure he was bleeding to death. She had explained the rhubarb had turned his urine red, and he was going to live!

The garden area was covered with weeds now. She had turned the soil and raked it smooth but had never planted this year. No time. She smiled as she remembered the first year of the garden when she had solicited advice from friends in her club. They told her they always planted by the moon. She mulled it over in her mind, wondering how they did that and finally asked, "Do you use a flashlight or what?" Not a farmer's daughter!

She looked back at Roger. She hated to see the hurt and feelings of worthlessness in his eyes. It must be so hard to deal with watching others do the things you had always enjoyed and taken pride in.

"You are a great supervisor. That's the tough job."

She gave him a kiss and went back to work after draining her tea. She wished she knew how to handle it better but was at a loss, so she would just hurry and finish.

Cory stood up, contemplating following her but decided, after a look at Roger, to stay and keep him company. He laid down next to Roger inviting some petting.

Chapter 7

That night, Roger handed her the papers they had prepared to put the house on the market. Before the surgery and subsequent stroke had occurred, they had been making plans for retirement and had purchased a condo two years before. They had been preparing to sell the house, figuring it would take awhile. Leah knew Roger wanted to go ahead with their plans, so she told him she would call the Realtor the next day and get things started. She felt rather sad to think of leaving Alaska with the three children there and the home they had been raised in. There were so many memories. However, she felt sure it would take a year or longer to sell as the market had been falling the past several months.

The right side of Roger's mouth drooped slightly as he smiled, though the paralysis seemed to have left some time ago. Leah wondered how long until his smile would be normal; however, she took notice of the confidence in his eyes. He had regained a little of his self-assurance, making a definite decision so Leah knew they would be selling the house. She was cheered to see the confidence return but sad to realize what had brought it back. She really didn't want to face any more changes just now and hoped she was right about the sale taking some time.

The next morning, Leah called the Realtor Roger had picked out and made an appointment. They met that afternoon, and the contract was signed. Roger asked several questions, which Leah translated for the Realtor. She explained Roger's health condition and requested he be sure to check all transactions with Leah to keep any stress off Roger and to eliminate the possibility of any misunderstanding.

That afternoon the sign was placed in the front yard, giving Leah a queasy feeling every time she looked at it. Melanie came by that evening and was very upset about the 'For Sale' sign.

"Why didn't you let us children know what you were planning before we had to see the sign? I feel like this is my childhood being sold!"

"We didn't realize all would happen so fast, and I am sorry. Dad made the decision last night, we called this morning, and the sign arrived this afternoon."

"Did they have to put it right up?"

"I must admit it was too fast for me, and I share your feelings, but Dad wanted to get going on it."

"Well, Mom, you have a say in it too."

"I feel like I'll be leaving a part of my past when we leave this house. I know I have a say, but your dad is so excited that he made the decision. I don't want to interfere. Besides, the warmer climate and more sun may be good for him and help him improve faster."

Melanie had a more sympathetic tone as she told her mother she did understand, just had to get over the shock of it.

"Where's Dad?"

"Upstairs asleep."

"Are you real sure he can take the stress of moving? And can you? It's pretty soon!"

They walked into the kitchen, and Leah poured them both some coffee and placed two muffins on a plate. They sat at the dining table and wrapped their fingers around the warm mugs.

"Be sure to tell Suzan, and I would appreciate it if you would call Dave and Cindy for me. I don't really care to discuss it right now, okay?"

"Sure."

Melanie agreed, and Leah explained to her what had transpired in the past few days since they had last seen her. They talked almost every day on the telephone, but it seemed so much was happening that they couldn't cover it all. Leah really enjoyed their visit and begged her to come again soon and often, though she knew the children kept very busy schedules. She was really feeling lonely these days with Roger unable to converse normally and lost in his own thoughts a large amount of the time.

"I wish I could change things, Mother, but it'll be alright." Melanie gave her mother a big hug and kiss and headed out the door.

The next day, Leah and Roger had an appointment with Roger's cardiologist and entered the waiting room to find the other stroke patient Leah had visited in hospital sitting there.

"How good to see you," Leah said. "Do you remember me?" He just stared unknowingly at her.

"My husband was in the hospital for the same surgery at the same time you were. He also had a stroke five days later. I visited you a few times. You can see he's doing quite well."

"I'm doing okay. Back at work," he replied confidently.

"That's fantastic! And your speech is so good. Roger still has some difficulty there."

"Oh, I can talk fine. I just wish I could keep thoughts together. I have trouble figuring things out and staying on one idea ... makes it hard to work." He looked down and rather sad as he said it.

Leah felt very sorry for him and also wondered why he was working again so soon if it put such a strain on him. Maybe he had to for the income.

"Well, you look great, and I'm very glad we met here. Do take care of yourself. Good luck."

Leah walked over and sat by Roger, seeing the puzzled look on his face and realizing he had no idea who she was talking to. She felt very sorry for the lost look in the man's eyes and hoped Roger didn't feel that way. She explained they had been through the same ordeal a week apart and that he was working again. Roger looked surprised and asked the doctor about him. He explained that his stroke had been different from Roger's in that it seemed milder, with no paralysis. Roger seemed to forget about it after that. The doctor did a few tests and said all seemed to be going well and repeated they would just have to 'wait and see.' That was the only answer to her many questions and she had come to dislike the phrase intensely.

It was only two days later when the first call came to show the house. Cory was intrigued by all the activity but seemed to be dismayed that so many changes were taking place. He had always seemed to know what was going on and could make his displeasure clear. Leah was just as upset as she had never expected any activity this soon.

That night, she called the girls and asked if they would take Cory if the house sold and they moved. Suzan and Melanie were thrilled as they had wanted him since the day they moved out of the house into the condo they shared. It was only a short distance away, but it might as well be in the next town as they were so busy with work and activities they normally saw Leah and Roger only a couple times a month. They called daily, especially since their father's stroke, and Leah knew they would do anything they were asked. She also knew Cory would be happy with them and would have good care. She would have been reluctant to have him left alone since they both worked and had active social lives had he been younger. But the advancing years had slowed him greatly, and sleeping during a large part of each day was on his agenda anyway.

Melanie had hearing loss that was discovered at age eighteen, just after Dave and Cindy's wedding. Cory had slept in her bedroom after that as he was a great safety alarm in case of any problem. Leah had often been concerned after she moved in with Suzan but felt they would help each other, though she knew it was only temporary. They each did their own thing and were very independent, and Leah fully expected one of them to be getting married before long. At any rate, Cory would have a good home with them.

Cory had been given to the family by a neighbor who had sworn he was un-trainable and a real nuisance to have around. Leah had fallen in love with him the instant she saw him but had told the dog he would learn to live with her as she had no intention of changing anything to live with him. He had been very easy to train in all aspects, needing only one or two times to be told or shown what was expected of him. He had brought so much love and pleasure to the family and had been great therapy for any ailing or depressed member. Now she felt she was doing the best thing for him, but it added to her feelings of losing the past.

Both girls expressed concern that they might be losing their parents sooner than they had anticipated. Leah assured them it was far from sold and could take years. She just wanted everything arranged in advance. That was Leah...always preparing well in advance. Last minute preparations for anything threw her into a tailspin. She knew she had better start the tedious chore of eliminating and packing soon.

She had a hard time sleeping that night and caught herself praying the house wouldn't sell for at least a year. It was now September...maybe next summer...or early fall...just in time to move before the weather was really cold. A shiver came over her, and she snuggled deep into the blankets and finally dozed off.

During the rest of the fall, Leah and Roger continued their drives around town and the speech therapy. Leah could see marked improvement, and Roger's writing was legible now, though she had to correct his spelling often. But, in truth, he had never been a good speller.

He had gone back to work late in August and made the decision to retire almost immediately. Leah had asked him if communicating with his colleagues was difficult, and he had replied it was not as few tried to talk to him. Leah felt a stab at her heart again as Roger told her about it as she had observed similar reactions from business people on the rare occasions when he attempted to convey his needs to them.

It hurt, but she realized almost no one knew how to react to stroke victims. Roger was often treated as if he was feeble-minded or had difficulty hearing, and sales people constantly finished his sentences for him, almost always getting it wrong. This really frustrated Roger, and he refused to try more and more. She had observed occasional angry looks and mutterings because no one wanted to wait to let him express his needs or desires. She had taken over the task of paying all the bills, something Roger had always done.

She had received a past-due notice from a bank in the northwest and had realized she didn't even know what it was for. She went through all their papers and laboriously educated herself on their business affairs. The bank in the northwest had been taking care of the condo payments from the rent payments and had failed to inform her when they hadn't come in. She arranged for a property management company to take care of it, mailing all rent payments to her, and then wrote the bank to close the account as she would make the loan payments herself.

During the next few weeks, she set up a system she could work with, and no more problems occurred. She had often been angry with herself for not keeping abreast of their finances but vowed she would never be ignorant of them again. She had taken care of the finances when they were first married and couldn't remember when she had relinquished the job to Roger; probably after the children were born and she was busy learning to be a mother.

She had loved having the children around as they grew up and could never understand the mothers who looked forward to school starting. Leah had spent the summers entertaining them and doing the ball playing, picnicking, hiking, and exploring the children loved to do. Roger's work kept him at remote sites during most of the long days of summer when work was done around the clock. The first day of school was always lonely and sad for her, so she would plan activities to keep her busy and away from the quietness of the house until time for them to be home. Then it was a joy to hear about their accomplishments and events at school.

She recalled the time she had been gone most of the first school day, leaving Cory alone in the garage. He was limping when she returned, making her feel guilty and wondering how he had hurt himself. She gave him some petting, and he seemed better until the first child came home. It then hurt terribly until their sympathy made it better. As the third child came home, Leah realized he was limping on the opposite leg and reprimanded him for 'faking.' He had tucked his tail and gone to the stairs with no limp at all. She wasn't the only one who enjoyed having them home!

There had been little activity on the house, so Leah was feeling quite settled when the call came that a previous prospect wanted to see it again. Three days later, they had an offer. It was almost twenty-thousand dollars less than the asking price, so Leah was sure Roger would refuse. She was extremely shocked when he countered only five thousand higher, and it was accepted. Roger managed to convey that he felt the soft market and falling prices made the price a really good one. Leah wondered if those were really his words or the Realtor's. He seemed to be processing information better at any rate, and that encouraged her. She gave him the brightest smile she could muster and told him she had lots to do. Grinning his mischievous grin he replied, "You...sure...do!"

Leah was really feeling panicky now as she had twenty years of accumulation to deal with. The under-house storage was also jammed with numerous boxes of mementos the children hadn't had room for when they moved out. She didn't know what they were going to do with them, but they would have to deal with their own things. She still had many mementoes of their childhood she would have to find room for. They would undoubtedly have to rent some storage space. Her inner voice began to reprimand her, telling her to slow down and quit getting ahead of herself. She would have time to cover each base as she rounded it. Just take care of each day's chores and stop worrying about all the rest. She said a short prayer that she could get through this. Hadn't God enabled her to deal with everything else?

The Realtor went over the terms with them and all seemed agreeable. It usually took close to a month to close, but they would need to be ready to move when it did. The buyers could insist on occupancy within twenty-four hours, although Leah couldn't imagine anyone being in that big of a hurry. She had never made such demands or even requests when they had purchased homes and felt the Realtor was being unnecessarily alarming. She would do the best she could!

Roger had mentioned updating the abstract a couple of times only to be told by the Realtor to wait as it probably wouldn't be needed. He again asked about it, informing him he had friends in the profession who would do it for him and was again told to wait. He couldn't understand him wanting to wait but didn't want to upset him so dropped it.

The following day, the Realtor called with some requests of the buyers, and Leah told him they could have first opportunity but she would not give all the appliances, garden supplies, and equipment with the sale. They seemed to think since they were leaving the state, they should leave everything with the house.

That involved a lot of money for all the things they had acquired over the years, and Roger took good care of his tools. She intended to have a garage sale and advertise the more expensive items.

That afternoon, she went to the grocery store while Max visited with Roger. She took a little extra time to do some mall shopping when she saw they were having a sidewalk sale. She found a shorts-and-shirt set as well as swim trunks and a shirt to match for Roger and then found shorts and a blouse for herself. They would all be great for traveling, and she hoped she could talk Roger into taking some extra time in southern California. She even took time to make an appointment for a haircut the following week.

When she returned, she learned the Realtor had called and talked Roger into more points on the loan. Leah was upset as she telephoned but managed to be congenial while informing him if he went behind her back over anything else, she would refuse the sale and remove him from any future transactions. She felt it was obvious he was taking advantage of Roger's stroke to talk him into what Leah had refused. Leah was rather surprised about it afterward as she wasn't accustomed to being forceful or aggressive.

The next couple of weeks were a whirlwind of phone calls from both Realtors trying to negotiate various changes, none of which were to their benefit. Since it was a buyer's market, both Realtors kept reminding them, they seemed to be catering to the buyers' every whim. Leah finally had enough and told them to cancel the sale. That got everyone into turmoil so she relented, but they no longer bothered her or Roger.

A week later the real clincher came. The Realtor called to inform them the buyers were demanding a current abstract, and he had taken care of making an appointment for that afternoon with a local engineering firm. It had to be done immediately. Roger was furious as he could have had it done months before by a friend at no cost. It was too late now, and the surveyor arrived shortly and spent about thirty minutes asking about changes and looking around outside then left.

The following week, a bill arrived for 350 dollars, and Roger really hit the ceiling. Leah calmed him down, fearful he would have another stroke; she was upset enough for both of them. She called the engineering firm only to be informed the Realtor had insisted it be done immediately, so they had charged the full amount. After Leah argued that was pointless as they were the ones paying the bill, they agreed to take one hundred dollars off; a bit better.

Leah managed to advertise the appliances after calling the Realtor to give the buyers the first opportunity. When she had heard nothing from them in ten days, she sold everything within a week. Then the garage sale went very well, considering a disaster was narrowly avoided.

Roger brought several things up from the storage under the house and put them out for sale. One item was a wooden chest he was about to sell for five dollars when Leah discovered it contained several lenses and cases to their thirty-five-millimeter camera, a telescope, and binoculars. After that, she carefully watched every transaction. One did slip by; the artificial Christmas tree they had decorated for sixteen years was sold for five dollars; Leah decided it was Roger's favorite sum. That was okay except that he forgot to take out the numerous strings of lights and several handmade ornaments they had been given, some by family members now deceased. Leah didn't realize it until they were gone but was too tired to let it upset her for long.

All in all, it was not a bad two days, and they had rid themselves of a lot of excess baggage for the move. The condo was less than a thousand square feet and could hold just so much. Leah wasn't even sure if there was room for the bedroom suite as it was rather large. They had purchased it before moving to Alaska, and it was good solid wood. She sure wasn't going to part with it.

The following week, Leah took Roger to his speech therapy session and ran some errands. When she returned, he was waiting, looking very proud of himself, and held out his hand with three fifty dollar bills in it.

"I just bought your snow blower," said the therapist.

Leah gasped. They had purchased it the previous spring on sale for four hundred and fifty dollars, original price six hundred dollars. It had been started and used one time for about thirty minutes. She had planned to advertise it that week for at least three hundred and take no less than two fifty.

"He said you were going to sell it, and I asked how much he wanted for it. He said you would store it until you move, so I can give it to my husband for Christmas."

Leah opened her mouth then closed it. She knew Roger had no idea of the value or memory of what had been paid, and she should make all transactions. However, Roger looked so pleased with himself, she didn't have the heart to chance hurting him so she smiled at him and said, "Sure."

If she had only known how often this would happen in the future, she might have been able to prevent some of the agonies in store. Unfortunately, she had no preparation for the trials she would be facing for years to come or the unkindness of strangers to someone different.

They drove home, had lunch, and Roger took a nap. Leah was still upset though she knew it was only money. She called Dave and discussed the incident with him. Dave could always calm her and make her feel it was no big thing. He rarely let small incidents get to him. He suggested he talk with Roger about staying out of the moving process, but Leah felt it would be unwise. Roger liked to feel he was making the decisions, though he looked to her to make most of them.

She poured herself a cup of coffee and surveyed the room. She would need to advertise the furniture as soon as they had a closing date for the house. The champagne-colored plush carpet still looked almost new, and the satin drapes matched perfectly. They had vacuumed beautifully and looked new also. The Thomasville sofa of teal blue and chairs of a teal and multi-print had worn well for twenty years and would still bring almost as much as originally paid, as should the Lane end tables of solid oak.

Good solid wood furniture retained its value, and she knew hers had many good years left. She really didn't want to part with it but knew it would never fit in the condo. The tables matched the oak paneling on the fireplace wall and should stay with it. She had heard nothing from the buyers so decided she would sell them too.

This was such a painful thing to go through—selling off one's things as if selling pieces of one's self. She had finished painting the outside the year before after Roger had been called out of town. She was afraid of heights, and the two story high south wall was all that remained. She had climbed the extension ladder, painting without looking down. Of course, she received several phone calls during the time she was up there so came down once and told the children to take numbers, and she would return calls when she finished. She was not going to climb that ladder one time more than necessary.

The house had rough siding, charcoal with salmon-colored trim in front when they bought it. She had immediately covered the salmon with moon-mist gray. Time caused the trim to crack, and she had lovingly scraped, sanded, and painted, giving her the feeling of putting some of her very own sweat and blood into that house. Leah felt very tired and alone. She needed Roger's help with all this as well as his easygoing manner but knew she would have to tackle it alone this time. She just couldn't burden his mind with unnecessary small concerns. Soon she heard him stirring. October had flown by and November wasn't slowing.

"How about a drive? It's a little cold, but the sunshine is beautiful and will be setting in about two hours. What do you say?"

"Okay," Roger replied and began to get ready.

Leah drove through the downtown area and then out to the new shopping center under construction on the outskirts of the city. A big, new welcome sign had been erected and landscaped around with shrubs and flowers. Roger gazed at it for several minutes, frowning and shaking his head.

"Don't re...member..."

"That's quite alright, dear, as I've never seen it before either. It must have been put up this fall. Lots of changes are taking place. This used to be the city limits, but it's now moving this way. Soon it will probably be the heart of the city."

They watched the sun go down as they returned home. The sky was bright red and orange, shading into pink and peach, and ultimately into pale pink and lavender as soft clouds drifted by and made way for dark blue sky. Leah loved the sunrises and sunsets in Alaska, most of all the ones in winter when ice fog froze in the air and looked like diamonds glistening. The frost on trees and bushes glistened with the colors of the sun—ruby reds, topaz orange, citrine, amethyst, sapphire and aquamarine, and gold and silver as the sun rose or sank behind them, making the atmosphere appear to be jeweled.

She would really miss the winters when she painted, sewed, knitted, and enjoyed the scenery. Skiing had not been mastered, so she spent the long winters creating and taking long walks through the woods with Roger. They had sighted moose and sheep numerous times and many different tracks in the snow. So many memories! It would be so hard to leave!

Dave called and said he and Cindy would be over the next day, Saturday, so Leah could get out for a while and do some shopping. Christmas was just around the corner, so she looked forward to getting a few presents. The move would take all her energy, so the more she could get done now, the better. She had been thinking about what each of her family members would like— now to find it!

Saturday dawned a beautiful crisp day; Dave and Cindy arrived shortly after noon. Leah took off after being told to stay all afternoon. Cindy would prepare dinner. She did appreciate them so much and all their love and help. She was thanking God for her precious family as she drove away. She headed straight to the shopping center.

She ran into several friends she hadn't seen for some time and visited as much as shopped. She did find several items and had Christmas almost covered. Then she decided to stop in the liquor store for a bottle of wine. Perhaps it would help her sleep better if she had a glass before bed.

"I'm not sure about this wine," she said to the liquor store clerk, a pleasant, middle-aged woman. "I like a medium-dry sipping wine. I thought a glass before bed would help me sleep."

"That one is a good choice, but I have a Johannesburg Riesling on sale that is very good. I like a medium-dry wine myself, and this is one of my favorites. I don't know a lot about wines but after my husband's stroke, I began to try some to help me sleep too."

"Really?" Leah said very surprised as her eyes opened wide. "My husband had a stroke four months ago. How long ago was your husband's, and how is he doing?"

"Oh, it was three years ago, and I had to put him in a home. He became violent after regaining some of his physical abilities, and he was so big, I couldn't handle him. His mind just didn't seem to work right anymore."

Leah felt faint as she paid for the wine. She was so shocked the woman could speak so candidly about it. She could never even imagine Roger becoming violent or putting him in an institution. He had displayed a somewhat volatile temperament after his first bypass surgery, but the frustration certainly justified the anger.

"I'm sorry," Leah answered, genuinely shook. "Mine is doing fine. He seems to improve each day. Good luck to you." She was more trying to convince herself than converse with the woman. With that, she hurried out and decided to go home. She was quite shaken and wished she hadn't gone in there. She drove home, still thinking about the incident in the liquor store.

Chapter 8

As she entered the house, she could smell spaghetti sauce and garlic and realized she hadn't eaten since breakfast. She was hungry!

Cindy had the table and dinner ready and began carrying in the salad, spaghetti, and garlic bread as Leah took off her coat and put down the packages. Dave had met her at the car and carried most of them upstairs to the spare room.

Dinner was delicious, and she and Cindy visited as they cleared the dishes. Cindy told her Roger and Dave had talked some as they watched the football game, and they thought he was talking a lot better. They left a short time later as Dave had a lesson to prepare for the next morning, and Roger seemed tired. He went to bed soon after, and Leah poured herself a glass of wine and went up to take a bubble bath.

She soaked and sipped for almost an hour and really let her mind wander and go blank. She felt much more relaxed afterward and forgot about the woman in the liquor store. There was no similarity to them; she was sure of it!

The next few weeks were very busy selling the furniture and packing. They had decided to store everything in Seattle, ship the car there, and fly down. They would stay with Dave and

Cindy until after the holidays and then pick up the car and travel down the West coast, across the Southwest to Texas, and up to Oklahoma to visit the families there.

Leah's mother lived alone and didn't drive, so she loved to have them visit and get her out of the house. Roger had always been very fond of her, and the feeling was mutual. She had been used to spoiling Leah's father and now gave all the attention to Roger. They would spend several months traveling seeing family and friends they hadn't seen for years. Roger seemed very enthusiastic about the plans and leaving Alaska. He had loved this state so much, but his health problems made it less attractive to him. The cold weather was much more difficult since the staples had been put in his chest and the darkness increased the depression he felt, so he decided he had spent enough time in the cold north country.

Leah had been reluctant to take Roger away from his doctor and speech therapy but had been assured he would be fine. She had observed him reading Reader's Digest several times and had spent time determining how much he understood and had discussed with the therapist how to use it to help him. The magazine had so many articles of help with speech and lots of humor, so Leah packed a dozen issues to take along. She had obtained numerous work sheets for Roger to complete while she drove. He rarely spent time holding his head in his hands as he had done the first months after the stroke. Leah felt sure he had been trying to pull things from his memory and put thoughts together to make some sense.

Now he had good and bad days but seemed to understand so much more. Each thing he did correctly made him appear to feel more in control and gave him more confidence. He couldn't talk well enough yet to really express his feelings or ideas, but he was getting there; Leah was sure of it.

The day of closing arrived gray and cold. They were kept in one office while the buyers were kept in another, never allowed to converse. They had indicated an interest in keeping all her kitchen appliances, but she had waited a week for her Realtor to inform their Realtor they were for sale, never receiving a reply. She hoped they understood she had to get things done in a timely manner. The whole procedure seemed odd, but it was finally over, and they had one week to vacate.

The movers arrived two days later, and all was packed and loaded before six p.m. Max and Lorene had come to help but had taken Roger to their house when it became evident he was becoming stressed.

Leah was very thankful he was not present when she was given the papers to sign. There were a few boxes Leah had packed; ones containing some of the more valuable things to be shipped that she did not care to have the packers handle or know about. As she read over the papers and examined the boxes she found the number of packed by owner boxes had multiplied drastically. Nearly every box was marked PBO and noted on the shipping papers. She kept her cool, though she was seething inside, called the manager who had given the bid, and stated she would only sign the papers with the notations that all PBO boxes were in error and markings were nullified. Otherwise, all was to be removed from the van and unpacked. He agreed to the packers' dismay and Leah signed after making several notations and making the packers initial them. What next? she wondered.

Lorene had dinner ready when Leah arrived to check on Roger, so she ate. Lorene's homemade stew and light rolls really warmed her inside, and she was so grateful. Afterward, she felt so tired she begged them to forgive her for eating and running, but they understood, and she decided to go to Dave's for the night and return to clean the house the next day. There was little to be done, but Leah wanted to clean windows and vacuum. It was late when they arrived at Dave and Cindy's, so she showered and fell into bed exhausted. Roger was already sound asleep, so she decided to look over all the papers and file them the next day. There was still much to do before leaving town, and she was making a mental list when she fell asleep.

She arrived at the house after leaving Roger with Max to find the new owner there with carpet layers. A roll of the champagne carpet was lying at the curb and puzzled Leah. She went inside to find the living room carpet had already been ripped up and must have been what was at the curb. A new beige carpet covered most of the living room now and a new wooden railing went up the stairs.

The new owner informed her they had been upset that no refrigerator remained and wanted the old one in the garage moved into the kitchen. It had been given to them when a friend purchased a new one and was used for overflow and garden produce. She had no idea how old it was or how long it would keep running. Leah told her she could have it if her carpet layers would move it in for her. She also informed her of her efforts to let them know the appliances were for sale. She said they had never been told.

She heard the woman tell the workman she wanted the oak paneling removed from the fireplace wall, that beautiful oak paneling Leah had lovingly kept oiled and polished. Leah couldn't believe her ears but decided the sooner she left, the better. She knew the new owner needed to make it into her own just as Leah had when she and Roger bought it.

She stated she had come to clean the windows but was told no need, so she bid farewell and left. She wished she hadn't come back at all and hadn't heard and seen the changes being made. Then she realized it was no longer her home, and maybe seeing it would help her say good-bye to the house, the past, and Alaska. Sadly, she walked over to Max and Lorene's. At the door, she took a deep breath, put a big smile on her face, and told Roger she was ready to go.

They stayed with Dave and Cindy for the next three weeks while running around town taking care of all the final billings and closing accounts. It was an extremely busy time, and many friends and neighbors had asked them to stop by or come for a meal before they left, which was impossible with Christmas and all they had to do. Leah constantly wondered what was in store for them in the future and caught herself talking to God a lot, asking him to help her know what to do and not make mistakes. He was the only one she could depend on: the doctors gave her very little help, always telling her to 'wait and see'. How she hated that phrase! She had so many questions: How would Roger fair with the long trip they were planning? How would they adjust to living in a condo? How would she keep Roger on his diet while eating in restaurants?

Dave set up a computer disc for Leah and showed her how to use his word processing program well enough to write some letters. There was some unfinished business, and Dave agreed to take care of any actions while they were out of town.

Christmas arrived, and they had a great holiday with the children. They all expressed concern for what the next holiday would be like without Mom and Dad. Leah assured them they would be together one way or another, if only by phone. One of their gifts was a catalog of bed and breakfast inns with prices, phone numbers, and close attractions listed. Leah was anxious to read it as they traveled south. The packing was almost completed, the car had been shipped to Seattle, and they could now relax. January first arrived, and they boarded the airplane to Seattle.

Their friends were waiting when they arrived and took them to pick up their car that had been shipped. After careful inspection, it was determined everything had arrived in good shape. They spent the night and next day with them seeing some of Seattle then began their trip down the coast, starting at Astoria, Oregon.

The first day was gorgeous, with the sun shining on the Columbia River as they drove along. Roger seemed at ease and happy to have all the previous months of work and worry behind them. Leah most certainly was. It had all happened so fast that she could hardly believe she had made it with almost no problems. The furniture had arrived in Seattle and was secured in a storage facility awaiting their call to deliver it to the condo. She finally felt like she could relax for a while and settled back to enjoy the scenery.

She had obtained a written statement from the doctor that Roger was well enough and quite capable of driving and was stored with the registration in the glove compartment. Roger was happy to be able to drive again, though Leah had seen him hesitate before starting the car several times. At any rate, he was doing fine; he just needed directions. She was his navigator.

Astoria was a very picturesque town with lots of history. Situated where the Columbia River joins the Pacific Ocean, it had many beautiful buildings and large bridges that were very old and nostalgic. They drove through the town taking in all the sights then located a lovely motel and checked in for the night. By the time they unloaded the car, it was dark out, and they decided to drive through the town again, enjoying all the lights of the bridges and shops.

They located a seafood restaurant and had a dinner of fantastic grilled salmon for Roger and grilled halibut for Leah, the best they had eaten since last summer. They had friends in Galena and Fairbanks who sent fresh salmon, and one of their neighbors in Anchorage was a commercial fisherman and supplied them with halibut each season. One summer, Leah had purchased two small halibut, though Roger was out of town, not wanting to miss filling the freezer for winter. She and Dave had wrestled them on the back patio, finally achieving the cutting of steaks and cheeks, wrapping and freezing them. They found sea gulls in the driveway the next morning. They were used to wonderful fresh fish right out of the ocean that was so good for Roger, and Leah hoped they would be able to find a good supplier stateside.

They returned to the motel which had a spa and indoor pool, so they relaxed and exercised in the pool, and then Leah enjoyed the hot tub. It was too hot for Roger, so he sat and soaked his feet and watched her. There was no one else in the pool, so they stayed until they began to look like prunes. They decided they had better get out even though they were enjoying it immensely.

Back in the room, Leah gazed into the mirror. She found several lines she didn't think had been there before 'The Stroke' as she had come to refer to time—before or after 'The Stroke'. She showered after Roger and put on her gown and robe. Roger was waiting for her, looking very relaxed and happy as he reached out and gave her a very passionate kiss. This was a bit of a surprise as he had shown little interest in sex up to now, but she recognized the kiss and the look in his eyes. He held her close and whispered in her ear, "Let's get...uncomfortable!"

Leah smiled and gave him a big kiss, knowing, once again, he had said the opposite of what he meant. Shortly afterward, they were in bed, and Roger had no problem there, much to Leah's relief. Leah let out a big sigh as she lazily stretched out on the bed. They had just overcome another hurdle!

After Roger's first open-heart surgery, he had been impotent for a while. They had watched a show on television sometime before about a man who had suffered a stroke and was left impotent temporarily. Leah remembered the film well and had unknowingly filed the information in her subconscious. His failure had resulted in fear, feelings of inadequacy, and ultimately anger. Roger had gone through similar reactions, leading Leah to think he was feeling many of the same emotions. His anger had led to numerous arguments and, finally, plans to move out into an apartment. However, each time he was scheduled to leave, some obstacle presented itself so that he could not. There had been many times when Leah was ready to move him out herself as he had attacked her femininity, personality; every facet of her character. Two years later, he had stated he didn't know how she had held their life together during that period and hoped she could still love him. That had been the end of it, and their problems as well as Roger's impotency, were over.

Not this time! Leah could forget the fear of reliving those trials. They both slept very well and awoke to another beautiful sunny day. Leah made coffee and toast in the room before they checked out and continued on their way. She loved her French roast coffee first thing in the morning, so they carried a coffee pot and toaster whenever they traveled. Roger needed to eat something in order to take all his medications, and toast served the purpose without much fat. Breakfast was usually difficult to eat out as most restaurants prepared high fat eggs, bacon, and sausage. He did, however, love pancakes and sausages; 'pigs in blankets' he called them, and he did have them regularly. They decided to head out and stop later to eat.

They were following the ocean route, and the deep-blue water of the Pacific sparkled in the sun. It was a rugged, rocky, beautiful coastline, and the waves tumbled into the rocks steadily. Huge trees lined the road and gave the area real personality. Peering through the larger ones thickly covered in hanging moss gave a feeling of mystique. They decided to stop at Tillamook, visit the cheese factory and wineries, and have lunch.

The factory was busy with sales on all the leftover Christmas items. They sampled cheeses, purchased several ornaments and half-price gift items, had lunch, and bought snack items to keep in the car. Roger spied the ice-cream counter, so they had to try the real old-fashioned double-dip cones. Wonderful! Of course, he should not be eating ice cream but promised to eat light for the rest of the trip. Leah felt like a warden, always on him about his diet.

They stopped at numerous scenic points and decided to stay at Newport that night. They hadn't gone many miles that day, but this was supposed to be a pleasurable vacation, and they had no time schedule. The motel overlooked the wharf and ocean with many ships docked there. They watched the waves come in until they grew too sleepy to continue.

The next morning dawned misty and cloudy, so they thought they would get farther. Little did they know the ocean and the Pacific coastline are just as beautiful when storms are on the way as when the sun is shining. The clouds continually changed the color of the sky from pale blue to deep gray with numerous combinations of the shades between. The high waves crashing against the rocks and the deep-set clouds were always moving and changing and somewhat eerie to watch, so they stopped almost as many times that day. They marveled at the size of the many rock formations and cliffs. They found a motel at Coos Bay and walked around that night, watching the storm clouds roll in. It was a little chilly but exciting. All the trees leaned to one direction, and most of their growth was on one side, casting many ominous shadows in the night.

They watched TV to keep up with what was going on in the world. Roger was getting out phrases and having much less difficulty letting her know what was on his mind. They still had to use a lot of sign language, and she had to do most of the talking in restaurants and shops, but they were thoroughly enjoying the trip. He had shown no problem with his driving, although he tired very easily.

It was on to California the next morning. They had visited the redwoods with the children many years before, and Leah was anxious to visit them again. At Crescent City, they decided to take a more inland route and turn east just outside Eureka. By the time they made the turn, the sun was going down, and it started to rain. It seemed to get dark very quickly, and Roger was getting tired. Leah took over the driving just as they were entering the mountains. She had difficulty seeing at night, and the rain and curves made the driving anything but pleasurable.

She was happy they had decided to keep the Blazer as it sat high and was great at times like this. They could make out a few of the larger trees but missed most of the redwoods.

Leah had begun to look for motels as soon as it was dark, but there were few, and the only ones she found were small. After they intersected and turned onto Interstate 5, she saw several that failed her expectations; she began to worry as she wanted to keep Roger from becoming overtired, and the dark, wet roads had her feeling very fatigued. They finally pulled into a small motel and decided it would do regardless. They were tired and needed only a place to sleep for tonight. Once inside the room, it was pleasantly surprising. It was old but spotless, and the furniture looked like very well-cared-for antiques. It was warm and cozy, and Leah found another surprise in the bathroom. A coffee pot and real ground coffee had been provided with a basket of toiletries. The outside appearance belied the warm, lovely room inside. Leah called Dave and Cindy to let them know where they were, and that all was well, asking Dave to call Melanie and Suzan and relay the message. He agreed and gave them all the news of Alaska; nothing earth shaking, so Leah could relax and not worry about anything. All was under control. They were quite relieved and comfortable, and they slept very well.

The next morning, they awoke to sun again and mild temperatures and continued on to the beautiful valley. They were awed by all the lush winter greenery after twenty years in Alaska and stopped to take in the specialty shops, several wineries, and to get recommendations of places to see and restaurants.

They proceeded south and found it also lovely stopping at a few more wineries. These were full of history and trinkets, and

Leah sampled several wines at each, shocked at all the fruit-flavored ones. She really enjoyed the light taste of the peach and blackberry and purchased a case of splits to enjoy during the rest of the trip. Everyone was anxious to tell them about their wines, vineyards and any other information they wanted. They took several pamphlets and papers on the history of the area.

They continued on across the border into Nevada and Las Vegas and decided to spend a few days there as it was Leah's first visit. Leah was enthralled by all the palm trees; the only ones she had seen before had been in Hawaii. Roger had been in Las Vegas several times before their marriage and wanted her to see all the night life.

Leah figured January was probably a busy month with lots of "snowbirds" in town and suggested they stop at a tourist information center they passed on the outskirts. The man gave them several pamphlets on motels, saying they should have no problems locating a nice place to stay. Then he asked how long they had and if they had lots of plans for their time. When Leah told him they had no schedule or set plans and were flexible on time, he told them about a condo unit for a phenomenal rate. The catch was that it was a promotion and to get the rate, you had to spend two hours visiting a development site and listening to a sales pitch during which they would buy you breakfast or lunch. Leah looked at Roger questioningly. He shrugged and said okay, so Leah signed them up and got a map to the place. Roger always left the talking, writing, and directions to her, but she wanted his approval regardless.

It turned out to be located just behind the Strip. Perfect! There was a recreation and exercise room with an outdoor pool and spa just across from the entrance to the condos. Inside, they found two bedrooms, a kitchen with a bar leading to the eating area, living room, and a bathroom. It was very clean and well furnished down to dishes, cooking utensils, and appliances in the kitchen. What a deal! It was even decorated in gray, mauve, and deep aqua—Leah's favorites.

The next day, they made the bus trip out to the site of the development. After a breakfast of steak and eggs, the sales pitch began. The entire trip out, everyone had noticed the wind was blowing fiercely and all the trees leaned to one side. Leah listened politely and then gently informed them she really wasn't interested. Roger smiled and nodded his agreement. She stated they enjoyed visiting but didn't care to live there and didn't want to waste the sales crews' time and energy. That was the end of that, and they and the rest of their group were taken back to the condo, where they enjoyed four days at less than was usual for one day. Roger squeezed her hand as they left. It was obvious he was tired and ready to get back to the condo.

The evenings were spent taking in all the casinos as Leah had never seen anything like the lights on the Strip at night. Such extravagance was a rarity in Alaska as most places had maintained a rustic frontier decor. Caesar's Palace was the most exciting sight she had ever seen. They walked through the casino, observing the high rollers in their expensive finery at the baccarat tables but learned quickly not to get too close or stop to watch a game. The Omni Theater was showing a movie with a plane trip down into the Grand Canyon that felt so real, Leah actually got motion sickness. The feeling of nausea was short-lived, so they played the slots for a while.

The next day, they bought tickets to dinner and a show. They spent the day downtown taking a bus to the Nugget and parleying a two-dollar roll of nickels they had bought for one dollar into over sixteen, plus two cokes for Roger and two margaritas for Leah. Then they returned to the condo and showered and dressed for the dinner show. It was great, and they both developed a great respect for the female star as a very talented lady. They had only seen her in a TV series previously and learned the lady had multifaceted talent. However, she had real competition from a baby elephant in the show. It was adorable, and Leah was amazed it could be trained to perform so well.

Roger was feeling frisky again, and again had no problem. However, Leah was wondering if it was good for him to keep up this pace. She thought she had heard or read that heart patients should curtail any strenuous activity, and passionate sex had been listed. She decided to check into it later. She relaxed and enjoyed the evening, not wanting to spoil the mood with talk of things of which she wasn't sure. There were enough changes to their life as it was!

They spent the next two days walking around the Strip day and night, taking in all the sights in all the casinos and all the gift shops. She enjoyed the bright lights at night very much but was ready to go when they packed up and headed for Lake Havasu. They had wanted to see several other shows but couldn't get tickets, so they vowed to come back another time.

Chapter 9

They checked in with the children again, giving them the details of the Las Vegas experience."We were about to put out a tracer on you 'Blazer Gypsies.' Grandma has called twice, wondering where you were and when you would get to Oklahoma."

"I'm sorry, Son. We should have called the parents but just didn't take the time. We're usually so tired each night, we just watch a little TV and fall into bed. As a matter of fact, we usually watch TV in bed."

"I know, Mom, and you really don't need to concern yourself with calling all the family. Just call me, and I'll keep everybody up to date for you. But do keep in touch with me."

"I will, and we are fine and having a great time. We love you and appreciate all you're doing. We plan to spend tomorrow in Havasu then on to New Mexico and Texas. We should make it to Oklahoma within the next two weeks. We'll call again soon."

Lake Havasu was warm even in January, and some of the cacti were in bloom. There were palm trees all over the town, truly giving it the appearance of an oasis. It was exciting to view and walk across the London Bridge and then take the cruise on Lake Havasu and learn the history of the founding of the city, which was all man-made. Even the whole grove of palm trees had been purchased in California, brought in, and replanted. They browsed the shops and stayed at a lovely inn across the lake.

The first night, as Roger was taking a shower, Leah decided to take a stroll around and find the convenience store she had been told was on the premises. As she rounded the corner of the building, she heard the sound of nails scratching the sidewalk and turned around just in time to see the tail of a skunk scurrying off. She must have scared it as much as it did her, but why didn't it spray? She didn't really care and counted it a blessing as she hurriedly returned to the room, deciding to investigate the grounds tomorrow by daylight. Roger laughed at the story of her encounter, turning on the TV as she went to the shower.

"Each day, I seem to find so many things to thank God for that are so different from what I've thanked Him for or even asked for in the past. We're definitely not in a rut!" she told him as she closed the bathroom door.

Roger definitely seemed relaxed and seemed to be speaking a little better, with words coming more quickly. It was still slow going, but it was progress. He did seem to get depressed when tired or unable to do something he wanted to do. He still tired easily and had to rest frequently. That was fine. He could rest while she drove.

The next day, they drove around the town section away from all the tourist attractions and were quite impressed. It was filed high on the list of places to return to on future vacations. They stopped in a local real-estate office and obtained brochures on motels, condos, and land prices. They purchased more supplies and continued on to Phoenix, intending to see friends there who had been neighbors in Alaska. However, they were not at home and all the motels were full, so they wound up in Prescott for the night. Leah kicked herself for not calling sooner as she would have loved to see them. Next time! The list was sure getting long.

The town was in the mountains, and the temperatures were below freezing, which they hadn't realized until they saw a pool with ice covering it. It was late when they finally found a motel, so they showered and fell into bed to watch the news. Refreshed the next morning, they decided to spend some time looking around the downtown section that was built around a square. Leah spotted some antique and gift shops and had to browse. She found several pieces she liked; a bowl of rose-satin glass, an unusual piece of Santa Clara pottery, some Deco period mirrors, and several pieces of the older Fenton. She wanted to buy them all but knew their chances of getting them to their new home in one piece were slim to none. They were already heavily loaded.

They walked around the square with its old metal benches and numerous plaques and monuments. The surrounding buildings were very picturesque, built in a time of ornate eaves and figures in the brick and concrete. Several wrought-iron eagles decorated the buildings. After a delicious lunch of chicken dijon over rice, they continued their journey through some Indian village diggings and headed on to Tucson. There was lots of Peridot jewelry in all the shops, and Leah learned it was plentiful in the area. A highway patrolman followed them from the time they hit the interstate, keeping Leah wondering if she had done anything to warrant it. She finally relaxed as Roger read his Reader's Digest and then tried to explain what he had read. Their escort seemed to tire as they exited the state, and Leah decided that the loaded Blazer probably made them look suspicious. Maybe it was the Alaska tag! That had proved a source of conversation, with many asking about the state and life there, making a quick stop into a lengthy one.

In Tucson, they toured a mission and bought an Indian-made basket woven tightly of straw and intended for carrying water. It was explained that the native grasses expanded when wet, making the basket so tight it wouldn't leak. Leah was fascinated and wanted several but settled on one small one to add to her native-made basket collection from Alaska. They leisurely enjoyed whatever the area had to offer. They found a factory that made hollowware called Armetale, and Leah bought several pieces for gifts. They needed a wedding gift for a friend, and these pieces wouldn't break easily during shipping. She would have it mailed from Oklahoma. The back of the Blazer would soon refuse to accept another item.

In Artesia, New Mexico, they stopped at a restaurant for lunch. The cook was from Old Mexico and had prepared a huge Mexican buffet. The food was wonderful, and they eagerly told the owner when he came over to greet them. Strangers in town were easily spotted, and they struck up quite a conversation about Alaska and the desert. Roger got way off his diet but enjoyed the food so much, she just couldn't say anything. The owner invited them to stay that afternoon if they could so he could show them around Artesia. They found a lovely motel with an indoor pool and spa and decided to stay. The owner of the restaurant and his wife picked them up and spent the entire afternoon driving them around town, teaching them many facts about the area, desert, and desert plants. They learned one could actually survive in the desert on certain cacti that were edible and stored water. It was a definite highlight of the trip, and they promised to return and keep in touch with their new friends. They invited them to use the pool and spa but restaurant management meant early rising, so they declined. Roger and Leah changed into bathing suits and found the pool water to be warm, so they exercised awhile before calling it a night.

They pulled into a service station in San Antonio, called Leah's brother for directions, and headed for his house for a visit. On the second circle around the town, they found the correct exit and, eventually, the house. Her brother had worried that they were lost but forgot about it as they began catching up on the years since they had last seen each other. Their conversation ran almost nonstop except for the few hours they slept until they left the next day. Roger joined in for a word or two but usually just motioned agreement to the others.

They were headed for Corpus Christie, and Leah's brother insisted on leading them to the correct entrance to prevent them circling the city again. Roger was driving and became confused in the heavy traffic, pulling into the wrong entrance that went the opposite direction they wanted to go. Leah told him he needed to get off the freeway; Roger became flustered and upset and pulled over, stopped, and asked what he should do. Leah was very frightened but couldn't get to the driver's seat as they were stopped on a very busy crossover shoulder with traffic constantly whizzing by. She spoke with all the calm she could muster and instructed him step-by-step in starting the car, driving to the first exit, and taking the frontage road to the next entrance going in the correct direction. He made it with her slowly giving each move as it was time to make it, and she was relieved to see he was in control again. This was the first time he had become so frustrated, and she felt certain he needed to rest a few days before they went on. She breathed a silent prayer of thanks, asking for strength and patience again. She had no idea how many times she would ask for the same things in the coming years!

She had driven much of the distance since California so Roger could read the Reader's Digest short stories to her. She would then have him explain what he had read to determine if he was improving in comprehension and retention. He could rarely remember to the end of a paragraph but was enjoying the humorous stories. He also worked on vocabulary sections and could remember three or four lines. His reading skills were improving steadily as was his speech. He was slow and had to think about what he read or said, but it was coming. The topics in the stories gave them numerous ideas for discussion, and Leah could determine how Roger's thought processes were coming along. They had left out six issues, but he needed only one as he couldn't remember the stories after he read them. He was remembering more of his past experiences and places, though, and that was very encouraging. Leah had found a packet of salmon-colored paper, the closest she could find to orange, and ran off exercises for him from the therapist's materials. These didn't interest him much, and he spent little time on them but would spell, try to match, and give examples of same meanings or sounds during their discussions. Leah would get him to try writing something each day, both to put the orange color in front of him and to get him to practice his writing skills. Now he seemed to be enjoying driving and taking his place back behind the wheel, and Leah was delighted that he seemed more confident.

They spent a week in Corpus Christie in a condo just across the highway from the ocean. They could see it from their kitchen, dining, and living-room windows. They found several great seafood and Mexican-American restaurants, and Roger was very good to stick to his diet, especially when they ate in the condo. They had been traveling so long, it was a real pleasure to prepare small meals. Most of the days were sunny, cheery, and comfortable with lots of green grass, trees, and shrubbery sprinkled with colorful and fragrant flowers. The wind was cool and the air heavy with humidity, but it was beautiful. Aransas Pass was a real treat, seeing all the cranes, herons, and pelicans they had never seen in numbers before. They toured the King Ranch and Padre Island and generally had a very restful and relaxing week. This was another place they wanted to visit again. They planned to travel extensively for the next few years. Roger had always wanted to visit Australia and stay a month or two. Leah planned to see he got to fulfill that desire as soon as his health was good enough. They marveled at the mild winter weather and the ability to see flowers blooming outside in January; this was a good place to spend the winter. They again gathered information brochures and pamphlets for a return. Their collection was getting rather large.

They had neighbors from Alaska they hadn't seen in at least ten years who were now living in Texas, and they wanted to visit them. They sat in their room the last evening in Corpus Christie and studied the map. They decided to visit a historic town for a few days and call their friends from there. They again packed up, which was beginning to become a chore for Leah. At first, it had been a challenge and fun, but a month out of a suitcase was getting very monotonous.

The next stop was a very old historical town with much to see. They learned about all the "Sunday Houses" owned by farmers of the past for the trips to town and church on the weekend. Many had been well preserved just as they had been when in use. There were numerous antique shops and a mansion to tour, which were all the things Leah enjoyed. She wanted to stay a week or more and see it all, but Roger was getting tired, so they called their friends the second day and continued on to see them the next morning.

It was so good to visit with old friends and reminisce about the years when they were young and raising their children. They had two boys; the youngest hadn't been able to decide whether to marry Suzan or Melanie when he grew up. He was now finishing college. There was a lot to see there, with many unique shops to browse. They spent two days with them, looking over and listening to plans for the house they were building. Leah and Roger hoped to build also but didn't know where as yet.

They arrived in Norman to Roger's parents delight and stayed with them for two weeks. It was a great rest they both needed from packing up and moving on every day or two. They saw many old friends and renewed family ties that had almost been lost over the many years in Alaska. The trips home had always been too short to see everyone. Now they had lots of time. Roger and his dad seemed to know what the other was thinking; they talked little but communicated a lot. His mother had hearing loss, and it was difficult for him to talk with her as she didn't understand his slowness and often began speaking or left the room before he could get his words out.

She and Leah cooked together as Pop was on a heart and diabetic diet, so he and Roger could eat together. Mom loved junk food, so Leah would take her shopping and stop for burgers, fries, and pie. She usually ate very healthy with Pop, so Leah figured it didn't hurt anything to treat her while there. They were both getting up in years, and Leah knew they would not have them forever. Pop seemed to be moving slower and with more effort than the last time they had been home; he was now eighty-four.

They all went up to visit Roger's aunt and uncle and had lunch with them; it was a wonderful day. Mom loved having Roger and Leah to drive them around as Pop's reflexes had slowed, and he only drove around town avoiding the heavy traffic times and routes. All in all, Roger seemed to be enjoying himself too. He was more at ease driving in Oklahoma as all the highways were familiar to him; he had traveled them many times.

Mom seemed more forgetful than on previous trips, but the years were passing for her too. She still had little gray hair among the dark, naturally curly strands. She kept it very short as the curls seemed to have a mind of their own and refused to stay where she wanted them to. The high humidity made them curl tighter, making Leah jealous. She was sure she would love naturally curly hair instead of her straight as a board, thick locks. Roger kept his cut very short also as it curled like his mother's. Pop had little hair left except around the edges; Roger had teased him in the past for paying a barber to trim it when there was so little to trim. His own forehead was getting longer, and the top seemed much thinner, so his dad gave it right back. They had always been great buddies, and Leah had always been extra fond of her father-in-law. She prepared many low-fat, low-sugar dishes for him as Mom wasn't very creative in her cooking, and he longed for desserts. Leah and Roger knew he would sneak off to the bakery when he could get away with it.

They went on to see Leah's mother and stayed there for another week before driving to see Leah's sister and her family. They spent a day with Leah's brother. He had begun his business in his garage and then moved it to a small town when he bought the airport there. They all enjoyed flying in his Breezy, an open airplane that looked much like a big bird and scared the real ones.

He lived in a lovely little town with lots of charm and named for the state's first governor. Set in the rolling hills of Oklahoma, known as 'Green Country', it is truly peaceful and slow paced. Several antique shops and resale shops got Leah's attention as she and her sister-in-law killed the afternoon looking while Roger and her brother spent time at the machine shop her brother operated. The shop turned out many parts for airplanes and had been very successful. During her numerous trips by air from Alaska, he had informed her there was probably one of his parts on any plane she flew. She laughingly asked if he was trying to reassure or frighten her. In reality, she was well aware of her brother's quest for perfection.

He was very special to her; he had almost died in a plane crash several years before, and no one had expected him to walk or work again. She was sure he lived with pain much of the time and forced himself more than he should, but he had always possessed that drive and knew no other way to live. He not only walked and worked, but he also flew, skied, and skydived. Of course, Leah didn't approve of the latter three and was afraid he was trying to prove to the world he was as good as before.

They took Leah's mother shopping and out to eat numerous times, which was a real treat for her. She always felt she was too slow and detained her friends so rarely got to leisurely shop, stopping for coffee or lunch when she got tired. Roger had always been fond of telling her he had nothing but time or more time than anything else. They had moved into a spare bedroom and unpacked and repacked for the trip to Tennessee, Florida, and the Bahamas. It would be nice to leave a large portion of their winter clothes here in Oklahoma.

They arrived in Tennessee finding the town had changed and grown so much, they hardly felt like they had been there before. It had been several years, but they found the office where Leah's sister worked, remembering it was on the main street. She was thrilled to see them, introduced them around, and then took them to the coffee room. It was only 3:00 p.m., so Roger and Leah walked across the street to a shopping center and looked around until time for her sister to leave work.

They hardly recognized the house as it had been remodeled extensively, but the atmosphere was the same. Jenna and Todd had lived in the South since they were married and were much in tune with the laid-back Southern lifestyle. Leah and Roger always loved to visit as it was so peaceful and relaxing. Jenna had lost a lot of weight through walking. Todd and Roger had always enjoyed each other and were now making plans to go fishing. Jenna informed them she was taking the following week off, so they must stay until she went back to work. That was not a problem as they didn't really need to be in Florida for nearly two weeks.

The week was spent checking out all the shops and Factory Outlet Malls around as well as the best restaurants for fish. They did splurge and get off the diet one night at a restaurant where barbecued chicken and ribs were the special. It was superb with all the creamy coleslaw, baked beans, cornbread, pickles, and peppers you could eat, along with generous portions of chicken and ribs. Roger stuffed himself, giving Leah a look that said,

"Don't say a word!" Leah was afraid the new shorts and tops she had bought for the cruise would be too tight.

They had such a great time. Luck was with them as the weather was sunny and warm the whole time they were there, but a storm was forecast for the following week that could bring ice, sleet, and freezing rain. They headed south, staying one night in Georgia, and then crossed over into Florida the next day. They had seen many signs advertising the tourist information centers and all the great deals they had to offer for tourists. They stopped and picked up lots of brochures, discount coupons, and pamphlets with information from where to stay to where to eat and reduced tourist rates for most attractions. However, they found the winter/senior rate at a chain to be the best value for the money and stayed in Orlando. The room was large and opened onto a patio, pool, and garden area. The inside door led into the hall and on to the indoor pool, spa, and sauna. The restaurant offered many delectable entrees, with several heart-smart offerings among them. They spent the next four days at Epcot center, Alligator Farm, Sea World, Cape Canaveral, and had one afternoon at Cocoa Beach before traveling on down to Fort Lauderdale. They had taken it slow, but Roger was having more difficulty speaking, and his skin was a little gray, which meant he was tired. The cruise should be just what he needed.

Roger had been driving most of the way and had done fine. But the highways were unfamiliar in Florida, and he became confused at a clover leaf and screamed at Leah to tell him which way to go. She had told him she didn't know which turn to take and would check the map, but he turned into the entrance curve, screamed at her to tell him what to do, and stopped the car on the shoulder. Leah was almost in tears with fear and anger. She didn't deserve to be yelled at as she was trying hard to take care of everything and hadn't been there before. She finally found the correct route, showing Roger the highway sign and directing him where to turn off to get back on route. It was the first real outburst Roger had made, and it unnerved her so she couldn't conceal the tears that silently rolled down her cheeks. She was shaking all over but tried to conceal it from him as she felt her insides doing flip-flops. She quietly offered to drive, but he ignored her and continued on. They were silent for several miles, lost in their own thoughts, when Roger reached over and patted her knee as if nothing had happened. This had always been his way of apologizing—something he could not verbalize—and all was forgiven.

They had reservations for a short cruise with three days in the Bahamas. In Fort Lauderdale, they took a day to look at some time-shares, thinking they might winter here for a few years. They were tempted as the accommodations were plush and would provide for home away from home. While talking with one of the personnel, Leah glanced out the window to see a large lizard run by. It frightened her at first, but her attention was quickly drawn to the tree it was climbing. Hanging from the branches were some oval green and yellow fruits with ridges and grooves.

"Are those star fruit?" she asked, expecting to be wrong as she didn't even know if they grew on trees. She had bought a couple in Alaska when on special and enjoyed their lovely star-shaped slices in her fruit trays and salads more than their taste; they were a little too acidic for her. She did like them in green salads more than alone, the dressings reducing the acid taste.

"They sure are!" the saleslady replied. "Do you like them? Most people aren't too familiar with them unless they are from this area. Didn't you say you were from Alaska?"

"Yes, but grocers obtained great produce from all over."

The cruise to the Bahamas was another adventure. The ship they were on had a large spa and lots of entertainment. There just wasn't enough time to take it all in. They passed several schools of fish, including flying fish skimming the water. Dinner was an affair, with your own waiter to see you had anything and everything you wanted. The food was the finest, and the wines were vintage. Leah told Roger they couldn't take it very long eating this rich fare, but she was loving the pampering. They arrived in port before dark and found a taxi to their hotel. There was a large pool in the center of the garden area, and their room had a kitchenette. They spent the next day wandering. Stopping at a local grocery store, they were shocked at the prices, which were much higher than the mainland. It was even more humid than Florida and had lots of tropical flowers amidst the tropical trees and bushes. Their hotel was in walking distance of 'Old Town', and they planned to see it before leaving. It was not supposed to be quite as touristy.

At the dock next morning, people were swimming with dolphins, and vendors were everywhere. They each bought a shirt sporting "Don't Worry, Be Happy" across the front. Boarding a ship for a day trip to an island, they reveled in the tropical landscape and the beauty of the area. The ship soon departed for a reef and snorkeling. Bathing suits were the proper attire, and a barbecue was to take place after drinks on the beach. The day was gorgeous, the sand warm, the company very friendly, and they hated to re-board the ship that evening. The barbecue was ready, and everyone stuffed themselves before the dancing began. Some of the ship's hands had come up with several large lobsters, which were cooked for all to sample. On board was a professional dance duo; the husband having worked on that very ship before going to Japan where he met his wife and partner. Watching them dance all the calypso dances was worth the price of the ticket alone. Then the limbo began, with most of the passengers feeling very warm, happy, and willing to try anything. Leah and Roger remained spectators and had a ball watching the merry-making. "Hot, Hot, Hot" and "Don't Worry, Be Happy" were played, so many times they actually learned most of the words.

Back on shore, it was late, and they went to their room tired and ready for a shower. They watched a little TV and then fell asleep. The next morning, they had breakfast at the little restaurant on the premises, not knowing what to expect. It definitely catered to the tourists as there were low-fat menus as well as the traditional hearty breakfasts. With full tummies, they walked over to Old Town; it was a good hike and a beautiful walk with flowers in bloom everywhere. The only discomfort was the heavy, dank air. They met a very nice man who gave them directions on what to see and do and where to find anything they wanted. He was a very tall Bahamian.

The next day, they saw one of the male passengers who informed them he had been told the ship would return to Miami rather than Ft. Lauderdale. The Super Bowl was in Miami and rioting was going on, so Leah did not want to go there. He told them he had won money at the casino the night before and would get them on a ship back to their original destination. He made arrangements and informed them later that day.

Back at the hotel, they ran into a couple they had met on the boat over and made plans to visit the casino together that evening. They all had dinner, watched a show, and watched people gamble for a while.

The next day, they lounged around the pool and relaxed before returning to Fort Lauderdale. They purchased souvenirs for the family and returned to the ship. Again, they had dinner aboard, and it was even better than the first one. A comedian was entertaining in the lounge and kept them laughing all the way back to port. Roger and Leah were sold on cruises, planning to take a longer one soon.

It was late, almost ten o'clock, when they arrived in Fort Lauderdale, and no rooms were available due to the Super Bowl in Miami. They had been warned not to take Alligator Alley (Highway 75 or Everglades Parkway) across to the west side at night, but it was late, and the next highway was almost an hour north so they decided to chance it. They drove all night, keeping their eyes peeled for creatures on the road. They didn't see a single one and were about to fall asleep when they arrived in Naples and stopped for coffee.

They drove on up to Sarasota and found a lovely motel and checked in early. After a swim and soak in the spa, they collapsed into bed and slept for three hours. Too tired to do anything else, they spent the evening reading the Sunday paper and watching TV, catching up on the news. Dinner was crackers, cheese, pickles, and fruit in their pajamas. Roger slept through the night in spite of their nap while Leah dreamed of alligators. They toured Sarasota before going on, passing a familiar jewelry company; there was one in Anchorage where they had shopped and learned it was the same owner. Summer in Alaska, winter in Florida - nice!

They enjoyed touring St. Petersburg with its picturesque buildings and then turned back west and traveled along the coast to Gulf Shores, Alabama. Leah loved the ocean, and this shoreline and scenery was very different from the Pacific. This was where they decided to spend a week. Most of the time was spent walking the beach and lounging around the pool and hot tub overlooking the ocean. They loved it and had a small kitchenette to make their breakfasts and a balcony so they could hear the waves at night as the tide came in. It was so peaceful, they didn't want to leave. The food was again fresh from the ocean, and they enjoyed clams, oysters, and shrimp. They spent part of each day walking barefoot in the sand along the Gulf, beach-combing and watching boats and birds. They called friends in Louisiana and promised to call again when they reached New Orleans.

Thinking they were arriving the week after Mardi Gras, they were shocked when they were asked to sign a form that promised they would leave the New Orleans motel by Thursday as the big weekend was coming up; it was Fat Tuesday! They called their friends the next morning and agreed to meet them for dinner. Never having been there before, Leah was shocked several times as they strolled down Bourbon Street. They were stopped by a policewoman giving Leah a real startle. She informed them she had been told Roger had smuggled a young woman into the Quarter who wasn't having any fun and would have to fine them ten dollars. Puzzled, Roger took out his wallet and gave her a ten, while Leah wondered who the young woman was. It bought them two hats and was actually a contribution to Meals on Wheels. They thought it was a clever way to raise money and wore their hats on the rest of the stroll.

They stopped in at all the famous bars they had heard about and then found a coffee shop and ordered coffee. Dinner that night was in a restaurant built around a French theme and actually contained parts from the Tower of Pisa, or so they were told. Just as they were finishing their salads, a parade came into view, and they rushed outside to catch some of the coins and necklaces thrown from the floats. Leah was too short to reach for most of the objects, but a young man took pity and practically threw them into her hands. She was busy catching, throwing kisses back, and having a great time. She really didn't care if they ate at all.

Roger attempted to converse with his friend, as they had grown up together in Oklahoma and his wife had worked with Leah. They had introduced Roger and Leah, and their children were close in age. However, Roger had difficulty keeping up. They enjoyed the evening and invited them to visit once they were settled in the Northwest and renew their relationship. The night was clear and stars shone brightly overhead as they passed the canal and watched the lights on the riverboats. Once back in their room, they donned bathing suits and went to the spa and pool. Roger swam while Leah relaxed in the swirling hot water of the spa.

The next morning, they checked out and continued on to Texas and down to Port Arthur. It was nearly eighty degrees when they checked into the motel at half past six in the evening. They had dinner, relaxed in the pool, and made plans to go on down the coast to Galveston as they watched the news before falling asleep. They heard the wind picking up but paid little attention to it. The next morning, they awoke to thirty degrees and snow and ice. What they had thought was wind had actually been sleet!

The decision to return to Oklahoma was no contest. Further travel and Galveston would have to wait. They loaded the car and took off slowly as the roads were icy, deciding to get as far as they could. They took Highway 69, hoping to avoid the fast, heavy traffic of the expressways. The farther north, they went the more ice and snow they encountered. They finally stopped to eat on the outskirts of Tyler after munching fruit that morning. The sun came out and made the scenery beautiful, but the roads were treacherous. The temperature warmed very little before starting back down. At Dennison, they decided to stop for the night and fell exhausted into bed. Roger had driven most of the way while Leah kept the route pointed out along with highway signs and dangers. Her eyes ached from straining them against the bright sunlight on the snow. It occurred to her she had never felt this drained after a trip in Alaska with all its ice and snow as she fell into a deep sleep.

They awoke early and continued on to Oklahoma, arriving in the late afternoon to find nearly everything also covered with ice. They unloaded and visited with Mom and Pop, hoping the weather would warm up. Shortly before heading to bed, they heard something falling outside and looked out to see it was sleeting again. The next morning, Roger wanted a Sunday paper after Leah made a big pancake breakfast, so she donned her boots and coat, grateful she had left them in Norman by mistake. She wrapped one of Mom's wool scarves around her head, put on a pair of gloves, and started out. The first frozen parking area was maneuvered slowly, the second almost twice as slow as she took two steps and slid back three. Her fine-tread Alaska boots were useless on this solid ice. The sun was leaving a wet glaze on top, which was difficult to traverse. She finally made it the half block to the convenience store at the corner and bought the paper. Now she wondered if she would get back without falling. After a short rest and a complimentary cup of coffee, she started off confident she would do fine, and she did until she was in front of the apartment, which is when she began to slip. She reached out to grab hold of the parked car in front of her, lost her balance, and went down on her butt—hard! She felt as if she had jarred her teeth loose and had thrown the paper, which landed in front of the door to the apartment as if by aim. She had grabbed, shifted first one way then the other before going down and now felt all bent out of place. Roger and his parents opened the door, afraid she was hurt, and Roger carefully ventured out to help her up. She could hardly stand she was laughing so hard. Once inside with the paper and all the outerwear removed, she began to survey her injuries. Nothing seemed to be too badly damaged, but she knew she would be sore later.

"Best enjoy that paper and appreciate it. I don't think I'll be going for another until this mess melts!" That was three days later, and they were about to go stir crazy not being able to get out, with only the TV for entertainment. As the ice melted, Leah did laundry and packed to go, taking time each day to take Roger's parents out to shop and have a meal.

The next three weeks were spent visiting with Leah's mother, brothers, and sister, shopping, and visiting museums. Leah's mother loved being able to get out and see things she hadn't seen for years. An orchid show being held at a local greenhouse, was a spectacular display, and gave Leah the courage to think about raising orchids. She was determined to try it as soon as she and Roger were settled. Unfortunately, it would be some time before Leah felt really settled again.

Roger was tired of shopping and flea markets and made the fact well known. He informed Leah he was driving to visit her brother while she and her mother shopped. He had never gone anywhere alone since the stroke, and Leah panicked, afraid he would forget the way. It was only thirty miles, but with several turns off and onto expressways; it was easy for anyone to make a mistake. When she asked him not to go, he became angry and yelled at her again.

"I'm so tired of shopping…I can…go wherever I want, and you keep your mouth…shut!" He had added a few swear words, which was so unlike him before the stroke.

Leah was shaking with shock, anger, and frustration. It seemed so easy for him to remember profanity, and this in front of her mother! She said nothing else to him, and he left. Leah's mother was upset, but she told Leah she needed to give Roger some slack and let him try.

"I understand your fear of allowing him to go alone, but he may fool you. At any rate, he wants to try, and how far off can he get? You will cripple him emotionally if you continue to guard his every move."

Leah began to cry as she was afraid of Roger's outbursts. It wasn't that he had never used a swear word before; it was the look in his eyes and the memory of the woman in the liquor store. He wasn't usually so easy to anger or quick to yell at her. It seemed the more often he did it, the easier it became, and Leah was unprepared to deal with this. Maybe when they were settled in their own place, it would be better. Maybe he was tired, and all the traveling had taken its toll. Maybe he was missing his children, and the trip to Alaska would help.

"Don't worry about me," Leah's mother said. "I love Roger, and I always will. He's a good man, and I'm sure the ordeal he's been through has him very frustrated. Just try to go along with him and give him a little space."

Leah couldn't resist calling her brother to let him know Roger was on his way over and obtained his promise to call if he didn't make it in a reasonable amount of time. It should take him approximately forty-five minutes, so they waited until an hour and a half had passed before leaving, calling to ascertain his arrival first. They were going to have burgers with her sister-in-law and niece before going to the shopping center. They spent the afternoon shopping for clothes and groceries. Several times, Leah wondered if Roger was on his way home but knew he had a key to the house, so she did her best to put it out of her mind.

When they returned that evening, the house was empty. As they were putting the groceries away, Roger opened the door and walked in as if he had just gone outside to get something. He grinned at Leah like a cat that ate a canary, and she knew he had done fine and was very proud of himself, as was she.

"Hungry?"

"No."

"Did you eat on the way home?"

"Yes."

"Where? What did you have?"

Roger hesitated then answered. "Barbecue! It ...... good!"

Leah thought to herself, When the cat's away..., but just smiled and said nothing. She did give him a look that let him know he hadn't fooled her. She had figured he would stop at some cafe and get as far off his diet as he could. She was well aware of how very tired he got of the diet and the small meat portions. He loved to eat, and barbecue was his favorite but only if he could have his fill, meaning a couple pounds.

They called Suzan to wish her a happy birthday. They were scheduled to fly to Alaska by the end of the month and would celebrate both girls' birthdays then. Suzan's was in March, Melanie's in April, Dave's in May, and Cindy's in August, so they would have a big celebration while they were all together. They would spend some time in the condo with the girls and some at Dave and Cindy's. It would be good to return to Alaska and see the children, if only for three weeks. They still had business to attend to, and Roger needed to see his doctor, so it would be a busy time.

Leah unpacked and put things in order before they flew off to Alaska. With only a forty-minute layover in Denver, they arrived twenty minutes late and hurried to their gate. Settled in their seats, they relaxed as the plane took off and were soon viewing snow-covered peaks, stirring Leah's feelings of loneliness and longing to be settled again. She missed Alaska, or was it the comfortable feeling of having roots and the ability to get on with life that she missed? She felt she had been in a state of limbo for the past four months and was getting tired of living out of suitcases. Roger never seemed to tire of traveling and wanted to go all the time. He seemed to want to see and do everything now.

As they landed, Roger squeezed her hand and smiled as if he had been reading her thoughts. All the children were there to greet them and had many plans for their stay. Leah decided they should stay with Melanie and Suzan at the condo for the first week, taking care of the bank accounts and anything remaining on the house. They still had some loose ends to tie up.

The first week was very busy, taking Suzan to work each day so they could keep her car to run errands and then picking her up. Leah had dinner ready each evening, much to the girls' delight, and they didn't want them to leave. They spent the next two weeks with Dave and Cindy as they had much more room. Both were working, so Roger and Leah took walks each day, sighting moose and ducks as well as many birds. Several days, Dave took Cindy to work, leaving their Jimmy for Roger and Leah to use. Roger saw his internist, having him review the blood work done in Norman. He had put him on Omega 3 (fish oil) before they left Alaska. The test in Norman had shown such an increase in Roger's blood lipids that Leah had immediately ceased giving it to him, and she informed the doctor what she had done.

"Yes! By all means, stopping them was the right thing to do," he said. Leah dreaded finding new doctors but didn't know when they would return to Alaska again.

They needed to find a new internist and cardiologist as soon as they settled in the condo. In the meantime, she would keep check on his blood lipids with blood tests in Oklahoma and adjust his diet accordingly. All the business was concluded, and the only reason to return would be to visit the children and close friends.

They shopped many of the familiar places, buying all the things they couldn't get outside, and took time to visit with merchants they had done business with in past years. Max and Lorene had been very happy to see them, and they had dinner together several times. They were planning to sell their house and move to Arizona sometime this year. They were their closest friends in Alaska. So many of the neighbors had retired and moved to the lower forty-eight!

Too soon, it was time to fly back, and Leah and Roger were sad to leave the children but anxious to get settled in the condo. They would call to have the furniture shipped upon their arrival in Oklahoma. The trip home was uneventful; it was just a little bumpy over the Midwest, and they had a rough landing that is frequent in spring when the weather is changing. It was already beginning to warm, usually getting into the high seventies.

Leah's mother convinced them to stay a little longer with her until the weather warmed in the north. Leah made arrangements for the furniture to be shipped during the middle of May, only a month away, and they would spend a week or ten days driving there, taking time to see all the sights.

Chapter 10

The furniture was scheduled to arrive on Thursday, and they planned to arrive Wednesday, cutting short the sightseeing but knowing they would probably travel that same route again. They had no idea how many times they would make that trip with no time to sightsee.

The scenery changed from wheat fields to mountains to desert, and now they were entering a land of trees and lakes.

After checking into a motel, they drove around and checked on the condo. Property management had said it was empty, freshly cleaned, and utilities were on. Roger and Leah spent the next day arranging to have all utilities in their name and making appointments to get the phone and cable turned on. They called Seattle to learn that the furniture was on its way and should arrive the next morning. It did!

The sewing machine had been shipped upside down and was badly damaged, the wardrobe hanging rods had fallen, and all the clothes were crushed in the bottom, the beautiful mauve chairs had been rubbed threadbare in several places, several pieces were broken, including the hand-blown crystal ornament the children had made for their twenty-fifth anniversary cake topper, and Roger's best white sweater had been wrapped around a metal clamp-on bed lamp and was now covered with rust.

Leah was sick. They had paid a good amount to have it packed, shipped, and stored with trip and storage insurance. Thank God she had caught all the little PBO notations and had them rescinded before shipping. They could have delivered everything in pieces, and she would have had no recourse. As it was, she felt sure she had a lot of work ahead of her.

She and Roger set up all they could, checked out of the motel, and called all their family members to give them their new phone number and to let them know all was well. Then they spent the next few weeks getting everything unpacked, finding several surprises as they did so. They spent a great deal of time finding receipts and getting estimates for all the damages.

They also spent several days looking for furniture as they had one bedroom suite, two chairs, one card table, and two folding chairs. Each store they visited, they asked what was available now. Each time they were informed the display items were for order only. Finally, they found a store, explained their situation and were told they could take anything on the floor that day. They found a sleeper sofa, end tables, and lamps they liked and asked how soon they could be delivered as the Blazer wouldn't hold more than one table and the lamps. Three weeks was the soonest.

"Three weeks!" Leah exclaimed. "Maybe I didn't make myself clear. I meant we literally do not have any furniture! We need it now. Can't you get it out any sooner?"

"Well, maybe in two weeks. We wait until we have several deliveries before we go over your way."

It was only forty miles, but Leah could see it was no use to argue. They paid for the purchases, which were good buys;

Leah picked up the lamps, asked them to call her the day before delivery, and started for the car. Roger and the salesman wrapped the table and carried it out. Roger was showing signs of fatigue, and Leah knew the past weeks had really been a chore for him. They could accomplish a little each day before he was too tired to go farther.

"Five stores order only and finally one with furniture to actually sell, and they can't deliver for two weeks. Oh, well, we can be thankful we decided to keep the card table and chairs. At least we aren't eating on the floor."

Roger looked over at her and smiled and then got a serious look.

"I'm…hungry. Let's…eat."

The words hungry and eat were always very clear. They saw a restaurant on the same side of the street just a few feet away and pulled into the parking lot. The building resembled the structure of a barn but was painted yellow and white with green trim. The sign boasted a buffet lunch. Leah dreaded buffets as Roger had a tendency to eat more than he should. They entered to find a very clean and nice decor with antiques sprinkled about. The seats were covered in cheery pink and green floral chintz. There were numerous paintings of people in turn-of-the-century attire and old buildings hung on white painted walls. The buffet turned out to be barbecued chicken, salads, and soup. Not so far off Roger's diet and all fresh and well prepared. They ate and then returned to the condo with lamps and a living room table and were quite comfy. They purchased a small TV their first day in town, so what more did they need? Roger had always teased her stating that all a man needed was a bed, a table and chairs, and a TV. They were learning those really were the necessities.

Sure enough, two weeks later, they received the call that the sofa and tables were on their way. In the meantime, they had found a recliner for Roger, and the furnishing was almost complete. The following week, Leah began the arduous task of trying to comply with insurance on all the repair estimates, statement of replacement costs, and appraisals on the items that could not be replaced.

This was a backbreaking job as several trips were required and lots of checking for retailers since she was unfamiliar with the area. She had a year to get it all done but managed to have it in the mail, with a backup file of copies for safety, within a month. It was almost two months before she received a letter asking for more data and refusing some items. They had paid for services and insurance in good faith, and she knew they had payment due.

It was on one of the trips that Roger saw a big screen TV and wanted to buy it, telling Leah they would put the smaller one in the bedroom. Finally, a sales clerk came over and asked if she could be of help. Roger started to ask a question, and she quickly finished it for him, not getting it right. Roger said, "No…wait…"

She began again to phrase the question. Again, Roger shook his head and tried to start asking her to wait. Finally, after three wrong tries by the clerk in rapid succession, Roger got visibly upset and said a swear word. That offended the clerk, who gave him a shocked and dismayed look and turned to leave. Leah tried to explain that Roger didn't mean to be offensive, but the clerk saw a supervisor and motioned to him. Leah couldn't hear what she told him, but as soon as they approached, Leah explained that Roger had suffered a stroke and was slow of speech, and the clerk wouldn't give him a chance to tell her what he was interested in. She said she was sorry he had used a four-letter word, but that was also due to the stroke. Profanity was much easier for stroke victims to get out than other, more difficult words. Leah continued. "No need to go any further. We are leaving and will purchase our new TV where they are more patient and allow one to inform the clerk what they want rather than the clerk telling them!"

That said, she took Roger's hand, and they walked out the door with clerk and supervisor staring after them. She hated episodes like this as she had never liked conflict, but people seemed so quick to assume Roger was slow-witted rather than just slow of speech. That attitude really upset her, and she wished there was some kind of education program for the general public to help them learn about strokes and their victims' need for patience and understanding.

During that summer, they found a heart specialist for Roger, only to be informed after the first appointment that they would need another doctor for anything besides a heart attack. The doctor was just too busy with his cardiology patients to treat a flu or virus. So Leah started all over again to look for an internist. Many of the doctors had closed practices, and she knew little about any of them. Finally, she began asking people she met at church for recommendations and was given several. She made an appointment, and she and Roger went in to see the one selected. He pleased Roger and got them in to see a speech therapist, so all seemed to be going well. The cardiologist had told Roger to walk daily, working up to two miles a day, and they began.

The condo was set in a small farming area that had once been nothing but farms and now was being taken over by developers. Just three blocks away, several farmers held on to their small acreages and a few cattle. Many gardens shot up as the spring gave way to summer, and corn was in most of them. Roger and Leah walked almost every evening, getting acquainted with a few of the residents and most of the animals within a one mile radius of the condo. Tall pines were everywhere except the prairie, which was surrounded by tree covered mountains. They were amazed at the roses, irises, rhododendrons, and numerous other species of flowers. The winters got very cold with lots of snow here, but the summer seemed to get just as warm. August brought a week of near one-hundred-degree weather. It was very dry, however, and didn't feel that hot.

From the deck of their condo, they could watch the gorgeous sunsets, and they did most evenings, sipping tea or lemonade after their walks. They drove to the mining areas just east of them, Canada just north, and the ocean to the west. Traveling almost two hundred miles north into Canada, they encountered rugged, tall mountain peaks like the majestic ones in Alaska. It was such a treat to be able to visit sand dunes, ocean, or mountain peaks within a days' drive, and they wanted to see it all.

Roger quickly tired of the speech therapist even though Leah had given her lots of material developed in Alaska. Soon he refused to continue telling Leah that she could teach him more than the therapist. Leah felt overwhelmed with all her jobs; nurse, wife, therapist, and teacher. Sometimes she felt Roger was putting more on her than she was capable of and made her feel more like a warden, but she knew she had no choice but to do the best she could. Some days when Roger was tired or not feeling well, he could hardly carry on a conversation and would stare at her with those big brown eyes, not understanding a thing she said to him. She felt that the move, all the changes and traveling had caused him to regress some. On the bad days, his skin had a gray tint that was too familiar and scared Leah.

She had met a few of their neighbors but didn't feel close enough to anyone here to confide in them. Her frustrations grew each time they dealt with some business person that treated Roger as if he was feeble-minded because he was slow and had to have time to think. Many tried to fast talk him into purchases that he didn't want, and a few succeeded. The few times when Leah tried to intervene, Roger became very angry and more profanity was hurled loudly at her.

She thought she was dealing with everything and doing okay until one day, she went into a beauty supply shop for hair color and shampoo, and the lady struck up a conversation, asking how long they had lived there, where they came from, and why they had chosen this area. Before Leah knew they were even near, tears were streaming down her face, and she could hardly talk.

She apologized, telling the shop owner she felt very alone as she had left all the people she was close to, and Roger was in his own world most of the time. She felt he could do more than he tried but was too dependent on her. The shop owner was very sympathetic, having gone through a stroke with her father. She told Leah she had better talk to someone and cry her tension out or she might end up a basket case. Leah did feel better and somewhat relieved when she left, though she knew experiencing a stroke with a father didn't begin to compare to going through one with a husband.

That September, Melanie called and asked if they would like to have her visit. Leah was overjoyed and could hardly stand the wait until her arrival. They met her in Spokane and made trips down into southwestern Washington on the wine country tour and up into Canada, showing her all the attributes of the Inland Northwest. Only once did Roger become confused and frustrated, stop the car, and angrily demand Leah tell him what to do. Melanie said nothing, but the look on her face was that of shock and surprise; however, the episode was quickly over and not mentioned. Melanie enjoyed all their excursions and liked the area very much. The day before she was due to leave, she and Leah went to lunch alone.

"Mother, we need to talk about Dad. I know you have spent the past year waiting for him to return to normal, and you need to face the fact that Daddy is handicapped and always will be. He will improve, I'm sure, but he will never be the way he was before, and you must realize that and stop working so hard to help him recover. You both need to relax and enjoy life. If Dad is never able to run another job, or create another form, or read another textbook, it really doesn't matter at all. He only needs to be able to get his needs and desires across, and he manages that pretty well now. I don't mean to upset you or hurt you. I love you, and I love Daddy, and I want you to both be happy."

Leah listened to her daughter and thought how wise she had become and brave to give her mother this pep talk.

"In my mind, I know you're right, but my heart keeps saying to try harder, and maybe he'll return to normal."

"Mother, that's impossible. He's had a serious stroke, and you know there is always some permanent damage. You're exhausting both of you trying to make him work so hard to recover. It's not good. You need to start painting again and doing the things you enjoy, and let daddy do what he wants. Right now, you're as handicapped as he is because you've made his recovery your only goal."

Leah knew she was right, and her eyes filled with tears. Melanie took her hand and squeezed it as the waitress refilled their coffee.

"Would you like a glass of wine?" Leah shook her head yes, and Melanie ordered them both a glass. As they sipped the mild white Riesling, she continued.

"I love you all so much and just had to tell you what I have observed. Just think about it, Mom. I'm worried about your health."

Leah did think about it; all that day and the next as they drove Melanie to the airport for her return to Alaska, and for the next several days, it kept creeping back into her mind, especially the part about her being as handicapped as her husband. She realized she was and vowed to loosen up. Roger was able to answer the telephone and the door but always waited for her, fearful he would make a mistake. So he did! It was time for him to start.

The next day, they went grocery shopping, and Leah stopped at a food demo. Suddenly, a light dawned, and Leah asked the lady who she worked for as well as all the particulars about the job. It required only two days a week with only six to eight hours each day and was at stores close to home. You could refuse any demo you didn't want or wasn't convenient. Perfect! Leah had many years of experience in customer service so this should be easy.

As soon as she arrived home, she called the number she had been given, only to be told they were so busy they had no time to train her and to call again in the fall. About to hang up, the lady asked what work Leah had done in the past. After Leah told her, she replied that Leah should be a natural and asked if she could work the next weekend.

The following weekend found Leah demoing a new snack cracker at a local store just minutes away from home. It was rather frightening as she wasn't sure how Roger would react. Returning home that evening, she found him glad to see her and eager to report all he had done during the day—answered several phone calls and took messages. Of course they were misspelled and the numbers made no sense, but he had taken care of himself just fine. Leah found herself busy each weekend and Roger developing more and more confidence as time went on.

Fall passed quickly, and December was upon them before they were ready. They were going to spend a month to six weeks with the family in Oklahoma and do some southern traveling away from the cold. It was snowing before they left in mid-December, and road conditions forced them to take the route through southern Idaho, Utah, and Colorado before turning east.

Roger's father seemed much more feeble and shaky than when they had left only seven months before. They decided they had better spend most of their time with him as they were concerned about his health. It proved to be a wise decision.

They returned to the condo in February to gorgeous sunny days and resumed the walks and demos and began to look for property to build a home on. Leah wasn't at all sure Roger was up to building but figured they could purchase the lot then build a few years later. They located a perfect spot overlooking a lake and with a large rock hill at the front of the property where it met the road, acting as a buffer for wind and noise. The lot was covered with wild flowers and seven large pine trees, so they bought it. That became the destination of most of their walks, and Leah began to feel settled once more. The condo was small and crowded, and she disliked living so close to neighbors but could cope until they decided to build.

Chapter 11

In March, they flew to Alaska for Suzan's wedding, staying only two weeks and actually anxious to get back to Idaho. They spent many evenings looking over their lot, planning their 'dream home'. Leah located many wild lilies, violets, and daisies, begging Roger to try to save them when clearing took place.

Early in June, they received a call from Roger's mother that his dad was being hospitalized, and the prognosis was not good. She was very upset and not able to tell them much, so they packed that very night. The following day, they made arrangements to be away for an extended period and took off for Oklahoma just before noon. They stopped at a motel that night but couldn't sleep, so they drove the rest of the way without stopping except for food. Roger was visibly exhausted and stressed when they arrived, and Leah was as concerned about him as she was about his dad.

It soon became apparent the end was near, and his mom was not handling it well. She became very depressed and would talk about her childhood and things Leah had never heard before. She was afraid of being alone again. A week later, Pop passed away.

Roger was greatly affected and seemed to regress more. It was very hot the day of the funeral, and Roger was exhausted. They helped Mom get her affairs in order and file the proper paperwork. Confident she would be okay, they left for home. They had been in Oklahoma almost a month and were very glad to get back to the cooler temperatures of Idaho.

The trip back was fairly uneventful as Roger needed to get settled at home and get some rest. They stopped only to eat and sleep, although the weather was lovely as they got farther north and into the mountains. The trees were green and fields full of ripe crops and wild flowers. Leah would have loved to spend more time exploring the natural springs and sights along the way, but Roger just wanted to get home, and she wanted to get him into a better frame of mind. His speech had grown slower and his color grayer as the ordeal progressed with his dad, and she knew he was feeling the loss, so they stayed on course and were home in three days.

They resumed their walks each afternoon, and Roger seemed to relax more daily and was talking much better, making fewer mistakes as time went by. He frequently said the opposite of what he meant and sometimes knew it was wrong, but most of the time he didn't. Friends from Alaska came through and stopped to visit on the way to attend a son's wedding. When they returned a week later, Roger asked how the 'funeral' had gone. It was at times like this that he seemed to have no idea he had said the wrong word. Leah couldn't help but wonder why his mind had made that particular error!

They had one week of one-hundred-plus degree weather that made their afternoon walks later and slower than usual. One such afternoon when the temperature had dropped from one hundred to ninety-four degrees, they passed a driveway that was visibly deteriorating and chipping badly in an area where the homes were only a few years old.

"I'll be. It's snowing already!" Roger exclaimed.

Leah looked at him puzzled, wondering what in the world he was talking about considering the temperature. She looked all around to see if anything was falling, maybe some ash or dirt. She soon realized he was looking at the concrete of the driveway they were passing. Then she remembered the first remote assignment he had been sent on after their arrival in Anchorage. The sidewalks had been constructed the previous summer and gone through only one winter when they had appeared to melt with the snow. He must be talking about the deteriorating concrete. "Just like the Alaska job, right?"

"Right!" Roger replied.

Leah felt she was getting pretty good at figuring out what he meant to say.

They went shopping for some things Suzan needed and in one shop, the owner was trying to talk Roger into something Leah didn't want. She emphatically said "no" but the sales pitch continued, so she walked out of the shop. Roger climbed into the driver's side of the Blazer and began to fuss at her for disagreeing with him and the store owner. She tried to defend her position, but Roger just ignored her, talking ever louder. The more he talked, the more upset he got, and he began shouting insults and names at her. It was hot and the windows were down, so Leah quickly put them up, which made him angrier. She pleaded for him to stop shouting as people in other cars were staring at them when they stopped at a stop sign. Roger was getting red faced, and she put her hand over his mouth to quiet him. Big mistake! Instantly, Roger slammed his right hand onto her leg and frightened her so much she began to cry. He continued to fuss the rest of the way home and then let her out and took off again. She had no idea where he was going, how long he would be gone, or what she should do.

She was shaking as she opened the door of the condo and went in. She felt faint as she collapsed into a chair with her head in her hands, too shaken up even to cry. Sometime later, she calmed down enough to think of what she should do. She needed help! She needed someone to tell her what was happening and what to do. Without giving it much thought, she picked up the telephone directory and turned to mental-health facilities. She found one in town and called, not really knowing what they could do but desperate for any advice. After a few rings, a receptionist answered and put her through to a counselor. She explained what had transpired, hoping for an explanation and some information on what strokes did to the nervous and emotional systems. The counselor listened and then suggested she get him in to see a psychologist for an evaluation. Their family doctor should be able to give her some names. After she hung up, she sat for a long time, contemplating what the counselor had said and wondering where Roger was and how he would react to this suggestion. It occurred to her, as she examined the bruise beginning to appear on her leg, that he had regained quite a bit of his strength back in that right arm.

A couple of hours later, Roger returned, calm and acting as though nothing had happened, not offering any information about where he had been. They had dinner and watched some TV with very little conversation.

The next morning after breakfast, Leah decided to approach the subject, and Roger surprised her by agreeing to see a psychologist with her if she felt she needed to. She said she did and called their doctor for a recommendation. She made the appointment for a week later, the soonest they could get in.

The day finally arrived. Leah had spent the entire week 'walking on egg shells', avoiding any offensive subject or cause for anger or frustration to Roger. During the session, Leah began to cry as Roger began to describe his feelings of anger and deep frustration about what had happened to him and his inability to return to normal. He felt inadequate and useless. The doctor offered little in the way of suggestions or advice but had started them talking about feelings they had been reluctant to express to each other. Leah was somewhat surprised to hear herself saying she felt trapped by Roger's refusal to continue with speech therapy, expecting her to do everything for him. Both had good reason to feel the way they did and needed to share those feelings. She had just been afraid of hurting Roger but felt maybe they were making some progress now. Roger refused to return to the psychologist, but the lines of honest communication had been opened for them, and they did continue to talk about it.

Roger found a Ford dealer who had several previous rental cars with low mileage and made a deal on a year old Lincoln Town car, which he had always wanted. Leah hoped it was a good one and the dealer trustworthy as Roger made the deal without even discussing it with her. The dealer also had a seventeen-foot motorboat for sale, and Roger made plans to see and take it out the next day. Fortunately, the transmission gave out that very night, so they did not buy the boat, but Roger informed her he intended to soon. Leah silently thanked God for his intervention. The dealer talked to Leah while Roger was out of the room, and Leah explained the situation and that she wanted Roger to take a boating course before he bought one as they had never before owned or operated a boat. The dealer was very sympathetic and said he had picked up on an urgency in Roger to buy and do everything right now. He offered to do anything he could to help.

Leah remembered the doctors telling Roger patients usually got six to seven years from by-pass surgery using the leg veins, but the second surgery they had used the mammary artery from the chest, and it usually lasted at least ten years. Roger seemed to feel they had given him ten years to live as he had adamantly stated he never intended to be cut on again, and the first by-passes had lasted exactly six and a half years. Leah wasn't sure how to react to his urgency or even if she should mention it. She pondered it awhile then decided to just 'wait and see'. She was surprised when those words crept into her thoughts.

The summer passed, and the fall was beautiful, with flowers giving way to colorful trees as the leaves turned. They made several trips over to the coast, always ending up in Lincoln City so Leah could browse the antique and gift shops. They both loved the coast and watching the ocean as it changed so often it never bored them. Leah was flabbergasted the first time she saw camellia bushes over six feet tall and covered in blooms. Camellias were her very favorite flowers, but she had thought they only grew in the deep South. Roger really enjoyed motoring around in his new vehicle, and it seemed to be a good one.

The weather grew cooler and days shorter so they curtailed their traveling and spent more time in the condo. October produced some snow though it didn't last long as the sun was out often. This area was known as the banana belt so had milder winters than areas nearby.

Chapter 12

They received a phone call about a homeowner's meeting and decided they should get involved. They attended and met some of their neighbors, amazed by how few attended. They learned many of the owners lived elsewhere and rented their property. That made changes most difficult, but Leah felt they could hardly complain as that was precisely what they had done.

The next week, Leah answered the doorbell to find a couple they had met at the meeting. They lived in a downstairs condo near the entrance and visited for a while. Leah liked her very much, but he talked so fast Roger couldn't keep up. They liked to play cards, so it was agreed they would get together the next week. Leah told them she wasn't sure Roger could keep up but would try. They did go, but Roger took too much time, and they soon ceased and spent awhile visiting. As they started to leave, they were told of the next homeowner's meeting and some issues to be discussed as well as elections. It was said to be a really important meeting; Leah was pulled aside to ask her not to bring Roger as he was too slow and would disrupt the meeting. Leah was surprised by the request and didn't answer. She brooded all the way home, determined Roger would attend as one of her objectives was involving him in every bit of their life that she could. She was determined not to let anyone or anything hurt Roger if she could help it. She again asked God to give her more patience, thinking he was probably getting tired of the same request over and over, but she needed it over and over.

They both attended the meeting the following week, and Roger gave some input on a project and was very helpful to the decision. It took him some time to get it all out, but it was obvious he had more knowledge and experience than anyone else, so no one hurried him or interrupted, and afterward thanked him and encouraged him to attend regularly. Somehow Leah was elected to the board, though she couldn't remember ever consenting to run. She actually felt drafted but decided it might be a good thing, and she was so happy Roger had participated.

During that meeting, she met another neighbor and was invited down for a glass of wine and a chat. Two days later, she called to reissue the invitation, and Leah went. Roger was tired and declined a 'hen' session, giving her a big grin and telling her she needed some female contacts. She found her to be gracious and kind, and they became close that first visit. Leah felt like she had found a long-lost big sister, and their chats became a highlight of each week, whether in the condo, the parking lot, or on a walk. Beth was also on the board and filled her in on some of the other owners and what had transpired previously. There were some problems Leah could have done without, but she decided if you wanted something improved, you had to be willing to work for it.

Through the lovely fall days, she met several more of her neighbors; two were older and more experienced, and Leah learned a lot about the area and merchants that helped her adjust. She finally felt she had someone she could talk to who cared and didn't judge. They were anxious to learn all she knew about nutrition, and she got them started on natural herbs. She had spent a great deal of time going to seminars and reading about nutrition and its role on one's health due to Roger's health problems. They also gave her an opinion of how the Homeowner Association was being run.

As winter approached, they decided to return to Oklahoma for Christmas as it would be hard for Roger's mother to face the first holiday without his father. She seemed to be adjusting well but was lonesome. Leah's mother had gone through a long period of depression, sleeping a great deal of the time after her father's death. She was afraid Mom would do the same.

They took the northern route through the Black Hills and visited Mount Rushmore on the way down. They picked up Roger's and Leah's mothers, and all had Christmas at Leah's brother's home. They had a great time visiting, took Roger's mother home, and headed for Tennessee with Leah's mother to visit her sister and family and then went down through Mississippi and Louisiana on the way back. Leah's mother loved the plantations and gardens they stopped to observe. They returned to Oklahoma and began repacking for the trip home.

It was now February, an early spring was budding, and their trip was an adventure, taking state highways they had never before traveled. They went through Yellowstone National Park and Cody and took the route through western Idaho and eastern Montana, getting just a little off route to check out a hot springs resort. It was a little rustic, but they decided it would be a good rest to spend a day soaking in the warm mineral water. Confident they had soaked up enough minerals to take care of their fatigue, they continued on the next day deciding to check out parts they hadn't covered before. They ended up discovering a cheese factory in a small town that made the most delicious mild cheddar and cheese curds. Leah was watchful, concerned that Roger was getting overly tired doing all the driving over new mountainous territory with frequent stops. It was beautiful country so difficult to hurry through, but they finally arrived at the condo and settled in.

They again took up the routine of walking each day. It was so beautiful with all the flowering shrubs covered with green buds, quickly opening to reveal yellows, reds, and purples. They slept late and lingered over coffee and newspapers each morning, not accomplishing a lot and not caring. Everything seemed to be going very well. Still, Leah occasionally felt a twinge of fear, not really knowing why or what for. She enrolled in a night course on writing your life story at the local college and kept busy with her assignments. She resolved many things about her childhood and learned much about her family and herself while working on them, plus she was developing many new friendships and new interests, and they each had a calming effect.

She and Roger often walked past new houses under construction and went inside, getting ideas for the home they would one day build. Roger began to have occasional bouts of impotence that put him into periods of gloom and angry outbursts, but Leah just did her best to convince him it didn't matter and that it would pass. A short time later, an article appeared in a popular magazine on impotency, stating that help was available. She showed the article to Roger, and he agreed they should consult a doctor. Their internist recommended a urologist just across the state line in Spokane, and they made an appointment.

After several tests, the urologist gave them a prescription for a drug. Roger took the entire bottle with few results and became even more frustrated. Leah did her best to help and tried even harder to make him feel loved and needed. Finally, she suggested they return to the urologist and see if anything else was available. She wanted him to regain his confidence but mainly wanted to avoid the terrible time they had experienced after the first heart surgery. Those memories were still too vivid, and she didn't think she couldn't take it again. They were informed of several devices available to help the problem, all of which had been successful for others. They discussed penile implants and self-administered shots as well as other apparatuses. Some sounded pretty difficult, and Leah was reluctant to try anything that could cause him any discomfort; he had just had too much of that already!

This time, they decided on one that didn't sound too bad and were given a prescription for a devise call Erect-Aide. Roger agreed to try it, and they went to a medical supply house and purchased it before returning home. This one worked, and Roger quickly regained his self-confidence and began to be in a better mood. Life became pleasant again. Leah was very grateful for the knowledge they had gained from the article, and the blessing of peaceful harmony once more.

One evening when they returned from their walk and roamed through an almost completed house they had watched from the ground up, Roger informed her he was ready to build. Leah wasn't at all convinced he was able and dreaded dealing with all the decisions to be made, although it had occurred to her that he needed something to occupy his time. She just wished he would wait a year or so to tackle anything so stressful.

The next day, he walked down to the house, met the builder, and informed Leah the builder would be coming by shortly. Leah felt the panic return and couldn't discuss it, keeping busy to avoid it. She spent the rest of the day in a deep depression, wondering what was ahead of her.

The builder came with plans drawn up, and Roger signed an agreement with little input from Leah. When she made a request, it was shelved to be considered later. The plans looked fine but didn't really give a lot of detail, and Leah could see lots of decisions would have to be made by her, but clearing had to be done first, so groundbreaking was a few months off. Also, Suzan's first child was due in July, and they were planning to drive up to Anchorage as soon as Leah's class was over.

Melanie's car was past its prime, and she wanted the Blazer. Roger had promised it to her, so they would drive both cars. Leah asked Roger to drive the Lincoln; it was very comfortable and rode smoothly; she would follow in the Blazer.

Leah spent lots of time looking for and buying furniture, clothes, toys, and anything else she could think of that the first grandchild might need or want. It was all loaded into the back of the Blazer with just enough room for Leah left in the front seat. She had convinced Roger to let her drive it as the Lincoln would be easier on him since he tired much easier and faster than she did. That evening, as she prepared to leave for her last class, she wondered out loud if she should take the Lincoln as the Blazer was loaded. Laughing at her own stupidity she told Roger, "I can't believe I just asked that. Tomorrow I begin a twenty-five hundred mile drive in that very vehicle, loaded as it is!"

Chapter 13

The next morning, they took off; Roger in the Lincoln and Leah following in the Blazer so she could keep an eye on him. June was 'bustin'out' all through the Okanogan, and the rivers sparkled in the bright sunshine amid varying greens and bright blue skies accented with billowing fluffy clouds. It was so peaceful driving through such natural beauty.

A short distance into the trip, Roger took a wrong turn. It took Leah almost ten miles of honking and turning on blinkers to get him to stop. When he did, she reversed the order and instructed him on a set of signals so he would know what she intended to do and could follow her lead. That worked well, and they did fine until they hit the ALCAN and some rain, hail, and thunderstorms that slowed them down. However, they encountered brown bears in shades of cinnamon and dark sienna as well as many elk and sheep, so they took time to enjoy the unspoiled scenery.

Unable to locate a good motel and not very tired, they elected to drive all night. The next morning around 4:00 a.m., Leah saw an animal in the middle of the highway. It remained planted where it was, staring at Leah until she was almost upon it, then bounded off just as she recognized it to be a bull elk with a heavy winter coat, it's antlers still covered with velvet. The winter in the north had been exceptionally cold and long that year, which accounted for nature's insulation this late in the season. Just as she passed the elk, a wolf, also carrying a heavy coat, ran from the side of the road. She may have interrupted its planned breakfast. Normally skinny animals, it looked quite fat with its' long fur.

Leah loved the feeling of freedom and serenity the drive afforded her in the early morning sunrise. The blue-gray mountains were peaked with pink, early-morning snow surrounded by wispy cottony fluffs slowly drifting by as if they were just waking up. Ever-changing foothills decorated with sparkling streams and budding willows and birch among the spruces made her feel right at home. Soon they would be hitting the curvy mountainous roads of gravel, and she wanted to relax as much as possible before she reached them.

They came into a small town, and she located a cafe that looked good and clean, so she turned on her blinker and pulled in. Roger followed, and they enjoyed a great breakfast of biscuits, vegetable omelets, and fruit. The cook was happy to prepare anything any way they wanted it as they were among the first few travelers that year. Before going on, she instructed Roger in the passing signals as the road ahead would be difficult to see if a car was coming due to the sunlight on the pavement. If she passed a car and pulled quickly back into the right lane, switching on her left blinker, he was to follow. If she hesitated in the left lane with only the right blinker on, he would know a car was coming. They practiced several times with no traffic until Leah was comfortable he could remember.

Traffic began to build as time went on, and they encountered many travel trailers that slowed everyone down and made many drivers impatient. Many had been taking chances and made Leah shake her head when suddenly she looked back and couldn't see Roger. At that very moment, she saw a black vehicle on her left passing her with a string of three RVs ahead and realized it was Roger. Gasping, she strained her eyes to watch him praying he would make it. There was almost no visibility with the sun in her eyes and the reflections from the metal and chrome on the RVs. It was some time later before she could see well enough to get around the traffic and catch up with him. Shortly afterward, she signaled for him to pull over and informed him how much he had frightened her and not to take any more chances but to follow her lead. They wanted to get there in one piece, even if it took longer than anticipated. Roger agreed reluctantly with a couple of retorts about her driving too slow; it was a real change from his usual accusation of her having a 'lead foot'. She had to laugh as she informed him he was driving a powerful luxury car while she was in a loaded 3.0 liter. He looked rather foolish, and they continued on.

They had picked up some fruit, cheese, crackers, and muffins at the little town grocery and picnicked that afternoon on a lovely mountain overlook pullout. As they got out of the car, high-pitched screeching was heard coming from the end of a log lying just off the road. A large furry creature scurried into the hollow of the log and must have had a nest nearby, maybe in the log, as it tried several times to frighten them away. When they failed to retreat, it left, and Roger asked Leah why she was driving so slow.

"Because the frost heaves have the road so bumpy my bottom feels like it will never again be fit to sit on. My muscles have knotted in rebellion to the punishment they are taking, and it hurts because that Blazer doesn't have the cushioning or stability of the Lincoln. Besides that, it's loaded, and that makes it slower. Stop complaining or just go on down the road, and I'll meet you in Anchorage when I get there!"

Leah was genuinely tired and in no mood to be criticized. Roger listened with wide eyes as she was not the one who usually got irritated and then muttered, "Sorry," and headed for the Lincoln. He waited for her to start off and then followed so Leah guessed they would continue on together as planned. She was sure glad as she hadn't meant a word she had said; she was just so tired. She had to shoot up another 'arrow prayer.' Pulling out, they heard screeching again. The log was being reclaimed!

They had decided to travel as long as they could and then pull over and sleep awhile, again not having much choice in motels. They made it until just after midnight when they found a pull out and stopped to sleep awhile. Leah put towels over the windows, donned her sleep mask and was out before she got her head down.

Suddenly, she jumped at the sound of loud noises overhead. Removing her mask and opening her eyes, she saw several large black birds sitting in a tree just above the car, staring at her. Yawning awake, she looked at her watch and saw it was almost five-thirty. The birds continued staring but had quieted down, so Leah decided they must have determined it was time to sound the alarm and awaken their visitors.

Roger opened his door and motioned to her to join him in the Lincoln. He had opened a couple bottles of orange juice, and she got out the muffins, and they enjoyed breakfast together. Giving him a kiss, Leah slid back into the driver's seat of the Blazer and threw the rest of the muffins and crackers to the birds as payment for the 'bed and breakfast'. They should be in a motel by 5:00 p.m. or close to it. How wonderful a hot shower and a bed were going to feel!

They arrived at half past four, checked in, and walked around the area to get a little exercise. It was situated among tall pines and birch with a babbling stream running through. Leah and Roger headed for the shower, too tired to care about much else, ate the last of the apples and cheese, and fell into the bed. The next morning, they enjoyed a delicious country breakfast.

Feeling very full and a little guilty about all the calories they had just consumed, they walked over a mile enjoying the beauty they had been too tired to care about the night before. Leah loved the streams and remembered outings they had taken with the children, fishing for salmon and picking wild berries for jam and jelly.

They arrived in Anchorage in the early afternoon and called Melanie, who was now in her own apartment and had made them promise to stay the first night with her. She was at work, so they settled into her spare bedroom before she arrived. Dinner was soon ready and was wonderful. Shortly after, Roger was sleepy leaving Leah and Melanie to visit and finish the wine.

The next day, they joined Suzan for lunch and made plans to deliver the baby furniture and other gifts that weekend. It was quite a shock to see her as she had gained almost seventy pounds. They knew she had been having problems and having to stay off her feet, but she had not told them nearly the extent of it. She had also neglected to tell them her husband was gone a great deal of the time and the marriage was in trouble. Leah took care of things, set up the nursery, and saw to it the baby things were readied for the arrival of Jessica Leah…a girl!!

They spent several days with Dave and Cindy, moving back to Melanie's apartment as the 'due date' approached. The morning of July twelfth, Suzan called from work to say something strange was happening.

Leah and Roger rushed to her job and drove her straight to the hospital, and Jessica Leah arrived at half past twelve the next morning. They were very tired but proud and relieved grandparents. However, the marriage appeared to be over.

Suzan was very weak, and Leah spent most of the time with her convincing her to bring the baby to Idaho and let them help her through this rough time since it appeared her husband was not going to be around. She had six weeks maternity leave, more if needed, and could fly down soon after they arrived home and got things ready. A change of scenery would do her good. She could come as soon as she was able and they were back home.

Leah and Roger again took the ALCAN, only slower and more relaxed, now enjoying the views and all the wildlife. They stopped often to take pictures, breathe in the fresh air, and be amazed at the breathtaking views. They encountered a female bighorn sheep, so Roger parked and began taking pictures. She seemed fascinated with the camera and began walking toward him while bleating to her young to stay hidden. Leah pulled out some crackers to distract her, and they did; they worked so well, the sheep tried to climb into the car, causing Leah to lose her balance and sit down hard on the gravel road. A short distance later, they came upon a porcupine and slowed to let him have the road, which he apparently felt belonged to him as he waddled in front of them for some time before continuing on.

Soon they were home again and had a ball setting up a nursery of sorts, finding a lovely port-a-crib at a garage sale. It was almost new with a matching changing table. Then Suzan and Jessica arrived three days later and stayed for a month.

It was like having baby Suzan all over again, and Leah was in grandmother heaven. Roger was equally enthralled. They took them on short trips around the area, and the time flew by. Soon it was time for Suzan and Jessie to return to Anchorage, and Leah and Roger sadly drove them to the airport, watching as they flew away. As they entered the lobby area of the terminal, they saw their builder and called to him.

"Where are you going? We just sent our daughter and granddaughter back to Alaska."

"My dad passed away last week, and I'm just seeing off some of the relatives."

"I'm so sorry to hear that. What happened?"

"He had a stroke and never got much better and then died a week later. I'm busy trying to settle my mom. She wants to sell the house and move in with her sister." He looked very tired and sad.

Roger told him to get some rest and call when he felt like it, and let them know if they could be of any help. Leah felt suddenly cold thinking how quickly he had passed away and how lucky she was to still have her husband.

They settled in to resume their life in Idaho while they missed their daughter and granddaughter terribly and had to keep busy to combat the loneliness. Leah planted large pots of flowers and vegetables on the deck, and they resumed their walks.

One evening as they walked, they were discussing the staggering bills that were coming in from their trips and all the motels. Leah agreed the Alaska trip prices were high but more understandable than the rates they had paid that winter in the South. Alaskan rates were always high in the summer, but the

Southern rooms discounted little, and the same price for their room as for her mother—a single and a senior.

"You would think they would discount at least a little for half as many."

"Yeah..." Roger answered. "And...I...half...a...man."

Leah stopped, stunned. It broke her heart to think Roger felt so inadequate.

"Roger, you are still better than any ten men I have ever known! I want you to remember how much I love you and need you, and never feel that you are in any way inferior to anyone. You started out way ahead of most."

Roger looked at her hard then walked over, put his arm around her shoulder, and gave it a squeeze. They finished their walk, holding hands and returned home to a gorgeous purple-and-pink sunset covering the sky above their deck. They sipped lemonade and enjoyed the view until it was dark and then went in to the TV and bed.

Their builder was busy finishing two other houses he had going and selling his mother's house, so it was decided they would clear the lot this winter and begin the construction next spring. Roger and Leah began looking around, getting ideas of what they wanted versus what was available and practical.

They made many trips into Washington to find kitchen, bath, cabinet, flooring, and lighting shops. They would have all their fixtures picked out before the construction began. It was a beautiful and warm fall, affording them lots of time to visit with acquaintances made around the area, and they had numerous invitations to play cards and visit. They had met the neighbors on each side of their lot and found themselves with not enough time to visit, travel, and do all the things they wanted.

Leah demoed most weekends and was asked to work for one chain exclusively, giving her a raise and lots of fringe benefits. Soon it was time to head for Alaska again to greet their second grandchild and spend Christmas there. This time, they would have no loose ends to tie up or problems to deal with and would fly, so they should be able to really relax and enjoy. They both needed that!

Dave and Cindy also had a beautiful little girl, so they had a full and fun holiday with the children. They spent a good deal of the time taking pictures. They took one day and drove to the end of the road up the mountain where the smoke from Redoubt volcano could be viewed oozing up and out of the snow-covered peak. They could also see the valley below with its stream and frosted trees. Beautiful! On the way back down, they stopped to take some pictures of a moose calf in a clearing. As Roger set the camera, Leah saw the mother eating in some willow trees between them and the calf. She continued eating, never taking her eyes off Roger, so Leah quietly warned him to make no fast moves. She saw the mother's ears go back in the charge position and knew they had better not get any closer. They got several great shots of both mother and calf and then returned to the car and continued down the mountain, leaving the moose still eating. Each incident of seeing familiar and beautiful scenery and wildlife made Leah happy and sad at the same time—happy to be back in familiar surroundings and sad to think of returning to the lower forty-eight.

While they were there, Melanie decided to put Cory to sleep as he had experienced a couple of strokes and didn't get around very well; he was now 17. She wasn't sure he could see much and was afraid of coming home to find him gone, never knowing how long or much he had suffered. She preferred to have him go in her arms, knowing he was loved. She felt it was the best thing to do for him, but it hurt her terribly. He was a member of the family, and Leah felt guilty for leaving him. As much as he loved the girls, the changes in his life had not been good for his health, and he seemed to go downhill fast in the past two years. She felt he had grieved for her and Roger and hadn't adjusted to being alone so much with the girls working. It also needed to be done when family was around to comfort Melanie.

They saw several friends, visited many of their favorite places, and shopped for the babies. It was so much fun to buy little girl clothes; Leah outfitted them both with Christmas pajamas, toys and several outfits. Roger teased her, telling her they had baby clothes in other states so she didn't need to spend all their time shopping. It was soon time to return to the condo and spend their first winter there.

Chapter 14

The winter brought snow but much milder temperatures than experienced in Alaska. The snow was beautiful but gone in no time and prevented nothing, so they drove to the Silver Valley and Sun Valley and took in all of Idaho as an early spring approached, bringing with it the groundbreaking for their new house. Roger seemed to be anxious to get started and had several outbursts, coming mainly when he made a mistake and reacted with the actions of a child...anger and tantrums. Spring was wet and gray, and Roger seemed to regress into despondency. He never articulated it but appeared to be resentful of Leah's working most weekends. He continually wanted to go somewhere, always suggesting a 'weekend trip'. Leah didn't feel she could quit her job as the store manager was so good to her and allowed her to take winters off when necessary. He had been exceptionally understanding when they had to leave for a month during their busiest time due to Mom's surgery. Besides, Leah loved working and had made many new acquaintances. The change of pace was very good for her, and the time away from Roger helped too.

Leah felt she needed time away from Roger though she hated to admit it. She had begun to feel very sorry for herself due to the stress she had to live with most of the time. Attempting to keep things from upsetting him, she often felt she was being manipulative. Other times she felt he was manipulating her and greatly resented it.

They returned home after Mom's surgery just in time to learn they were going to have to blast for the foundation of the house. The feeling of pending doom returned, giving Leah many hours of uneasiness trying to determine why. Hadn't enough problems come their way? Roger's mother called often; she was lonely and unhappy they had left after only a month. Only a month! Leah and Roger needed to get the house built and regain the feeling of being settled. Will that time ever come? Leah wondered. It seemed they had been living out of suitcases or 'camping out' in the condo for such a long time.

The house was held up by rain for two months as cement trucks were not allowed on the roads due to the saturation. They had been told that spring and fall in Idaho were frequently gray with lots of rain, but they had experienced such beautiful early springs the previous three years it was hard to deal with the wetness now. They spent much more time inside and shopping around for light fixtures, carpet, tile, and cabinets. Finally, the foundation was poured with hot sunshine, necessitating Roger hose it down several times each afternoon.

The previous spring, they had lunch in a great soup-and-sandwich shop and found out one of the partners was a previous acquaintance. Soon after, they were approached to invest and become a silent partner as the group was contemplating buying a fourth restaurant. The three they had were doing well, and Roger liked the other partners, so Leah encouraged him to invest, and he did. She had felt they needed to invest some money, and Roger needed something to occupy his time. They had taken the paperwork to their accountant; he said it looked good, so they were shocked to learn one of the restaurants had been sold just before they had returned to town. The park location had been sold in order to finance the lake purchase. Leah was asked by the other partners to work at one of the locations and become familiar with operations and determine any problems. With the house, her weekend demos, and Roger, she was running in all directions and doing her best to keep it all under control. She found herself getting very impatient with Roger for expecting so much from her. Her questions or suggestions regarding the house were usually ignored. It seemed to be progressing very slowly but surely, and she had no time to move right now anyway.

The financial reports on the partnership had not been entirely accurate, and the business was in trouble; there was nothing Leah or anyone else could do to save them without pouring lots more money into them. She developed a great friendship and a good deal of respect for the other partners, some of whom were being hurt much more than she and Roger as ultimately all restaurants were sold, and the partnership dissolved. The others expressed a lot of gratitude to her as her working and learning about the discrepancies had kept them from losing even more, and a disaster could have occurred if the sale had not gone through. Leah fell into a heavy depression as it seemed nothing had gone right for some time, and she feared what might come next. She felt so guilty for encouraging Roger to invest. She now had more time for the house, and it was almost ready for the finishing projects. It had grown considerably since the plans were drawn up.

Suzan and Melanie had decided to leave Alaska and move to Idaho, so Roger had enlarged the lower floor adding an additional living room, fireplace, and kitchenette, making it almost two houses. Leah was happy to have them and looked forward to having sweet Jessie but knew it was temporary. She wondered what they would do with that large house when the girls ultimately moved out and wondered how long they would stay. Roger had requested the girls make the move before winter as they were planning to drive the ALCAN, pulling a U-Haul behind the Blazer. Leah flew to Anchorage and brought Jessie back, giving them freedom to have garage sales and pack without upsetting her. She took time to visit with Dave and Cindy and their precious little girl before she left. It would be crowded in the condo until the house was finished, but they could make it, and it should be a short time with any luck at all. The girls made the trip in late September with no difficulties, and both found jobs quickly. Of course, they had many hair-raising tales of the long journey on the rough road!

Winter was on the way, the air was crisp and smelled clean; the turning leaves painting the hillsides in breathtaking colors. Then the call came that Leah's mother was to have hernia surgery, and the doctor was fearful of colon problems so Leah wanted to be there during the pre-op tests to give moral support and encourage her to do what was needed. She made arrangements to leave the next week, leaving lots of food and instructions with the girls.

The tests turned out much better than hoped, and the surgery went well, so Leah was hopeful of getting home before Christmas, but ice storms and the inability to get outside caused her mother to fall into a deep depression. Leah determined she should stay until after the first of the year and get her through the holidays as Dave and Cindy were planning to visit Roger and the girls in Idaho for some skiing. He would definitely not be alone. She booked a flight home for the first week of January. There had been several scary incidents involving flight so many new security precautions had been adopted. An attempted hijacking occurred making it scary to travel, so Leah's mother talked her into staying one more week. Also, her sister, Elaine, was coming.

Entering the airport with all the new security was rather frightening as it conjured up ideas of what could occur. Leah was instantly sorry she hadn't gone home when originally planned but that was only considering herself as her mother was in much better condition to be left now.

"Call your mother as soon as you get home."

Leah's aunt planned to stay a couple weeks and care for Leah's mother after Leah left. Leah's mother looked close to tears, but it would have been worse without her sister there.

"Soon as I walk in the door, I promise."

They were at the sidewalk as only ticketed passengers were allowed past security, and Leah had convinced them there was no reason to park to go inside since they couldn't wait with her. That had upset her mother but also made them more comfortable that all precautions for her safety were being taken.

Leah gave them both a hug and turned away to the revolving door. Turning for one last wave good-bye, she saw her mother and aunt wiping tears from their eyes, and she waited until they returned to the waiting car parked at the curb.

The first leg of the flight was a little turbulent causing her queasiness then became downright nausea. Leah couldn't wait to land in Denver and get her feet on the ground. She was feeling really tired and light-headed when she entered the airport lobby and made her way to her next gate. She had only a few minutes to relax when it was announced that the flight was overbooked and the airline requested any passenger who could to please take the next flight. That sounded pretty good to Leah; more time on the ground to get herself psyched for the last leg to Spokane. Denver was always crowded it seemed, especially so now. All seats in the waiting area were full, and she dreaded the crowded flight.

"When will the next flight be?" she asked the attendant.

"We have one leaving in two hours going to LA, and then it will be continuing on to Seattle and Spokane. I can give you a voucher for a free flight."

Leah declined as two more stops and she might get real sick. She wanted to get home asap. She boarded the plane glad she had requested an aisle seat; having learned on a previous flight after being wedged in the middle between two very large men. She felt a little guilty now as she had more than enough room for her five foot, 100 pound frame. A little guilty! She settled back to try to nap a bit before landing in Spokane and making the forty-five minute drive home. It seemed she had just closed her eyes when they were preparing for the landing.

Gathering all her belongings, she inched down the aisle behind the many passengers that had been packed into the plane. She saw the girls and Roger as she rounded the last curve in the walkway. Stepping out through the gate, she heard a squeal and saw Jessie running toward her. Scooping the two year old up in her arms, she finally felt at home.

The girls and Roger had moved everything into the new house, and it was wonderful, even though she couldn't find anything. They had done a great job, and Jessie seemed to feel right at home, having made the move as easy as changing clothes. Soon they were all settled, and life was good again.

Roger seemed to love having the children around, and the little things that needed to be done kept him busy and seemed to make him feel needed. Leah continued to demo and began working with seniors, helping them with the new food pyramid, food labels and low-fat and low-sugar cooking. All seemed to be going well indeed.

Leah's brothers and sisters decided to get together in Oklahoma in April, and she and Roger made the trip with Jessie, wanting to show her off. It took all of Leah's energy to keep up with the little girl, but Jessie had a ball as did all the adults. The Azalea Festival was taking place in the town where Leah and her siblings had been born, so they all made the trip to the park and reveled in the many-colored blooms.

As expected, Suzan met a man who seemed to adore Jessie, and they were married the following fall. Jessie stole the show, telling everyone she and her mama were getting married and calling her new peach taffeta her wedding dress. Leah had major surgery that winter and had a terrible time getting her strength back. Dave, Cindy, and their daughter came for Christmas and stayed until she was on her feet, a tremendous blessing for both she and Roger. One afternoon, she was lying on the sofa, almost asleep, when she felt warm, wet kisses planted on her cheeks and forehead. She opened her eyes to find two smiling, precious little girls standing over her. Amazing how much better it made her feel!

Her immune system seemed to be shot; she just couldn't manage to stay well. She had pneumonia six weeks after surgery and then rhinitis, shooting her temperature to 102 degrees. Then she was diagnosed with asthma. Melanie stayed through the spring to help out and then moved into Spokane to be closer to her job. Depression was the next thing to overcome.

Leah wasn't sure why she was so sad—probably a combination of things she hadn't fully dealt with too busy to take the time. Life had seemed to whirl by rapidly the past few years, and she felt so tired that she was afraid of what it would take to make her feel really rested again. She would cry at the drop of a hat, and it often happened in church. She was so tired, she contemplated quitting work even though she loved it. Her life just seemed to be out of control.

Then, on July first, Leah's mother fell and broke her hip, requiring surgery and a prosthesis. She was worried about leaving Roger alone, but both girls promised to keep check on him daily, so Leah left for Oklahoma again. She called every other night to give a report and see how he was doing. After just a week, he complained he couldn't get anything done as the girls were calling all the time. The second week, he informed Leah he had bought a boat but promised not to take it out alone. He had successfully completed a boating course earlier in the year, but Leah had thought they would buy one together. Her mother agreed to go home with her, so at the end of three weeks, they flew back to Idaho.

The boat looked like a new one, and Leah was pleasantly surprised at the good deal he had made. She had been fearful he had been taken advantage of, but the price was well under what the boat was worth. Her mother moved into their bedroom on the first floor with the walk-in shower, and she and Roger moved into the downstairs bedroom. They showed her the sights around Coeur d'Alene, but riding very far made her sore, and she disliked using the walker. She progressed to a footed cane and decided it was time to return home. Leah arranged for wheelchairs and assistance, and her mother flew back alone.

The house was much too big only two years after moving in, and the area was building up so fast that they decided to sell and look for another small town in the Northwest. Leah had lots of muscle pain, making it especially difficult to navigate the stairs. They decided to take that summer to finish the lawn and landscaping and put it on the market the next spring. Moving would be a chore, but keeping that big house was too, and the area had become so crowded, some of the charm was gone as had the white tailed deer Leah loved to watch. The Chinese pheasants still nested in the knoll below the house, but they would probably leave before long also.

The roses Melanie had bought for the front yard were thriving as was the lavender miniature Leah had brought home from the grocery store. Its leaves had been yellow; it looked very sick and neglected, so she bought it for a dollar and nursed it back to health. It grew too big to keep inside, so last summer she decided to try it out front with the other roses. This year, it was close to four feet around and tall and covered with clusters of small lavender blooms. The hydrangea didn't fare as well and was moved to the back, hoping to revive it. All in all, the yard looked very nice and even the rock hill was blooming with the phlox, marigolds, and daisies they had planted. Neighbors had observed Leah watering the tiny shoots and wanted to know if she was trying to get the rock to grow.

They really loved it there, and things were going well in spite of the past problems. They were really sorry they had built such a large house. The stairs were becoming almost impossible for

Leah to climb and vacuum, so she decided to see her doctor. She was sent to a rheumatologist with a very busy practice and a great reputation. He told her she had developed a problem called fibromyalgia, whatever that was, after the surgery, and her muscles hurt a lot of the time. Joining a support group and attending seminars with Roger, they learned a lot about the disease, which greatly helped her overcome her depression. The anti-inflammatory drugs made her stomach hurt, so she finally began a nutritional supplement regime that seemed to be rebuilding her immune system, and a slow but progressive exercise program. She was coping but still depressed often!

Then an article came out in the paper about a suicide stating the deceased had fibromyalgia. Of course, there were other factors, but Leah decided she had to get more involved with the support group and overcome her depression once and for all. She was well aware that there were many other reasons besides her health, but it was a biggie as she had always depended on her good health. Now she hurt a great deal of the time and had so little energy.

She became very active, never missing a meeting and picking up many different types of treatment. Some worked for her and some didn't, but she was armed with knowledge about the syndrome and the fact that depression was a part of it. As one doctor put it, "The FMS patient grieves for the loss of their former life and health as one grieves for the loss of a loved one." That described Leah's feelings precisely.

Her sister, Jenna, flew out from Tennessee on her two-week vacation; it was her first trip to the Northwest, and they had a great time showing her the wine country and the West coast. She loved the area, especially southern Canada, and wanted to return soon with her husband. She especially loved the boat trips on the beautiful lake with its many coves and intriguing shoreline.

They spent the summer traveling again to all their favorite spots when they could take time from the yard and garden. The Oregon coast seemed to call them frequently, and they loved to take Jessie for a few days to the aquarium at Newport and the wildlife safari near Roseburg. They now walked with neighbors, stopping often to visit or play a game of cards. So many new homes were going up, the town was becoming crowded. A new theme park was going strong just ten miles north, and Jessie loved it. There was so much to do, time seemed in short supply. Roger had a couple of angry episodes after Leah's sister left, so she decided he tired with too many people around and kept company to a minimum. They only entertained or visited one couple at a time, avoiding parties. She had little time for it anyway. Her energy was building slowly, but she still hurt.

Fall was lovely and crisp, and they were enjoying the leisure when Roger's mother called that she had to have another surgery. She was now eighty-three, so they made plans to leave for Oklahoma the next week to care for her. It was nearly six weeks before she was strong enough to be left alone with neighbors and close friends to check on her. Roger was very tired of being away from home and in cramped quarters; he frequently had difficulty speaking. His frustration led to a couple of outbursts, which Leah quickly stopped by leaving the room and returning with a new focus for his attention.

Returning home, they took a week and made it a vacation, taking back roads and state highways and seeing scenery they hadn't had time for before. They checked out more hot springs and some mining areas they had seen on the map and returned as snow was falling in the passes, getting home just in time to avoid winter ice.

Leah was active in the church and civic groups, so the year flew by, and the house was put on the market. Roger rarely participated as he had difficulty keeping up with conversations, leaving all the talking to her. It was rather hectic at first with all the Realtors touring and calling, but it soon slowed, and they settled into the gardening chores. Returning from a trip to southern Idaho, they learned buyers were eager to make an offer on their house, and their Realtor was out of town. An associate made an appointment, and the next day, it was sold.

Jessie was going to have a little sister sometime in October, so Roger and Leah decided to rent for a year or two and continue looking, giving them some time with the new grandchild. They would have three granddaughters, so Leah had plenty of sewing and crocheting to do, and she loved it.

They found a newly completed house to rent and moved soon after. It was only a mile from their old neighborhood, so it hardly felt like a change except that the yard had to be put in. That was soon completed, and they again felt somewhat settled. Roger again kept busy doing the little things that a new house needs to make it home, and Leah worked in the unfinished basement that housed the laundry and office area as well as the storage and crafts area. The house was split level with just four stairs up and down that they could maneuver just fine.

Monique was born in October and was a real delight. The girls stayed with them when Suzan worked occasionally or when Roger and Leah could talk her into a night out with her husband. The girls soon felt it was their second home.

Christmas was a real joy with the new baby. Dave and Cindy were now in California and flew up with their little one so the family was all together. The weather couldn't have been better, and the children all skied, leaving the three little girls with the grandparents. They loved having them all to themselves.

Leah's mother was to have back surgery in March, and they made plans to go to Oklahoma the week before. Then Roger's mother called, saying that she was also having surgery a week before, so the trip was moved up, and they ended up staying for five weeks until both had recuperated enough to be left alone. They hurried home, taking only three days as the trip had definitely taken a toll on Roger again.

Leah waited until he seemed to be rested and back to normal—for 'after the stroke'—then approached the subject of moving to Oklahoma to care for their mothers. They seemed to need more medical care each year, and they had been keeping the road hot between Oklahoma and Idaho, and Leah was also feeling the strain. They discussed it some over the next few weeks, though Roger didn't want to live in Oklahoma again.

Dave called saying that he, Cindy, and their daughter would drive up in May. After their arrival, they all drove to Victoria for a week, taking Jessie with them to keep her cousin company. They had great fun, and having tea at the Empress Hotel with the royal family look-alikes greatly impressed the girls. They loved swimming nightly in the hotel pool. It was wonderful weather, and Leah, Roger and the girls walked the wharf, taking in all the artists and craftsmen while Dave and Cindy visited the beautiful gardens a short drive away. The visit went much too fast after they returned to Idaho with boating, skiing, and swimming. Soon the children returned to California, and the couple was alone again.

The lease on the house would be up in July, and they had some land in the small town where Leah's brother lived that they had purchased several years before just in case. Now seemed to be the right time! After mulling it over several times, they made the difficult decision to move again. This time, it would be another major move, requiring garage sales and the heavy-duty packing that Leah dreaded. It seemed they had just finished unpacking, but she couldn't keep caring for everyone without getting them closer together. They would store everything until they found or built a house.

They began the task of packing a little each day since they had almost a month and were toying with the idea of staying until fall. When they learned the owner was raising the rent fifty dollars a month when the lease was up, it made their decision, not because of the amount but the principle. They had put in the yard, tended it, and done all the little things that made it homey, and it now seemed they were expected to pay more due to the improvements. They called all of their doctors and picked up their records, deciding Roger should have a blood test to check lipids before they started out. Three days later, they learned the lipids were high and, more alarming, so was his glucose. He was now diabetic. They received information on the new diet, giving Leah indigestion just thinking about trying to maintain it while traveling.

Roger was depressed for several days and irritable, growling at her when she got in his way, so she finished getting things ready with as little exertion on his part as possible. She never mentioned the diet and noticed he seemed more depressed after the grandchildren had visited. She knew he was dreading leaving them as much as she was. It was awful being torn between children and aging parents.

Blake called to tell them they had a big house, and he and his wife were rarely there and insisted she and Roger stay with them while building theirs. He had been insistent, convincing her they would be an asset, so Leah agreed they would give it a try after Roger had okayed it, feeling it would be a great place to keep watch on the construction. It seemed to be decided that they would build, though Leah wasn't at all sure she could do it again and hoped they could find something they couldn't pass up. Blake made it clear he was hoping they would build on the lots they owned across the street from him and had a place for them to store their furniture, so everything seemed to be arranged and ready.

On a trip for records, Roger pulled into the dealership where they had purchased their last two cars. They had discussed selling Leah's Buick and the boat as the truck and car were going to be enough to take. Roger insisted he would drive the U-Haul and tow the truck while Leah drove the Town Car. Roger wanted to look at a Continental but was encouraged to drive a Mark VIII also. He picked the Mark VIII.

They advertised the Buick the following week and got a call the next day, wanting them to drive it to the prospective buyer. They had to go into town again so made plans to take it by that afternoon as they returned. While in the city, Roger again drove into the dealership, and before Leah could stop him he had traded the Buick, Town Car, and boat for the Mark VIII. Leah knew it was not a good deal, but his look told her not to argue or he would make a scene. She could do nothing, so she waited while papers were signed. Roger had learned she hated his scenes and the threat could manipulate her into giving in to his every whim. She resented it and was in turmoil inside as they left the dealership.

They made arrangements for movers and left the day after their lease was up, not realizing they were moving on the busiest holiday weekend of the year. The trip was slow with many motorists staring at her doing thirty-five and forty in the Mark VIII behind the U-haul and uneventful until they reached Kansas. They blew in amidst a rain shower that escalated into a full-blown thunderstorm minutes after they were in their room. The wind almost blew the trees over and broke limbs, threatening everything in its path. They were hungry and ran across the parking lot to a restaurant during a lull in the storm, giving several other tourists the courage to do the same. Soon several booths were full of dripping patrons discussing the weather. Returning to the room sometime later, they learned they were under a tornado watch, and that chilled Leah to the bone. They were back in Tornado Alley!

The next morning, they awoke to a rain-washed sunny morning, ate a light breakfast, and continued on, arriving at Leah's brother's house in early afternoon. They found the key where it had been hidden for them and unloaded their bags. Her brother and his wife had to be out of town for the next two days and afforded them time for some rest. They drove around the small town, found a restaurant then went back to spend a quiet evening.

Chapter 15

The following day, they went to see Leah's mother, watching dark clouds move in quickly soon pelting them with hail. It hit the windshield with such force, Leah was sure it would come through. Slowly they made their way to a partially occupied underpass and waited it out with several other unfortunate motorists. After the heavy rain and hail passed, they stopped and surveyed the damage, amazed there was only one dent in their new car, and it was just on the chrome trim around the window. Some homecoming, she thought. The storm put her in a gloomy mood, wondering what was in store for them in the future. It was better she didn't know!

They spent a few hours with Leah's mother and sister and then ventured back to Blake's as the dark sky was still threatening, and they hoped to prevent being caught again.

Leah's brother and his wife returned two days later with lots of stories about their trip and wanting to purchase property in Arizona. Blake loved the desert and the warmth with all the cactus, and they had brought back several for their sunroom. Blake was always working, rarely taking time off other than Sunday. That was his day to rejuvenate, although he often went to his office early before going to lunch and a movie or drive to watch eagles or explore different areas.

He was four years younger than Leah, and they had grown very close though they had lived far apart. As adults, they had learned they had shared many characteristics and understood each other. Leah marveled at how handsome he was, considering the near fatal plane crash he had survived some twelve years before. He walked a little crooked and she could often see he was very tired, but he would never admit it.

Roger said he was going to build the house himself; they could sub it out, but Leah wasn't at all sure about going through all the hassles again. It had only been four years since the Idaho house had been built, and all the decisions and conflicts were still much too clear in her mind. She began to hand him the real estate magazine section of the Sunday paper and secretly called an agent to inquire about a house she saw. It was just twenty miles north and halfway between her mother and her brother. It was on a corner lot and had been built by a contractor for his own family. It was supposed to have many extras and was a little over what they wanted to pay but was still within their budget. Roger refused to even look at it, stating he was going to build one himself!

They spent the next month getting plans drawn up and making inquiries about contractors. Roger seemed to be excited and happy about the prospect of contracting it, having spent many years in construction for the government and state. Leah felt genuine panic return. Was this what her premonition had been warning her about? She couldn't believe he was serious, but he just ignored or put down her fears. Blake tried to quiet all her concerns, assuring her he could recommend many of the subs he had done business with in the past.

The foundation was poured at the end of August, and framing began in September. Roger insisted on doing so many things himself that Leah was getting little sleep. He told her what was needed, and she made the contacts, lining up all the subs and picking out the hundreds of necessary items a new house requires. Roger gave her explicit instructions about several of the larger and more expensive items. She could readily see the budget would be shot before it was halfway through. He attempted to instruct the subs, but it was soon clear he could not make them understand him. Leah was forced to convey his instructions. The only problem was that Roger wasn't always able to tell her what was satisfactory, and she often felt she was losing her mind.

It became the norm to spend Sundays lunching with Blake and Annette, spending the afternoons and evenings visiting and relaxing together. They took in more movies than Leah thought she had seen in all her married life and explored places she had never been before. She began to long for Sunday to roll around because she spent the weekdays running. They spent many hours planning all the trips the four of them would take together: cruises and car trips through all the areas Leah and Roger told them about along the Pacific Northwest coast into Canada. They wanted to spend at least a month in Australia and New Zealand together. Blake continually told them he was planning to retire soon; however, Leah wondered if he could really leave his business for anyone else to run. She hoped he was grooming his son to take over as he had worked so hard for so many years and needed to reap his reward while he was able to enjoy it. Soon it seemed the days ran together, and she was never sure what she had done when. Blake had encouraged her to keep a phone log, noting all conversations and pertinent facts from each that proved to be her salvation many times. She would never have remembered many things had she not been able to refer back to the log.

They had planned to have Christmas in the new house but one problem after another arose. Roger began to have episodes of irritability and irrationality, and the anger returned. Leah told him after an especially bad day that insisting on building was the meanest thing he had ever done to her. She had tried and done many things in her life but had never even considered nor desired to be a house builder. She would spend hours checking on prices and deciding on items, only to have him tell her they were not right or too expensive. One evening she showed him the total already in the house, and he just shrugged and said, "It's out of control."

Out of control! She thought he was the one out of control as he had insisted on the expensive uneven buff brick, trim, and outer doors of a material that never needed painting and solid oak interior doors. She went for a long drive alone so she could get out the emotions she was feeling and have a good cry. She was afraid to cry or show her true feelings to Roger as she never could anticipate his reaction. Sometimes her tears could be disastrous, and she wasn't sure her nerves could take anymore. The cry did help, and she promised herself some time alone now and then.

She spent a lot of time walking and searching her soul for her real feelings because she was having many days when she felt she couldn't go any further. Roger wouldn't stay on his diet, but she couldn't stay home and cook while running all over the area hunting for things for the house. He had stopped speech therapy, stopped walking, and refused to do much to help himself. He had even stated that he had taken care of her for thirty years, now she could care for him. Just what did he think she was doing all those thirty years? Raising children and keeping a home, car, yard, and garden while he was away on remote sites was certainly no picnic. She suddenly came to the realization she was very angry and feeling sorry for herself, and she was very ashamed.

She asked God to please forgive her; she did know he would not put more on her than she could bear even though she had let doubts creep into her mind from time to time. Prayer was about all that had kept her going the past months. She felt she and Roger were growing apart, and she was so tired all the time that she didn't have the strength to do anything about it.

Christmas was celebrated at her brother's home with all the family there. The house was brightly decorated and a large tree was covered with aircraft ornaments. Blake was so into aircraft of all kinds and had collected miniatures for years. Many of the ornaments were ones Leah had found on their travels. Thank goodness for her sister-in-law's patience and understanding or Leah wouldn't have made it. She came down with a four-day illness and was flat of her back in bed unable to eat or drink or do anything but hurt and chill. She was finally able to be up Christmas Day and wasn't sure that her body hadn't simply rebelled against all that was going on in her life. She was still weak and dizzy but managed to stay up most of the day

As usual, all the family was invited to Blake and Annette's for dinner potluck style, and Leah hoped she wasn't contagious.

It was a very festive day and all made a tour through the new house, giving it lots of compliments. Leah hoped to have the next Christmas dinner there. She wondered how her sister-in-law could still speak to her after spending the busiest time of the year in bed. Annette seemed to take it all in stride, never concerning herself with minor details. Everything seemed to take care of itself and all got done.

The following week through New Year's Day, Leah rested a great deal while the inside of the house was painted and the trim finished. By mid-January, they began to move and had the furniture delivered. Leah was still feeling tired and decided there was no hurry to unpack—just find enough to get by with. She had kept a ledger by number on all the boxes so she knew where linens and kitchen supplies were, which were needed first.

The foundation had looked too small, but standing inside looking down the long hallway made her feel it had grown considerably. The hall began at the door to the master bedroom and continued through to the garage door just beyond the two bedrooms and bath on the west end. The master suite was on the east end with the living area in the middle. She could stand in the master doorway and see anything going on in most of the house, which would be great when caring for the mothers. Little did she know the mothers would use it very little, but used it would be!

They spent the first night in their new home on January sixteenth, their wedding anniversary. Slowly they did the little things a new house requires, always needing more hours in the day. Leah discovered, while getting taxes ready, that Roger had overpaid one of the subs by more than a thousand dollars. This revelation shocked and dismayed her as he was supposed to let her know before any payouts were made. How many more had been overpaid? When she tried to question him about the books and receipts, he always seemed to feel like the question was an accusation and would immediately become defensive and often angry. Tantrums became a frequent occurrence during the rest of the winter while straightening out the records, and Leah asked him to please let her set up the files and books. He agreed but wouldn't stay out of them, getting papers scattered all over the office. He seldom remembered where he had filed anything, much less which pile of papers anything was in. Leah felt really helpless but couldn't talk to anyone, afraid it would influence their opinion of Roger. There was really no one she felt close enough to confide in anyway. She could talk to her mother but then she would just worry. She could talk to Blake, but he was like a little brother to Roger as Roger had none, and she didn't want to chance endangering that relationship. He had begun screaming that he wanted a divorce again whenever he got angry.

Lots of little things needed to be done as is always true of a new house; however, some things the subs needed to finish. Roger refused to make any of the phone calls to them, leaving all the contacting to Leah. He did have trouble getting the words out, but she figured he would never be able to if he didn't start trying. Some days when he got upset and shouted he was getting a divorce, she actually wished he would. She knew it was an idle threat, and he knew as well as she did that he needed her help with so many things. He didn't even know what he was supposed to eat. He was supposed to check his glucose level four times a day but rarely did more than once and sometimes skipped that. She had put him on a vitamin and mineral supplement while in

Idaho, which seemed to be building his immune system. She had to ask him to look at her when she spoke as he frequently ignored her. He seemed to be doing fairly well and frequently told people he never felt better in his life. If only his temperament would improve.

He was reluctant to meet new people or go anywhere without her, not seeming to understand when she wanted to go somewhere alone. She began to wish for some time with no one making any demands of any kind on her. She really wanted to just be responsible for herself for a change and for everyone else to take care of themselves for a few days! She got very tired often and was having difficulty sleeping. It was past time for her to get a medical checkup herself, and she vowed to do it soon.

She inquired around, finally decided on an internist, and went to see him. Roger insisted on going with her, though she really wanted to go alone but couldn't come up with a good excuse. On the way, she realized they would be a short distance from the garden store and talked Roger into shopping for some supplies they needed while she saw the doctor. He needed some tools to level the yard, so he reluctantly agreed. She took all her records from Idaho with her, and the doctor quickly read through them. He admitted he knew little about FMS but said he had heard quite a lot about it recently and was open to learning more. He examined her thoroughly and then had her come into his office where he asked a lot of questions about her home life and Roger. She filled him in on her situation and both of their previous health problems. She found it difficult to talk about her situation and came close to tears several times but managed to hold back. He sat back and looked at his notes for a while and then looked straight at her and told her most of her problems were due to the stress of being the caregiver for her family. She needed to get away to relax for a week a couple times per year to rejuvenate herself or she would be incapable of caring for any of them.

"Terrific idea," she replied, "but just how to do it is the problem."

She could just imagine Roger's reaction if she said she wanted to go away by herself for a week. He always seemed hurt if she went somewhere without him or wanted to stay home when he needed to go somewhere. It sounded great and the thought conjured up warm, sunny beaches in her mind, but she couldn't imagine being able to do it. It would be such fun if her sister could accompany her, but she was working and spent her short vacations with her husband on the coast. She couldn't actually think of anyone who was free to join her.

"If you don't figure out a way to have some time for yourself, you may not be able to even keep yourself well much less anyone else. You seem to have lived with stress for so long without really dealing with it that you will have to before long. It would be best for you to decide when rather than have your body force it."

She left knowing she was basically healthy, but the stress would eventually cause the FMS to flare again. The nutritional program she was on seemed to be doing well, and her immune system seemed to have been strengthened, but there was no doubt that FMS, as well as so very many other ailments, were triggered by stress. Stress...was that the constant feeling she needed to be alert and ready for anything? She seemed to be always waiting for the next crisis. Boy! Would a vacation far away be wonderful?

She had been given a prescription to help her sleep and could get a tranquilizer if needed. She had an adverse reaction to one after Roger's first surgery and didn't care to chance a repeat. She did sleep well that night and felt great the next morning. She made breakfast while Roger went for the mail, and they settled in to enjoy scrambled eggs and biscuits while looking it over. Her work with Idaho Partners in Health through Nutrition had left her with numerous low-fat recipes, including the biscuits Roger loved. Her FMS Network quarterly had arrived, and she skimmed through several articles on recent successes with new meds and therapy treatments.

Suddenly, she decided to go to the library and see what they had on strokes. Roger seemed so moody at times and withdrawn at others, she felt there must be some information that would help her know how to react. That afternoon she went to the local library and got a card.

"I'm Leah Kerry, and we're new to the area. My husband had a stroke a few years ago, and I would like to get any books you have on the subject."

The librarian was a friendly lady, short like Leah with a beautiful smile, expressive eyes, and a genuine desire to help. Leah liked her immediately. She sat down at the computer and began looking for anything on strokes. After a minute, she said, "Bingo!" as she turned back to look at Leah.

"We have one book here, and I show two more books, but they will need to be ordered from another town. Should be here in two or three days!"

"That's great. By the way, do you have anything on fibromyalgia?"

"Why, I had a lady in this morning asking about that same disease. What is it? We didn't have anything except a paper I ordered for her."

Leah explained the syndrome and told her about the seminars and conferences she had attended in the Northwest. She offered to bring in some of her information to be copied and kept at the library. The librarian was happy to have anything and gave her a name of a patient who needed information badly. Leah also got information on a father whose daughter had FMS and was eager to learn more about it!

"What brought you to our little town?"

"My brother lives here, and we like a small town, having lived twenty-two years in Alaska and another eight in Idaho. We've been away such a long time, it's taking some effort getting used to the weather."

"I'll just bet it is. Who is your brother?"

When Leah stated his name, the librarian knew him well and told her how much they appreciated his efforts on behalf of the town and that she was very glad Leah had chosen this town also.

"I'll be glad to run off a copy of any information on fibromyalgia you have and set up a file for the library. We seem to have several suffering from it."

Leah left thinking she should find out how many had it and organize an informational meeting with them. Two days later, the librarian called to tell her the books were in. When she went to pick them up, she discussed an FMS meeting with her and the idea was met with enthusiasm and an offer to use the library for the meeting. That would be someplace everyone in town knew and an ad in the local newspaper should let people know about it. Leah set a date and went immediately to the newspaper to get it in that week's edition.

Back at home, she browsed the book on strokes she had checked out. It was put out by the American Heart Association and had been written by three doctors. It certainly had enough credentials so she was sure she would gain valuable knowledge from it. She digested the first dozen pages or so, thinking she had needed the book so much for so long.

She prepared a salad and washed two potatoes and baked them halfway and then sat down to read more. There were numerous stories of experiences of other victims, and she could recall Roger going through most of them and knew his were not unique to him but actually the typical reactions to a stroke. She found episodes of rage and tantrums and realized that as bad as they were, they were rather normal—if any of it could be called normal. There were many suggestions she wished she had known before now—if only she'd had this book ten years earlier. However, checking the copyright, she found it had been published fairly recently. Oh, well, it was helping her now! I feel grateful for anything, she thought to herself.

Roger had been working in the yard and came in hot, dirty, and sweaty. He looked very tired, and she was sure he had to be hungry.

"Why don't you take a quick shower, and I'll finish lunch."

"Good! What ....having??"

"Salad and stuffed baked potatoes."

"Stuffed ....what?"

"Spinach, onions, and cheese."

"No meat?"

"I'll shake some bacon bits on both. Or I could add tuna to the salad. Which sounds better?"

"The...tuna...good and the bacon....too. I like...tuna in salad. I'll...be...few minutes."

His speech was still slow but he got his desires out clear. He headed down the hall to the bathroom, and Leah put the book aside to finish lunch. It was now half past one, so he would probably just have cheese and fruit for his supper, so Leah dumped the whole can of white albacore tuna into the salad, added some sunflower nuts, and grated the white of a boiled egg. She threw out a great many egg yolks, using only the fat-free whites. She cooked the onion and fresh spinach while the potato finished baking and then stuffed them into the center and sprinkled a tablespoon of grated cheddar cheese over the top.

Roger walked in just as she set the salad on the center island and got out the salad dressing.

"This looks...good!" Roger was always very hungry after working in the yard as a new lawn took so much effort. Leah wanted to put some kind of flowering bushes around the drive as soon as the weather permitted and get a garden ready. It would be so good to get out and dig in the dirt again, even though this would be the third yard they had put in within five years time. It was getting to be a drag to both of them, and she hoped they wouldn't do it again ever. This house already seemed too big when she cleaned it but was built for privacy when company came. The office opened into the entry, allowing for bill paying and piles of papers without piling up the rest of the house. Leah was very proud of their design and hoped the yard would turn out just as good.

Roger ate hungrily, remarking how good it was. Leah finished first and asked if he felt like going for the mail and ordering flowers in the local shop. Their daughter-in-law was ill, and flowers would make her feel better. He agreed, and they set out after the dishes were taken care of.

The mail was full of the usual bills, so they proceeded to the flower shop. Inside, the owner welcomed them cheerily, and they placed their order, deciding on a live azalea that could be put out later. The florist introduced them to several townspeople who came in as "Blake's sister and her husband." She no longer had a name of her own, just "Blake's sister." That was fine as that title immediately made them part of the town and gave them a connection.

A book review group had formed to review several books on Oklahoma history, and Leah attended the next week. She met several more of the town's residents and enjoyed reliving some of the things from her own childhood there. The following week, she received a phone call asking her to join the local women's service club. She was beginning to feel at home once again.

She scheduled the first few FMS meetings the next week and took the information to the local newspaper. The organizational meeting was held with seven people attending. They seemed eager for information on a number of illnesses besides FMS, and Leah had to stress she was not a health care professional and that the meetings were for resource sharing only. She wanted all participants to provide input and to share any materials they came across. She also stressed they needed to confirm any diagnosis and treatment with a doctor. She wanted to share experiences, successes, and the newest research; that was all.

The meetings continued for several months with several guests speaking on various treatments. In the spring, she had a seminar, bringing in seven professionals on seven methods of dealing with chronic pain. It was well received with twenty-eight people attending from the area. Leah had been pleasantly surprised and encouraged with the number of health professionals willing to come to participate. She felt her time had been justified and continued until Jessie came to spend the summer.

Roger loved having Jessie there, and they bought a supply of games and toys for her birthday, hoping to keep her occupied. Her bike had been shipped down, so she was able to keep active. They made many trips around the area, and Jessie helped pull weeds and work in the garden, eager to assist her grandparents with the new house she loved. The only problem was the distance between the bedrooms, and she soon moved Grandpa into the spare bedroom after several sleepless nights with her joining them in their bed. It was usually because of a cricket, an owl, or some other sound she wasn't used to having lived all of her seven years in the Northwest.

They made trips into Arkansas and Missouri, and Jessie swam, played, and had a great time. She adored her great-uncle Blake, and they had several Sunday dinners together and celebrated birthdays together as Blake's was only three days after hers. She learned to tolerate her grandmother's shopping in flea markets, antique stores, and thrift shops, developing a pretty good eye herself. The summer was over much too soon. Leah took her home and spent two weeks in Idaho visiting friends, children and grandchildren.

She and Roger flew up together for Christmas, arriving just after an ice storm had made a mess of the trees and power lines. It was cold, but the holidays were enjoyable, and they visited lots of friends and saw all the new shops and subdivisions going in. Roger informed her on the way home that they would do future visiting in the spring and summer as he didn't care for the ice and snow anymore.

Back at home, they set about exercising and getting themselves in shape to start the gardening and yard work as it would soon be upon them. Leah frequently called Blake's office to inform him she was close to having lunch prepared and to come up as soon as he could. He always came if he could get away and seemed to really enjoy eating her cooking. She made cinnamon rolls, cakes, and pies he loved even though she would have to limit Roger and make sure most of the goodies were sent home with Blake. She would stop in at Blake's office to make copies or send a fax and was always encouraged to stay and chat awhile. She really began to look forward to those chats and depended on Blake for advice and help with any project or problem. They grew closer than ever, and Leah could see Roger responding to Blake more than anyone else. He seemed to give him confidence, and Roger began conversing with more people in town.

Soon it was time to plant the garden, and they set out many plants before heading back to Idaho for the birth of Suzan's son: their first grandson. Joshua weighed just over ten pounds, and Suzan needed help with two babies since Marie was only twenty months old. They stayed most of the time with Melanie and kept the two girls with them most of the time, giving Suzan and the baby time to bond. Her husband was still in school and working, so Leah did most of the shopping and caring for the family and loved every minute of it. They stayed until Jessie was out of school and then packed her up to go home with them.

They both agreed they were too old to be caring for little ones and were glad to be getting some rest. They decided to go through Glenwood Springs and take in the mineral baths as well as the beautiful scenery and picturesque town. Jessie went down the slides, sat in the spas, and had a ball, not wanting to leave. The trip was great fun, and Jessie loved every minute.

They arrived home to find the garden producing an abundance of weeds. After a few days getting it in shape, the okra, tomato, and eggplants showed through and began to bloom. Soon they were harvesting goodies, and Jessie was enthralled. She never minded helping weed until the evening a group of tiny toad frogs jumped out of a hole onto her feet, scaring her almost into hysterics. She refused to go into the garden from that time on but continued to pull weeds out of the yard. As the hot days arrived and the okra began to bear, they would have fried okra nearly every day, Jessie and Roger never tiring of it.

All too soon, the summer wound down, and it was time to take Jessie home again. Leah only stayed a week, wanting to get back to keep up with all the yard work. Flying through Denver, she gave up her seat to a handicapped person who had been left at the gate after seating had closed. She would have a three hour delay, so she called home. There was no answer, so she called Blake at work and asked him to locate Roger and give him her new ETA. When she finally arrived, she was met by Roger, Blake and Annette. Roger had left early to see a movie before meeting her, so Blake couldn't locate him and decided they had better meet her flight in case he didn't wait. Roger had learned of her delay from an agent, so they all went for dessert, laughing at the mix-up. Leah entertained them with her explanation of the airline's grateful gifts; an upgrade to first class, a free round-trip credit, and coupons for free drinks.

Fall arrived, and Roger and Leah made a trip to California to spend Thanksgiving with the children and grandchildren there. Dave and Cindy now had two of the most beautiful blonde little girls anywhere, and they adored them. The youngest insisted Leah sleep with her, and they became real buddies before they had to head back home. They enjoyed all the games and school programs, but it began to get pretty cold so they decided to take the southern route home, going through Tucson and spending a day looking around at possible winter homes.

Christmas was a family gathering, with both mothers, Leah's sister and brother, and close friends. Blake and Annette went to his daughter's home to watch the grandchildren open their gifts and then came by for dessert later in the day. Leah was tired but happy to have all together for the day as they had done many times before moving north to Alaska.

Winter continued, giving some really cold weather before submitting to the warmer temperatures of the approaching spring. Blake had obtained his helicopter license and certification that previous fall and purchased two before spring was in full swing. He had infected Roger with his love of flying and had involved him in the remodeling of some old commercial properties Blake had purchased. He and Roger spent a great deal of time together, and it seemed to be helping Roger so much. Several workmen remarked to Annette that Roger was a very intelligent man; Leah had always known that, but after the stroke, he had rarely had a chance to show it. With Blake, he seemed so comfortable and spoke and worked with ease. Blake was very patient when he needed extra time and was always informing Leah of near mistakes Roger had caught and saved him both time and money. Leah was so glad to have Blake's help with everything that she began to feel they had made the right move in coming back to Oklahoma. Roger was developing self-confidence and getting better all the time; his anger seemed to be subsiding also. He rarely had outbursts that spring, not even when Leah did something he disapproved of.

They began planting the garden and caring for the yard, making reservations for Jessie to fly down in June soon as school was out. She had informed them she was old enough to fly alone, and Leah had made arrangements for someone to care for her during the layover in Denver. She was very excited each time they called her, and Roger and Leah were counting the days until she arrived. Life was good again, and Leah rarely had the feelings of foreboding doom she had been plagued with for so long.

Leah's mother was scheduled for surgery June third, Jessie was to arrive June seventh, and Leah's aunt came to help her mother. All was working out well, and they were busy getting ready for the summer by planning trips and making reservations. They made numerous trips in to shop and lunch with the mothers and Leah's aunt before the surgery, knowing it would take awhile for recuperation. Leah promised to take her aunt to several of the small towns around specializing in antique shops as they both loved wandering through the items most of the family considered junk. Leah had also become fond of auctions, purchasing many vintage items for the house, and promised to take her to some of those also. This summer promised to be a lot of fun, and she was ready and anxious for it to begin.

Chapter 16

Leah and Roger were lingering over coffee and the newspaper before dressing for church when the phone rang.

"Hello."

"Hi, Sis. What's happening over there?"

"Just the usual coffee and news before church. What's happening where you are?"

"I just talked to mother and Aunt Elaine, and they've agreed to come down and go to Fin and Feather for lunch. I want you and Roger to join us on one condition."

"Oh, yeah? What's the condition?"

"I'm buying, and there is to be no argument either here or there. Otherwise, you can't come with."

"Well, aren't you the bossy one? We would love to join you but would really rather split the check with you. Please!"

"No way! It's on me or not at all!"

"Your way or no way?"

"Right! You agree?"

"Hold on and let me run this by Roger." She repeated the invitation and demands, and Roger nodded.

"Some....choice! Tell ....we'll go, take care....him later." Leah relayed the message.

"Good. We'll need both cars. Why don't the women go in my car since the mothers can get into the four-door easier, and Roger and I will take your two door."

"That sounds like a plan. What time?"

"The women said they would be here around ten-thirty, so we should leave here by eleven. We'll come down there as soon as they get here."

With that settled, Leah hung up the telephone and finished her coffee. It was only nine, so they had plenty of time. She and Roger finished dressing and made the bed just as her mother and aunt arrived. Aunt Elaine decided to leave her car at Roger and Leah's house and all women piled into Blake's Cadillac and the men in Roger's Lincoln. On the way, Blake took them on a side trip and stopped at the huge oak tree that had been the scene of the first Oklahoma governor's inauguration for whom the town had been named. It was hot by this time, and they lingered only long enough to get a roll of film taken of the family under the tree.

"Blake, thank you so much for showing us this place. I didn't know about it, and I was born and raised just fifteen miles from here." Aunt Elaine was enjoying herself very much despite the heat.

They arrived at the restaurant ahead of the church crowd and had to wait only a few minutes until they were surveying the buffet tables. The food was terrific as usual (they were frequent diners on summer Sundays when the resort was open). Leah got to the dessert table first and saw only one piece of lemon meringue pie, which she picked up. She reached the table and set the pie and her plate down at her place.

"This pie is for you, Mother. It was the last piece so I latched onto it, but you have to clean your plate first. No deciding to have dessert first." Leah knew her mother loved sweets and would live on them if allowed. Any pie would do, but lemon meringue was her undisputed favorite.

Blake picked up the pie and put it by his place and stated, "And I mean it too."

Their mother had always finished each instruction with the phrase when they were children. They laughed, visited, and ate until stuffed and had a great time. Leah was very glad they had come and could see Roger was having a great time too. As they finished, the women wanted to check out the gift shop.

"Shopping," Roger groaned.

"How 'bout we let the women shop to their heart's content while we go and get the helicopter to take it in for Memorial Day tomorrow."

"Good.... idea," Roger answered.

Blake had his choppers in a hanger in Muskogee until the one he was building was ready. They would leave the Lincoln in the hanger, and the women could pick it up on their way home. It was agreed, and the men left. Leah found a carousel pony doorstop to go in the grandchildren's room and some pins for the girls, and Annette bought some other jewelry for her granddaughter. They decided to shop in Muskogee for flowers for Memorial Day and stopped at a few shops before finding one open with wreaths they liked. They made their purchases and headed home after Leah picked up the Lincoln at the airport.

Roger and Blake were there just finishing the remains of angel food cake and strawberries.

"You're out of Cool Whip, Sis," Blake told Leah as she came in.

"I know. I'll get more tomorrow. We had the cake with peaches this week, and Roger really liked it."

"I wouldn't know. I've never had any," Blake whined, looking forlorn and deprived. Everyone knew he loved peaches and talked his mother into making peach pie every holiday and family dinner.

"I'll take care of that this week and make another angel food," Leah said, laughing.

"I have a tape of us when we were kids. Want to watch it?" Blake asked his aunt and mother.

"I think we had better do it another time. I want to drive back before dark; I'm rather tired, but we sure had a good time. Thank you very much," Aunt Elaine replied. She was as short as their mother, and it tickled them to watch her behind the wheel of her 1986 Lincoln Town car. She avoided heavy traffic and driving after dark, so they said their good-byes and left.

"Roger and I were thinking about taking the chopper down the river one time before putting it away for the night. Any objections, Sis? Do you mind?"

"Why...no." Leah couldn't really figure why he was asking her as Roger went with him often. Blake loved to fly and Roger loved to be with Blake. Blake had asked Roger why he didn't learn to fly himself and get his license. Roger had given him his sly grin and replied, "Why...should I... I have .. brother-in-law... fly me around?"

They headed out the back where they had landed the chopper in the pasture behind the house. The A-frame ladder to their pool was just the right height to get over the fence, and they prepared to climb over.

"Oh, Sis. Roger snagged his dress pants coming over. Do you think you can fix them?"

"I'm sure I can."

"You haven't been up for a while. You want to go first, and I'll come back and get Roger?"

"I don't think so. I need to put my purchases away and clean up your strawberry mess. I'll take a ride tomorrow."

"Okay. You had your chance."

They climbed over the fence and started the engines. Leah could see Blake going through his checklist and ran in to get the camera. She had only four frames left and took them all as they lifted off. Suddenly, Blake came back down and removed the doors as it was hot. She and Annette loaded them into the trunk of the Cadillac, and the men took off.

Leah and Annette sat in the sun room for some time, looking at catalogs. It began to get dark, and Leah turned off the TV to be sure they heard them go over. They were to call when they landed so Annette could pick them up at the local airport.

"It's getting pretty dark. They should be back by now."

Annette agreed, and they went outside to look at the sky. Leah took the phone so they could see and hear. At nine o'clock, Annette told Leah she was going to the airport.

"They might be down there working on something and forgot to call."

Shortly after Annette left, Melanie called and was filling Leah in on her new job. Leah told her about the glorious day they had enjoyed, how she was tired, and that the weather was hot. They were still chatting when Annette came back.

"Get off the phone! I need to talk to you," Annette snapped.

"I need to go, honey. Aunt Annette wants to talk to me."

"Okay, Mom, but call me back."

"Get off now!" Annette demanded.

Leah looked at her, stunned, as she replaced the phone and walked into the hall. Then she saw the policeman and started to shake.

"What is it? What's happened?"

"There's been an accident. Roger's being life-lifted to a hospital, and I'm taking the policeman's car back to the station, and then I'll drive you in with him following."

Leah was suddenly freezing as her mind tried to understand what she had been told. Suddenly it hit and she screamed, "No! No!...How is he? What about Blake? How is he?"

Annette just stared at her for a moment.

"I don't know how he is. I only know they've taken him to the hospital, and we need to get there."

"What about Blake?" Leah repeated.

Annette just stared at her.

"Annette, what about my brother?" Leah shouted at her.

Annette shook her head;..finally said, "He didn't make it."

Leah felt her legs go limp, and the room grew gray. She couldn't be hearing it right. This couldn't be happening. She began to shake harder.

"We're going to take the police car back to the station so he can follow in my car, and I will drive you in your car so you'll have it with you. I'll be right back. You stay here and wait for me. Don't try to drive yourself!"

Annette and the policeman left. She tried to think, but her mind wouldn't focus. She couldn't cry; she was numb. She stood in the middle of the room trying to decide what she should do. Finally, she ran to the kitchen and grabbed the phone book. She called the hospital and explained who she was and that she wanted to know the condition of her husband.

"Just a minute. The life-flight nurse is here, and I'll let you talk to her. We have his Medic-Alert and know he's had a stroke and is diabetic. Is he allergic to any medication?"

"Not that we know of."

"What insurance does he have?"

"He's on Medicare, and we have a supplemental policy."

"Could I have your group number?"

"I need to know about my husband's condition. I'll give you the information when I get there, but I'm at home; it will take some time; I need to know now!" Leah was close to hysterics.

"Here's the nurse now."

"This is the life-flight nurse, and your husband is badly injured. You should get here as soon as safely possible. We are just learning the extent of his injuries, but they are bad."

Leah choked and couldn't catch her breath. She just held the phone and stared into space.

"Are you there? Is anyone with you? Do you have someone to drive in with you? Are you okay?" The nurse was getting louder with each question.

"Yes...s...s. I...have...someone to drive me...I'll be there as soon as I can." Leah hung up the phone and reached for her purse. She went out the door and got into the truck, which was still in the driveway. Just as she reached the street, Annette and the policeman arrived and made her stop.

"Let me see if the house is locked." It wasn't so she took the keys from Leah and locked it and then made Leah slide over so she could drive. Leah just sat there in shock. She couldn't think; she couldn't cry; she couldn't feel; she didn't know what to do. She just sat there, unable to move.

Annette drove silently for a while then started talking, saying she hoped various items had been done and named them off one by one. She continued talking until Leah wished she would shut up. Then she realized it was her way of dealing with the tragedy. Blake gone! No, it just couldn't be. She couldn't accept it. She needed him. Roger needed him. They had so many plans to do things together! No! No! No! her mind kept saying over and over. The pain of it was choking her, and she had difficulty breathing. Leah saw lights going by in the distance but had no idea where she was or what the lights were; she was aware of nothing except that Roger was badly hurt and needed her, and she had to get to him.

Finally, they arrived at the emergency room. Her mother and aunt came in right behind them. Leah kept asking how Roger was, but everyone seemed unsure. After what seemed like hours, a nurse came into the room and asked Leah if she wanted to see Roger and if she thought she could handle it. She told her his face was cut and his breathing was shallow as both lungs had been punctured by broken ribs. She also informed her that she should call any family home right away. Leah insisted on seeing Roger to let him know she was there and would call the children afterward. She prepared herself.

Aunt Elaine insisted on going with her as she had worked in hospitals and had seen accident victims before. Leah walked in and saw the gash in his left cheek first, and then she saw the protruding left eye out of its socket, all purple and red. He was so swollen. She began to go down, her legs refusing to hold her. The nurse grabbed her and helped her out of the room.

"I'm okay…I'm okay…I want to let him know I'm here!"

She walked back in, aided by the nurse, and slid her hand into his badly swollen one. He indicated he knew her but couldn't talk due to tubes in his mouth. His chest looked very strange and out of shape. The rest of his body was covered, but Leah knew there was more. His forehead was covered with blood, she knew he must have had a blow to it too.

"I'm here, darling, and I'm not leaving until you do. I love you."

Roger lifted a finger slightly to let her know he had understood. She could tell he was in terrible pain and having a hard time breathing. She hurt all over for him and felt terribly helpless. The nurse put an arm around her shoulder and steered her out of the ER and back to the waiting room.

"You should call your children home as his situation is grave."

Leah stared at her in disbelief. Roger had to get well! She needed him; she couldn't lose him too.

Her mother and aunt took her hands and held them until she seemed to understand. All color drained from her face, and she shook her head. This couldn't be happening. The room was spinning slowly as Leah sat down by the phone and reached for her purse and calling card. She waited until she felt steady and the room stopped spinning then dialed Dave's home number, focusing on the telephone to keep calm as Melanie answered. She had babysat for Dave and Cindy and was spending the night.

"Melanie, it's Mom."

"What's happened? You sound awful."

"There's been an ...accident...Dad and Uncle Blake were in a helicopter crash. Uncle Blake is gone, and Dad is in very bad shape." Leah's voice kept breaking as she hurriedly blurted it out.

Melanie groaned then whimpered.

"No," she cried. Then she said, "I'll get Dave."

"Mom?" Dave took the phone after just a minute, "we'll get the next flight out. Where are you and how can I reach you?"

Leah looked around for someone to give her the number and address. The nurse took the phone and gave Dave the necessary information. Dave promised to call his mother as soon as the reservations were made and promised to call Suzan also. Leah was glad to only have to make one call. By now it was 12:30 a.m., and she thought of Roger's mother. She would be asleep by now. She had undergone open-heart surgery just eight months before and was eighty-nine, so Leah wasn't sure what she should do. She knew the nurses did not expect Roger to make it but didn't want to call as his mother was hard of hearing and understood little on the telephone. Someone needed to tell her in person. It would frighten her to be awakened at one or two in the morning, and it would be difficult to make her understand.

"Do you think I could wait to tell his mother first thing in the morning? She needs to be told in person as she can't hear well and is a heart patient. I don't know what to do."

"It's risky, but maybe you should wait rather than scare her due to the hour and her health," the nurse said as she left the room.

"If you think it will be all right, I'll go over and tell her first thing in the morning," Aunt Elaine told her. "I will bring her back to the hospital with me."

"I'm so afraid of her health if we wake her at this hour with such bad news. I need to wait. I can't deal with it all now." Leah felt near collapsing.

Leah's two brothers and their wives came in. Everyone was showing strain and shock. They all informed her they would be staying through the night with her, and she was so glad to not be alone. Annette made several phone calls while everyone waited.

"Where is Blake?" their mother asked Annette.

"I don't know. I guess he's still out on the sand bar."

"Sand bar?" Leah asked. "Where did it happen?"

"On the river near the bridge. That's all I know," Annette replied. She was very pale but going strong.

"Surely they've taken him to the medical examiner," Aunt Elaine said. "Can you find out where?"

"I don't know." Annette seemed upset by the questions and decided she needed to go. She came back and told Leah that Roger's wallet and personal items had been placed in the hospital safe by the highway patrol.

"Since you have lots of family here, I'll go. I have lots to take care of."

"That's fine. Thanks for driving me."

The phone rang, and it was Dave.

"We got a flight at nine-thirty a.m. on American and will be in at three-thirty p.m. Hang in there, Mom. Dad's a fighter."

"Someone will meet you, darling. I'm so glad you're coming. Did you call Suzan?"

"She's got to make arrangements for the children but will get out as soon as possible."

"Thanks so much, Son.

Soon the nurse came in to inform them they would soon be taking Roger to ICU. The doctor would be in to see them soon.

Leah began to shake again. What would the doctor have to tell her? She was so scared, more than she could ever remember. How could Roger possibly get through this? He had come so far after the stroke, and it had taken so much work on both their parts; would this undo all they had accomplished? She shook her head and tried to stop thinking. Her mother moved over and put her arms around her.

"It's chilly in here, and you're in shorts. You're cold aren't you?"

"I'm not sure," Leah replied. She didn't really feel much; though she was shaking, she wasn't sure it was from cold. She hadn't thought about what she had on but looked down at the black shorts and red house shoes. How dumb! She should have changed shoes. And the tank top she had kept cool in this afternoon was hardly enough to see her through the night.

"It's okay. I'm fine," she told her mother.

"No you're not and don't try to fool us. We can see you're far from fine, and you need a cup of coffee. I'll go get us all some." Aunt Elaine was taking control as usual and started out with Leah's brothers to get coffee for everyone.

Just as the door closed behind them, the doctor came in.

"Mrs. Kerry?"

"I'm Mrs. Kerry," Leah said.

The doctor stood before her, looking grim. He was a kind man with dark hair and beard; Leah only cared to hear how Roger was.

"Your husband has multiple injuries and is going to need extensive surgery to repair a ruptured artery in his left leg. However, he has lost so much blood that we will have to transfuse him to get him ready for surgery. Also, both lungs are punctured by the broken ribs and have collapsed. I'm not sure he can endure the long surgery, but he sure is a fighter."

"Will you be doing the surgery?"

"No. I'm an internist. I have an orthopedic surgeon and a plastic surgeon as well as a pulmonary specialist checking him now, and they will determine when he can go to surgery. They will see you up in ICU."

Leah was dazed, considering the injuries and the surgeries awaiting Roger. Could he make it? Leah began to beg God to see him through this. Don't let him suffer and please don't take him. Losing Blake was tearing her heart out, and she needed Roger to help her get through this. Please, please give me the strength to get through this, she thought. She really didn't want to face this but knew she had no alternative.

Her aunt and brothers returned with hot coffee, and it did taste wonderful and warming. Suddenly, she thought of Blake and was obsessed with whether or not he had suffered. How had he died? Was it immediate? She began to shake again and grew very pale. She walked to the door that led to ER and opened it, catching the first person she saw. She asked if the nurse or pilot that had been at the scene were still here.

"What is it you need, dear?"

"I need to know how my brother died, and I need to know now. I can't wait for this information. I must know now. Was it immediate? Did he suffer? I have to know!" Tears began to trickle down her cheeks; she was again close to hysterics.

"Let's go back in the waiting room and sit down. I will get in touch with the attending nurse and have her come to talk to you. I'm sure she is still here." She guided Leah back into the waiting room and gave a signal to her brother to watch her. Elaine followed the nurse into the hall and closed the door.

"She's close to breaking so keep a close eye on her, and I'll get the flight nurse back here as soon as I can. Call me if you think she needs a sedative."

Leah was whimpering softly and staring into space after she sat down and scared everyone. Elaine related what the nurse had said, and Leah's mother took her hands, which were like ice, and held them to warm them. Leah's brother, Ralph, sat on the other side and put his arm around her shoulder.

"Geez, sis, you must be cold in those shorts. Aunt Elaine, see if you can get a blanket to wrap around her."

As Elaine opened the door, a nurse walked in and took Ralph's place as he stood.

"I am the flight nurse. Did you have some questions? I'll try to answer as best I can."

"How did my brother die? Was it immediate?" Leah's voice broke as she was engulfed in another attack of shaking.

"I'm sure it was, and I don't believe he suffered. He sustained a blow to the head, and that was the probable cause of death."

"Oh..." Leah uttered softly as her lip began to quiver. "Th... ank...you."

Elaine had returned with a warm blanket that the nurse wrapped around Leah, then stood to leave.

"I'll be around here for a while yet, so have me paged if you think of any more questions. The pilot and I will be checking on you and your husband."

As the flight nurse left, the ER nurse came to the door and gave a questioning look at Elaine. Elaine knew she was ready to get a sedative or tranquillizer, but she smiled and shook her head no. She felt Leah needed to keep alert and deal with the situation without being drugged; her niece had always been strong, dealing with what life threw at her, and would do it again this time. The nurse gave a long look at Leah and then asked if she could get anything for anyone in the room. The boys took a long look at their mother who had started to cry silently as the flight nurse related her information about the cause of death. This was the second son she had lost in five years, and she was still in shock. They all indicated that they needed nothing, so she left. A few minutes later, she came back to tell them Roger was being moved to ICU, and they could see him before long but should stay here until they came for them.

Chapter 17

The minutes seemed like hours before they were informed Roger was in ICU and one or two at a time could visit him. Aunt Elaine decided she should accompany Leah first, and then her mother and a brother could go in. ICU was on the floor with the Cardiac ICU, with a reception area and waiting rooms separating the two. The group took over one waiting room with a couch and several chairs all in a beige and brown tweed fabric with almost identical carpet and cream-colored walls; it was very bland. A table and a telephone sat at the end of the couch and across was a kitchenette with sink and coffee maker.

Leah and her aunt walked down the hall to the room where Roger had been taken, just behind the nurse's station. It was cold and uninviting with machines everywhere. He had tubes in his mouth, nose, and chest. He had an IV in one arm and was being given blood in his other one. He was very swollen and had sand in his hair and on his back. The nurses had cleaned as much as possible off him, but he was in too bad a shape to be moved around much. He was being given pain medication but opened his one eye when they went in. Leah walked to the side of the bed and slid her hand into his, careful not to hurt him but let him do any movement he wanted. She was so afraid of adding to his pain. He had so many bruises, it was impossible to find a place on his body that looked normal. She softly told him how much she loved him and how they were strong and would make it together. She wasn't sure he heard her or understood, although the nurses said he did. She told him the children would be here the next day, and his eye opened at that, and the semblance of a slight smile curled the side of his mouth. She ached at the sight of him in so much pain and sat a long time with her hand in his.

The TV was on in his room and one of the nurses said, "There it is! That's it!"

Leah turned to look at the TV and saw Roger's cap, the one he had been given the previous month in Georgetown, in the foreground lying on the sand. She gasped and covered her mouth, afraid she would scream and turned away shaking uncontrollably.

The nurse grabbed her, put her arms around her, and held her. "I'm so sorry. I didn't think. It must have been quite a shock. I'll change the channel." She turned to CNN so as not to chance another local news cast.

Leah's brother and mother came to the door, and Ralph reached for her hand.

"Why don't you go down to the waiting room with the others, and I'll stay with Mom? I'll let her stay just a little while but you should get out for a few minutes."

"Okay, but don't attempt to touch him as he is in so much pain. Just speak to him and let him know he's not alone."

Leah joined the rest of the family in the waiting room, where they were all trying to figure out what might have happened. Blake was a very capable and careful pilot and had flown that river many, many times in various aircraft and should have known everything on the route. It was doubtful Roger would remember much, and it seemed impossible that this could have happened. There were so many questions and no way to get answers. They sat somberly, trying to deal with their pain and shock. Elaine pulled Leah over on her shoulder and tried to get her to close her eyes. She was so cold.

Soon Ralph and her mother returned to the waiting room and informed them some tests were being run on Roger, and they had been run out. It was now after 4:00 a.m. and the stress was showing on Leah's mother, so she asked her aunt and mother to go and come back the next day for the surgery. They weren't sure just when but as soon as the doctors were ready, it would begin, probably around 10:00 a.m. or so.

They agreed to go for a while and then go over to tell Roger's mother shortly after seven and return to the hospital as soon as she was ready. Leah's two brothers and their wives planned to stay with her until they knew more then would take turns going home for showers.

Leah saw machines leaving Roger's room and figured the tests were done, so she returned. Shortly, a nurse pushed a recliner into the room, telling her she should try to get some sleep. That was impossible as she couldn't stop her mind with all the questions swirling around in it.

Through the next few hours, the nurses continued to give Roger blood, explaining to Leah he had lost too much and had to be built up for the surgery. That would determine when it could begin. They neglected to mention the ruptured artery in his leg that continued to bleed.

At half past six, charts were reviewed, preparing for the coming shift change, and Leah listened intently to the list of injuries. It was hard to believe what she heard and very difficult to listen to. She choked up again; she couldn't cry. The pain was too great for crying. She couldn't express it, didn't know how; it reached down through her body to the bottom of her soul. There was no way to put her feelings into words or deal with them or get the pain out of her body or mind. She felt she would come apart but shoved the thoughts back to be dealt with later. Now she had to keep control and get through the day of surgery. The children should be on their way soon. She began to pray again.

"Mrs. Kerry?" The tall man took her arm and led her out into the hall.

"I'm the plastic surgeon. I'll be doing the reconstruction on your husband's face. Let's walk down the hall a bit."

They walked away from Roger's room toward the waiting room as he continued filling her in on what was to come.

"Your husband has been given five units of blood, and we should be able to take him to surgery around ten a.m. The left side of his face and his nose were crushed, and many small bones have numerous fractures. I will be using pins and wire mesh to put it back in place and expect it to take six to eight hours. That is a long time to be under anesthesia in his condition, and we will be keeping you informed of his progress every hour. Do you have any questions for me?"

"Not at this time. I don't know enough to question, I'm afraid."

"We'll try to give you information as soon as it's available but don't hesitate to ask anything you think of. I'll be talking with you later."

Leah was impressed with his easy-going attitude and hoped he was very good in his field. She knew none of the doctors and had never been in this hospital before, so she had no idea how good anyone was.

Soon the orthopedic surgeon came in and informed her that Roger's left femur had ruptured an artery, causing the huge blood loss and had to be repaired as soon as possible. His left ankle was crushed with numerous breaks and fractures they would attempt to repair, and the right ankle had been badly dislocated, turned completely backward; the worst dislocation he had ever seen. He would be setting it also. Roger had open wounds on his left ankle that were of serious concern as they were pressure wounds from the inside, and diabetes made healing difficult. They would have to be monitored carefully.

How much more? Leah thought to herself. Can he possibly make it through all this? She began to pray again, beg actually, God to stay with them and oversee the doctors and nurses and guide their hands.

Soon they sent her out so they could begin preliminary tests and preparations for surgery. Leah walked to the waiting room, more scared than she could ever remember. She sat down and began to shake, her face pale and drawn.

"I just made a fresh pot of coffee. You look as if you could use a cup. May I bring you one?" Another waiting family member touched her arm and asked.

"That would be very nice," Leah replied. "I would like a cup."

The lady brought a steaming cup of coffee and asked Leah who she had in ICU. Leah told her as best she could.

"Oh! Dear God! I saw it on television. You poor dear. We are praying for you and will be around if you need anything."

"Thank you. My husband is being prepped for surgery now, so we need lots of prayers to get him through it. Do you have a family member here?"

"My son was in a motorcycle accident four days ago and is in a coma. However, he showed a little improvement yesterday, so we're optimistic."

"I'm so sorry to hear that. I'll pray for him also. I guess there are lots of sad stories here."

"Many. And new ones come in each day. This is a very sad place. But you get to know each other, and it helps the time pass. Do you have any family here?"

"Oh, yes. They were with me most of the night and will be back soon. I sent them home as they had been up all night and needed to contact other family members."

Leah sipped the hot coffee and visited with her new friend, learning some of the other stories of the ICU. The elevator arrived, and Aunt Elaine and her mother stepped out with Roger's mother. Leah was shocked to see it was almost 9:30 a.m. Roger's mother was upset no one had called her the night before and told Leah she should have.

"Mom, we were all in shock, and it was well into the morning before I knew enough to call and didn't want to tell you on the phone, knowing you couldn't hear well and might get it mixed up. I knew it was taking a chance but decided it was best to wait until morning and send someone to tell you in person. I'm sorry, but I did what I thought was best at the time."

Roger's mother didn't seem very satisfied with the explanation, and Leah was sure she would hear more about it later but was too worried about Roger to spend any energy talking about it anymore. A nurse came out to find them shortly after 10:00 a.m., informing them Roger was being moved to surgery and gave them directions to the surgery waiting area.

Leah's mother handed her a bag with a fleece pants set inside and some socks.

"Put these on before you catch pneumonia. I hope you haven't already. It's too cold in here for those shorts."

Arriving in the surgical waiting area attired in the purple fleece outfit, Leah felt much more comfortable than wrapped in a blanket the way she had spent the night. However, she was reluctant to leave the blanket just in case. Around noon, a nurse came out and said the ruptured artery had been repaired and a rod inserted in the left femur. Roger was holding his own. Leah knew that was good, but it was far from over.

The waiting area was a mezzanine above the main lobby, open and airy with a view of the whole front side of the hospital. Leah saw her two brothers arrive and motioned to her aunt to let them know where they were. Soon all were in the waiting area with her, and Ralph told her he would pick up the children at the airport at 4:00 p.m. She was very anxious to see them and just wished the circumstances were better. Time passed slowly; the family kept trying to get her to go eat or let them bring her something, but she couldn't. She wasn't sure she could keep food down. She would eat when Roger was out of danger.

Each hour, a nurse or doctor came out to report on his condition, and all seemed to be going much better than they had anticipated. Then the orthopedic surgeon came and told her that the left ankle was so badly crushed and there were too many breaks to repair, so they would just have to see what happened. The open wounds were the big concern as infection could cause amputation. Leah refused to consider it.

"He's going to need both feet when he is well."

The surgeon explained what he had done and about the braces Roger would be wearing for the next few months. Leah prayed it would be just a few months. Soon the plastic surgeon came out and told her what he had done and how it was going. It was now nearly 4:00 p.m., and Roger had been in surgery for six hours.

"I told you it would be six to eight hours, but I am going to rescind that. I don't want to be held to a time as I want it right the first time."

"I want it right too. And the only time! I'm not concerned about the time if his lungs are doing okay."

"So far so good!" The doctor went back through the door, and Leah knew the next time she saw him it would be to give her the information that the surgery was over and successful. She knew in her heart that Roger was going to make it through this. God wasn't ready for him yet—she was sure of it.

Ralph arrived with Dave and Melanie, and Leah was relieved to see them. They received updates and explanations from the rest of the family, sparing her the need to go over it again. Dave explained to Leah that Suzan had made arrangements for her children and a way to get Jessie to and from school. She was scheduled to come in the next day.

"Mom, I see you've become quite the snappy dresser. Red shoes with a purple pants suit. Say, are those house shoes?"

"They are, and they are very comfortable, Missy. Afraid I didn't have much to choose from this morning," Leah replied as she looked down at the red cloth shoes. She had left so fast the night before she had taken no notice of what she had on.

The family kept her occupied with light chatter, pictures of the grandchildren, and tales of Melanie's new job. She had just started with a new company a month before, but there had been no question she could have time off for her family. Leah felt very grateful and made a mental note to send back a thank you note to her employers.

Shortly after eight o'clock, the doctor came out and explained that the surgery was finished, that it had gone well, and that Roger was in recovery. The whole group breathed a sigh of relief, and smiles were visible where lines of concern had been moments before.

"Thank you so much, doctor. I am very grateful for your concern and expertise." Leah took the doctor's hand in hers as tears of joy trickled down her cheeks. The doctor touched her shoulder, nodded and replied, "He's not out of the woods yet. He's got a long recovery ahead of him, and there are still many things that could happen."

"I know. But I believe God isn't ready for him yet or he would not have made him suffer through last night and today's surgery. He's been in excruciating pain, and I believe the worst is over. I just feel it in my heart." The doctor smiled, turned, and left the room.

Dave and Melanie put their arms around their mother, and all wept tears of joy and relief. Leah asked her aunt to take her mother home as the long night and day were telling on both mothers. Roger's mother wanted to stay, so Dave agreed he could take her when he and Melanie left. Leah's brothers decided to follow their mother home and make sure she was alright. Now that Roger was doing better, the grief over the loss of Blake would be heavy. Leah couldn't allow herself to think about it; it was too painful, and she had to keep control. She would have to deal with it later.

Soon a nurse came to tell them Roger was being moved back to his room and to give them some time to get him set up and stabilized. Leah thought about the children going home to the empty house and about the wallet and keys in the hospital safe.

"Let's find the safe and get Dad's things," she said. She asked the receptionist where to go and told Roger's mother they would be back shortly to take her to ICU to see him. She knew she would have to prepare her for what he looked like but wasn't sure how.

Leah, Dave, and Melanie made their way to hospital records where the safe was, only to be told they had nothing for a Roger Kerry. They were then sent to the admitting office where there was another safe.

"I'm Mrs. Kerry. I was told my husband's wallet and keys are in the safe. He was admitted late last night by Life Flight. The... helicopter...crash...victim."

The young lady on duty looked and returned empty handed.

"We have nothing for a Roger Kerry. The only thing I have from last night is for an Oscar Corey."

"My husband was in shock, swollen, and delirious. I'm sure his words were slurred and hard to understand as he had a stroke several years ago. May I see the Corey package? There will be identification in the wallet."

"There is no wallet. Just a coin purse and a pocket knife."

"Those are my husband's but where are his wallet and keys? I was told the highway patrol put them in the hospital safe."

"I don't know. This is all I have."

Leah turned to Dave and Melanie after signing for the articles and putting them in her purse. She decided she had better call Annette and went to a phone. A friend answered the phone, stating Annette and her family were gone. Leah explained the problem and asked to be called in ICU as soon as she returned.

"You two can look for them when you get home. They had been working in the garage so the wallet and keys could be there or in the bathroom, either one or on the dresser or his chest in the bedroom. We need to find them!" Leah told her son and daughter.

Returning to the plaza, they retrieved Roger's mother and went up to ICU. Nurses were still going in and out of his room as well as several machines, so they waited for the activity to stop.

"We need to find his wallet and keys. It worries me that I don't know where they are. He never went anywhere without his wallet, and I thought it was in the safe."

"They're probably laying on his vanity at home. Don't worry, Mom, we'll find them." Dave tried to soothe his mother's nerves. She had enough to worry her without the concern about a wallet and keys.

"It looks like it's finally quiet in his room, Dave. Why don't you take Grandma back, and you two can visit for a few minutes, and then Melanie and I will go back. We shouldn't all go at once and be careful not to touch him. He's so sore everywhere."

Dave took his grandmother's arm, and they walked down the hall to Roger's room. Dave saw his father first and was shocked by the swelling. Roger looked like he had doubled his weight, and his hands looked like risen loaves of bread. Dave's shock must have been visible because the nurse quickly told them he had been given lots of fluid while in surgery, which had produced the swelling and would gradually go down over the next few days. The left side of his face and nose were totally covered with bandages and some blood was seeping out. Dried blood on his forehead showed another cut, though it was difficult to tell how big or deep it was. Tubes were coming out of his chest and stomach, and his left leg was in a cast. The right ankle was in a brace, and he looked terribly uncomfortable. Roger's mother did surprisingly well but forgot about his pain and patted his arm, which produced a flinch. Dave just talked softly, telling his dad they were there and would be until he was well again. Roger responded to Dave with a half smile; two tubes in his mouth made it difficult, but he attempted to say something in spite of them.

"Don't try to talk, Dad. We'll do it for you. Just work on getting well." Roger nodded yes and closed his one visible eye.

Dave could hardly contain his feelings; it hurt so bad to see his dad in this condition. He had been through so much with the two heart surgeries and stroke that it was hard to fathom his surviving this too.

"We'd better get back and let mother and Melanie come back, Grandma."

"I guess so. I love you, son. I'll be back soon." Roger's mother spoke loudly as she was hard of hearing and didn't realize how loud it sounded. She reluctantly let Dave lead her out of the room and down the hall slowly. She had recovered from her heart valve replacement but still tired easily, and stress made everything difficult. She hardly looked her eighty-nine years, with only salt-and-pepper gray making her dark, curly hair a light charcoal. Her olive skin wrinkled little, having been oily like Roger's. She had lost her only daughter some thirty-five years before and her husband just a few years ago. Roger was now her only living immediate relative.

"How is he?" Leah inquired of Dave.

"He's awake but very swollen and still in lots of pain. You had better go on back as they are sedating him, and he will probably be out before long."

Leah and Melanie walked the hall arm in arm, neither sure of what they would encounter but eager to see that he was alive and recovering. All the tubes and machines were upsetting but neither let it show.

"Hi, Dad." Melanie slid her hand into Roger's, and he winked the one eye at her. "I'm going to be here as long as you and Mom need me. My bosses both told me to come and take care of my family. They believe in family first."

"You did so great, darling. You really are as tough as you always said you were!" Roger squeezed her hand slightly. She was very careful to just rest her hand in his with no pressure, allowing him to make any movement he needed. She was so afraid of adding to his pain. His hands looked ready to burst from all the fluid and swelling. Her heart ached to see him like this. He had been through so much that it just didn't seem fair. She remembered Blake asking her if she wanted to go first, and she felt horribly guilty.

"I need to change his dressing. Why don't you all step out while I take care of it?" his nurse asked.

Leah took Melanie's hand, and they walked back down the hall to where Dave and Roger's mother were waiting. Melanie put her arm around her mother's shoulders as a tear fell. She felt wiped out and knew the rest of her family must be also.

"It's getting late and by the time you take Grandma and drive home, it will be long past bedtime even in California. Why don't you all go on and look for the wallet and keys and get some rest?"

"Why don't you go home for the night, and I'll stay?" Dave asked.

"Oh, no! I couldn't rest if I did. I want to be right here with your dad as long as he's on the critical list."

"I could stay too," Roger's mother said.

"Mom, you need your rest. It hasn't been that long since your surgery. I promise I'll call if there's any change."

Leah managed to convince them only she need stay through the night and that she would be fine. Her brothers had picked up a toothbrush and toothpaste for her, and she had a comb in her purse. She made a list of things she wanted from home and sent them on their way. She had the truck at the hospital, so they would have to make do with one riding in the backseat to take Grandma home, and they should bring the Lincoln the next day. After they left, she checked on Roger, washed her face and hands, and brushed her teeth in the rest room and then made herself as comfortable as possible in the recliner the staff had brought in for her. The television stayed on CNN so as to avoid any local news. She had been told there were articles in the papers but had avoided those also. She didn't need any reminders of the horror. It was constantly with her.

Part of the night, she watched television and during the other part, she walked the halls, visiting with a few of the people in the waiting room when tests or something else was being done for Roger. She couldn't remember how much coffee she drank. The long night finally passed, and a new shift came on.

This shift asked her to leave the ICU while reviews were being done, so she went to the cafeteria, feeling a little hungry. She looked over the breakfast tables and decided on scrambled eggs and a biscuit with gravy. She opted for juice and water and decided to call the children later to bring her some filtered water. The tap water tasted bad after drinking filtered for years. The juice tasted bitter, and the eggs had no flavor. The biscuit and gravy were better, so she ate that, which was plenty. She knew it wasn't the food but rather her taste. She finished, put the tray away, and went back to the room.

A nurse was removing Roger's cast, and Leah got her first sight of his ankle—three hideous wounds with the flesh gone, exposing bone. They looked angry and discolored, and she almost fainted. The nurse took her arm.

"Are you alright?"

"I've never seen anything like those," Leah replied.

"Actually, these look better than I expected, considering. We have to be very careful and watchful of infection, especially since he is diabetic."

"Are you almost finished? I need to give him his insulin." Another nurse had entered the room with a needle in hand.

"Insulin?" Leah was surprised and concerned.

"The liquid nourishment we have to give him has pushed his blood sugar up, so we have to counteract with insulin shots."

"Oh, no! We've worked so hard to control it with diet."

"He should be able to get off the insulin shots once he recovers and can go back to a regular diet. This doesn't mean he will have to have them permanently."

"Thank goodness," Leah replied. "He has so many meds now, or did before the accident." Roger looked up at her and winked the one uncovered eye. His swelling seemed a slight bit better, but he still seemed to be in a lot of pain. Leah slid her fingers into his left palm, and he tried to close his fingers a little. It was too much, and he just let their hands rest together. He continued to try to mouth words, but they were inaudible with the tubes in his mouth and nose. He seemed very fatigued after the nurses finished and closed his eye. Leah sat down in the recliner and closed hers also. She couldn't rest as too many memories and questions haunted her.

What had happened? Blake was such a careful and capable pilot and had flown down that river hundreds of times. He knew where all the lines, towers, and everything else on the route were. Why hadn't he seen the lines? Tears filled her eyes once more. Blake's smiling face flashed through her mind, and she could hear his voice asking her, "Do you mind if we make a quick run up the river before we put the chopper away for the night, Sis? Do you want to go first?"

What if she hadn't said no? What if she had gone first? Could she have changed anything? Suddenly, her body shook with the sobs within, and she jerked her eyes open, and rose. Leah walked out and down the hall until she could catch her breath. No! Blake couldn't be gone. She couldn't stand it. She needed him, she loved him, and she didn't want him to be dead. She wanted to give him a hug and tell him how much she loved him. She felt like she would explode. She wanted to break something, hit something, or scream ... but that wouldn't bring him back. How could she deal with this? How could she get through all of this?

She needed to talk to him, needed to get answers to some of the questions, but she knew she never would. She felt her throat tighten and had a hard time breathing. The tears slid down her cheeks, but she quickly checked them and tried to get control. She had to hold on; she couldn't fall apart here. Why did this happen? She felt so empty inside. Hadn't she and Roger been through enough? Hadn't Blake worked very hard his whole life and deserved at least a little of his enjoyable retirement? Why now? Why? Suddenly she heard a voice in her mind asking her, "Who are you to question me? My authority? My control? My power?"

She had just finished reading the book of Job the week of the accident, and it was as if she could hear the voice of God rebuking her for her questions. She began to pray, asking God to forgive her. She knew he was in control. She knew he would give her the strength to get through this. Then she thanked him for causing her to read the passages that were strengthening her now. She sat in the waiting room for over an hour, lost in prayer, memories, and dreams that would now never come true but thankful for what time they had spent together.

"Who do you have in here?" Leah turned to look at the person who had just sat down beside her.

"My husband was in a helicopter crash Sunday night," Leah managed to get out before she choked up.

"I saw the report on TV. The pilot didn't make it. Did you know him?"

"He was my brother." Leah's voice broke, and she could feel the tears choking her again.

"I'm so sorry," replied the man softly, his voice taking on a degree of concern and sympathy. "I'm a pilot also, and I hate to hear of fatal crashes. There have been several this weekend."

"I'm afraid I haven't watched news reports or read a paper since Sunday."

"Of course not! Can I get you a cup of coffee?"

"That would be nice. Black, please."

The dark-haired man returned shortly with two cups of coffee and handed one to Leah. He looked to be around fifty with a deep tan and kind eyes; he was genuinely trying to lift Leah's spirits.

"Thank you. My name is Leah, Leah Kerry."

"You are welcome, Leah. I'm Steve Michaels."

"My father-in-law has just had open-heart surgery, so we will be here for a while. Just let us know if we can do anything for you. You must be completely drained emotionally. I can't imagine what you must be going through with a double tragedy like this. Please let us be of help to you."

"You are very kind. Two of our children came in yesterday afternoon and should be here soon. There really isn't anything I need. I'm not really sure what I feel. I can't really think about it all right now."

"You look exhausted. There's my wife now. Marge, this is Leah Kerry. Her husband and brother were in the helicopter crash Sunday night."

The bright-eyed lady sat down beside him and looked at Leah

"You poor dear. My heart goes out to you. We will be around here for the next several days, so please let us do anything we can to help you. My dad is still in recovery but is expected to do fine, so we'll be available."

"Thank you so much, but there is nothing I need, and my family will be here soon."

Chapter 18

She was learning that there were many nice people around, and she didn't feel quite as alone. She went back to the room to check on Roger just before Dave and Melanie got there. They had not found his wallet or keys. Roger roused when he heard their voices and looked hard at Leah and tried to mouth something. Leah thought she saw him mouth, "Blake?" and her heart filled with fear. She wasn't sure how to respond, so she just said softly, "I understand, dear, and don't worry. It's going to be okay." Roger seemed satisfied and closed his eye again.

Dave and Melanie gave him a gentle kiss on the forehead and talked a little about their night in the house and how good everything looked. It was the first time Melanie had seen it, and she liked it very much. Soon Roger appeared to be asleep, and they went to the waiting room.

"I called Annette's house, and her friend told me there had been looters at the scene of the crash. We have to find Dad's wallet and keys. Maybe if I go home, I can find them."

"I'll drive you, Mother. I don't want you going alone. Is that okay, Melanie? Do you mind staying here alone?"

"Not at all. I'm sure some of the family will be here soon. Why don't you pick up Grandma on your way back? I'll give her a call and tell her so she'll be ready."

Leah called the highway patrol to see if there was any further word, and they were to call her back. She and Dave went to the parking lot and got the car. As they pulled out of the area, Leah suddenly heard Blake's voice saying, "Sis, Roger snagged his pants on the fence. Do you think you can fix them?"

"We've got to find the pants dad had on Sunday! I'll bet that's where the keys and wallet are. Blake just reminded me!"

Dave glanced at his mother and started to ask what she meant but decided to drop it and not question her. She seemed in a very fragile state, and if she thought she heard Uncle Blake, well, they would deal with that later.

Dave drove on home. The sun was shining brightly, and Dave told her they had met the man who had pulled Roger from the wreckage and given him CPR. The family lived on the river just above where the accident had occurred. He and the girls planned to go see him and visit the site.

"I'm not ready for that," Leah said, "but I do want to meet him and thank him. He saved your dad, and we must find a way to show our appreciation. The grass needed to be cut. Dad was going to cut it on Tuesday just after the holiday. I hope I can find someone to take care of it."

Her mind seemed to be jumping from one thing to another.

Arriving at the house a few minutes later, they were shocked; the lawn was mowed, weeding done and looking great.

"I wonder who...?"

She would check into it later. Leah went straight to the laundry room, figuring Roger would have put his pants near her sewing machine, but they were not there. Then she went into the bathroom—not there either. Finally, she thought of the hooks in the closet where Roger kept his robe and pajamas. There she found the slacks; the wallet and keys were in the pocket. She felt so relieved that she began to cry. She washed her face, grabbed some clean underwear, cosmetics, and other necessities and then headed to the kitchen for a drink.

"We need to get back."

"Why don't you take time to eat something or make some coffee? You need some time away from the hospital. Melanie will call if we're needed."

"I can't relax away from your dad. His health is too shaky right now, and too many things could go wrong."

They were about to leave when Leah noticed several messages on the recorder. She played them, learning the news had spread throughout the state and that relatives and friends were expressing their sorrow and concern. She didn't attempt to make any notes, knowing no return call was necessary.

"Let's head back. I can stop worrying about the house now, and I'll get coffee at the hospital. I was panic-stricken thinking you children were sleeping here and someone could have the keys and address if they had taken dad's wallet and things. Such a relief to have them!"

"I called Melanie, and Grandma will come with Aunt Elaine, so we can go straight to the hospital if you want."

"Let's do that, Dave."

Leah was so relieved to have Roger's wallet but needed to be near him, so they drove back to the hospital, arriving just in time to see his cardiologist leave.

"He's doing very well, considering," he told them as he went on to his next patient.

Considering, Leah thought, yes, he is doing very well indeed. She slipped her hand into his and could see him trying to say something.

"Don't try to talk, darling. Those tubes make it so hard. You can talk all you want when those are out of your mouth."

Roger seemed to relax, and then more technicians and nurses came in for more tests. It seemed they always arrived just as he was settling down. It was evident he was still in a lot of pain.

She and the children went down to the waiting room where fresh coffee had been made. Several people had been there all night also, and they all asked about Roger and exchanged updates on their family members. Aunt Elaine, Leah's and Roger's mothers came in, and Dave took over bringing them up to speed on Roger's condition. They all went down to the cafeteria and were soon joined by Leah's two brothers and their wives. Leah's two sisters had come in from Tennessee and Oklahoma City and details were repeated. Ralph informed them he had talked with Annette, and the funeral was planned for the next day.

"Why so soon? I can't leave Roger yet; too many things could happen. I won't leave as long as he's on the critical list. Why couldn't she wait until Friday? With his friends and business associates all over the continent and Monday being a holiday, it only makes sense to wait."

"I agree, Sis, but she insists on tomorrow. I asked to do the eulogy, and she said she would think about it. Think about it! I'm his brother for goodness sakes! What's to think about? I don't know what's gotten into her!"

"I wish she would wait, but I'm sure she is just as torn up as we are and wants it over. Maybe someone can record it for me so I can feel a part of it later. Roger will need it also."

"We'll see to that."

Questions dominated the conversation the rest of the meal. Everyone wanted to know how it had happened. What had caused the accident? Discussions led to more questions and no answers. The shock, pain, and grief were evident in all of them. Leah's mother looked so tired.

Suzan arrived at 6:30 p.m., picked up by Dave and Melanie. She gave her mother a big hug and kiss and then hurried back to see her dad. Leah went with her and could see the shock and dismay on her face. She talked briefly, telling Roger about the grandchildren, and then they went back to the waiting room as she was close to tears.

"He looks so miserable with all those tubes and needles in him. But he is so strong to have come through this. Jessie was having a fit to come with me as she was sure she could help Grandpa. I promised to call tonight and let her know how he is."

The rest of the family took turns visiting Roger, giving lots of time in between, and Leah felt better just having family around but worried how seeing so much family from out of town would affect him. He was sure to wonder about it, and she was so afraid to tell him about Blake.

The hospital chaplain came to sit by her and took her hand as he sat down beside her. He had been by several times each day, keeping an eye on her.

"You look tired. Is there anything I can do for you?"

"Not unless you know where a shower is. I'm beginning to feel really grungy."

"Well, my dear. I can supply that. You can take a shower in the sleeping room I use when I'm here overnight. Get your things, and bring your daughter to stand watch. There are several keys and someone could come to use the room while you're there, but your daughter can tell them it's in use."

"Mom, that would make you feel so much better. I'll get your things."

Leah and Melanie were led down to the first floor to a bedroom and shower, and Leah took a long, hot one. It felt wonderful and warm—so warm she didn't want to leave. Much of the hospital had been cold most of the time, even the cafeteria. She changed into clean clothes and returned to her family in the waiting room feeling like a new person.

"You look pale, dear," her aunt told her, brushing back a hair from Leah's forehead.

"Well, I just took a shower."

The family all laughed, and Aunt Elaine gave her a big hug. As the day passed into evening the mothers and Aunt Elaine left to try to get some rest before the funeral the next day. Ralph told Leah they would be up after it was over to check on her. Leah told her children to stay home the next morning and come in after the funeral. She asked them to mix her nightly tonic of one-fourth cup each of honey and cider vinegar and she would find warm water as her allergies had been causing sneezing and coughing, and she didn't want to let them get too far. She tried to assure everyone that she would be alright alone; she just needed the honey and vinegar. She sent the children home shortly after nine o'clock after the rest had left, hoping they would get a good night's sleep.

She felt very alone and went back to Roger's room to watch TV. It was still on CNN, so she watched for a while and then closed her eyes and pulled the blanket over her. She was so cold! Two nurses came in to discuss Roger's injuries and care and gave Leah a report on his progress.

"He's doing far better than I expected, but he has a long way to go. I don't want to sound pessimistic, but we have to be watchful of his grafts. One could detach due to the impact of the crash."

"How long do I have to worry about that?"

"Each day gives him a better chance, but it will be at least two months before we can be sure."

Leah groaned, and the nurses quickly tried to reassure her he had beaten the odds up to now and was a real fighter. He tried to say something each time he awoke, and Leah wished with all her heart she could know what it was he was saying. She felt her ankles and wrists aching and looked down to find they were quite swollen. What in the world would she do if she couldn't walk or use her wrists? She rubbed her wrists, which only made them hurt more. One of the nurses noticed her and asked to look at them.

"You are exhausted, and exhaustion and stress can do strange things to your body. You must get some sleep. Do you have enough blankets?"

"I could use another one and a pillow."

"I'll be right back with a warm blanket. Close the curtains so maybe you won't be disturbed for a while."

Leah stretched out on the recliner, lay back on the pillow, and covered herself with the warm blanket the nurse brought. She remembered the Vanquish in her purse and took two and then fell asleep. She awoke only once in the wee hours to find a doctor tiptoeing around Roger's bed, checking him with a small flashlight and trying very hard not to wake her.

"Good morning. It's time for shift change and review. Why don't you go get some coffee and breakfast?"

A male nurse had entered the room, and the movement woke Leah. She rubbed her eyes and looked up at him as she threw off the blanket. She put on her shoes and rose to leave, moving first to Roger's side.

"I'm going to brush my teeth and comb my hair, darling. I'll be back shortly."

She left the room and walked down the hall to the restroom and then the cafeteria for fresh coffee and a newspaper.

As she sat sipping her coffee, she remembered today was Blake's funeral. She had never felt more alone; she couldn't bear to leave Roger, and she couldn't say a proper good-bye to her brother. All the family would be going, and she would probably be alone until late afternoon. She felt her eyes fill with tears, her lips wouldn't stop quivering, and she felt as though she couldn't breathe. She sat there with tears rolling down her cheeks without the ability to stop them. She dropped her eyes to the paper as though reading, hoping no one would see or say anything. She knew one word from anyone would cause her to lose it completely. She sobbed inwardly for some time until she was exhausted and felt totally spent. She finally gained control and went back to the ICU.

As she headed toward Roger's room, the nurse at the desk told her Ralph had called and wanted to speak with her. She went back to the waiting room and made the call.

"I got a report on Roger, Sis, from the nurse on duty. I sure hate for you to be alone today but wanted to read you the eulogy."

"Please, go ahead."

"My brother," Ralph began, "was a devoted family man. He was a loving father, grandfather, husband, and son. My heart is heavy for those members of our family who are now suffering that loss the most. I'll leave it to those more qualified than myself to define Blake's contributions to his community as well as the aerospace industry.

A little over thirty years ago, I gave my brother his first flying lesson, and he was immediately hooked. He was a natural. His love for flying and enthusiasm for sport flying influenced thousands through his unselfish contributions to the air show circuit. Unfortunately, it took his life. But the good Lord, in his infinite wisdom, made sure that he left us doing one of the things in his life that gave him the most satisfaction. I could not ask more from our Savior.

My brother's physical presence will be missed, but my family and I can take comfort in our belief that Blake has his own pair of wings now and is flying into realms that our finite minds cannot comprehend. He is finally soaring into those high, un-traversed sanctities of space. How glorious it must be to put out your hand and touch the face of God. I love you, my brother."

Leah listened with tears streaming down her face and then told him she couldn't have said it any better. His voice had broken several times, and she could tell he was very emotional.

"Are you sure you can do this?" she asked as she wiped away her own tears.

"I've already asked Dave to deliver it for me as your representative. I've got to tell you, Sis, if you and Roger never did anything else good in your life, you have a son to be very proud of. He is one fine boy that anyone would be proud to call their son."

"Thank you. We are very proud of him."

"I wanted to let you know there will be a flyover at the cemetery, so if you can get to a window looking toward the southwest, you might be able to see it."

"I'll see what I can find, and do me one favor. Please be sure someone tapes it for me. I know Roger will need to see it later. We can watch it together. Maybe it will help the pain."

"You bet, Sis. We'll be up this evening, and you be sure to call if there is any change. You can get me on the cell phone."

Leah hung up, feeling so alone. She walked back to Roger's room, putting a smile on her face as she entered and slid her hand into his. He opened his eye and smiled the pained attempt he had been making since the surgery.

"I love you," Leah told him, and he nodded his head.

Leah pulled the chair over to the bed and sat with her hand in his for some time. She watched TV some but watched him most of the time. His chest was so sunken in and his breathing was so labored, but it did seem to be a little easier or maybe he was getting used to the respirator and relaxing a little. It must hurt so much, she thought, and it must be so frightening to have all those tubes, making it impossible to talk.

"Mrs. Kerry."

Leah jumped as her name came on the page.

"Yes."

"We have a call for you at the desk. Can you take it?"

"I'll be right out." She slipped her hand out of Roger's and went to the phone."Hello."

"Mom, it's Dave. We wanted to check on you and Dad. Did you get any sleep?"

"I did. Five hours straight. I feel much better, and Dad is breathing a little easier I think."

"That's great! I'm concerned about your being alone today. Why don't I bring one of the girls up to stay with you?"

"That's thoughtful, Son, but I'll be fine. I want you all to visit, relax, and come up after the funeral. Grandma is going to need lots of support. Keep an eye on her for any sign of a problem. This is so hard on her, losing the second son in only four years. Uncle Ralph called and told me about the flyover. He read me the eulogy and said you were going to give it for him. He also said he would try to get it taped for me. Don't worry about me. Just spend time with all the family that's here."

"Okay, but call if you want or need anything. We love you."

"I love you all too, and I'm so glad you're here. You have no idea how much help and strength you all are to me."

Chapter 19

Leah hung up and went back to the room. Roger seemed to be asleep, so she walked down to the nurse's station on the other wing where she wouldn't disturb him and asked about a waiting room where she might see the flyover, explaining the reason.

"I think the best bet would be the tenth floor. It's cardio rehab, and the waiting room is on the south side. It should be quiet there, so you can watch undisturbed." The nurse was so kind and understanding. Leah felt good just looking into her pretty smile and smiled back as the nurse patted her shoulder.

"Let us know if you need anything."

Leah felt sure she must know about Roger even though she was on another wing. She caught the elevator and went up to the tenth floor. She found the waiting room and some magazines and sat for some time, peering into the cloudy sky and wondering if anything would be visible. After a short time, she took the elevator back to the ICU waiting room. There were a number of families there and most looked as if they, too, had been there all night. It was midmorning, and several newspapers were scattered about. She had left hers in the cafeteria so picked up another and thumbed through it. There was an article on the accident and funeral that hurt, so she put it back.

It was still cloudy when the time for the funeral came, but Leah went back up to the tenth floor and sat with her eyes glued to the gray sky, tears choking her until her eyes ached from the strain. She stayed for two hours then gave up, figuring visibility was too poor. Loss and grief were suddenly overwhelming, and she couldn't stop the tears any longer. She ran to the restroom and burst into sobs that had been suppressed for too long. Her whole body shook as the fear, grief, and sense of loss pushed to the surface. People came in and asked if they could help, but she shook her head and then went into one of the stalls to be alone. She cried and cried, but it gave little relief. The pain was too intense to be eased by tears. The fear of what was ahead was too deep to be overcome in a short time, but she knew she had to go back down. She cried until no more tears would come and then washed her face and went out to the elevator.

An X-ray machine was just coming out of Roger's room when she returned, and the nurse was waiting to check his left ankle. Leah stood by the bed as she removed the covering and exposed the wound. Leah felt faint as she looked at the exposed bone and dying flesh, putting her hand over her mouth to keep from expressing her shock. The nurse looked up at her and began to explain.

"His being diabetic is a real problem, and we're just trying to keep down infection right now. The dead flesh will be removed and replaced with new flesh if we're real lucky. He has too many other things more important to deal with right now. We'll do our best to help him keep this foot."

Leah couldn't think of removing a foot. He just had to get well and walk beside her again. He had been through too much trauma to deal with something like that. She waited a minute and then walked the hall to the waiting room. She was so depressed that she could hardly make her body move. She knew they had come through a lot and should be very thankful but just now, she was overcome with a sense of loss. She remembered some years before wishing she could wake up and find it all to be a nightmare, but here she was in a worse nightmare. How could she find the strength to go through it all again? Would he be able to walk? How would not walking affect his diabetes? How would he react to the loss of Blake? Did he know? When should she tell him? It was too much!

She fell exhausted onto the sofa, thankful no one she knew was around. She couldn't talk about any of it with anyone without falling apart, and she was too tired to fight the feelings. She lay back against the sofa and closed her eyes. It was sometime before she opened them to see her children coming off the elevator.

"How did things go?"

"The service was very nice, Mom, and it was taped for you. It was in the high school gym and was hot as it was packed, and Grandma almost fainted. However, she was fine when we left. Were you able to see anything?" Dave looked tired as he set the jar of vinegar and honey on the bed table.

"No, the visibility was too bad; possibly the fires around had something to do with it. There is so much smoke in the air. I did go upstairs and watch but couldn't see a thing."

"There was lots of family at the funeral and some will be up to see you, but some had to leave town right after. We all met the missionary who pulled Dad out and gave him CPR. He prayed for them both immediately after he found Uncle Blake was gone and solicited God's help ASAP. We plan to visit with his family tomorrow before we come up and view the site of the crash again. We went by on Tuesday but just for a few minutes before the water covered the sand bar."

"I'm anxious to meet them and thank them. I've been concerned about what your father will think if out-of-state family flocks in to see him."

"Aunt Annette said she would stay away, so he wouldn't wonder what she was doing without Blake."

"What? That's absurd! As bad as your dad is hurt, he wouldn't expect Blake to be walking around!"

"I thought the same thing, but you know Aunt Annette. She'll do as she thinks best. She said so much food has been brought to her house by your friends since no one was home, the freezer is full as well as the refrigerator."

"You can all go out together and visit. You don't get to see that much of each other with Suzan in Idaho, so get some enjoyment out of being together. I think I have a cake and some cinnamon rolls in the freezer. I also made gumbo and some is there also."

"We'll be fine, Mom. We're grown now, so you needn't worry about feeding us," Suzan interrupted.

"I want to give you my Visa and put your meals and gas on it. Okay?"

"No! It's not okay. We can take care of our own meals. You and Dad are going to have big enough bills as it is, and we have money. Stop worrying about us! Please!" Dave hugged his mother as he refused the card, and the girls agreed.

"I just wish I knew how much your dad does remember and if he knows about Blake. They were so close. I really dread having to approach that."

"I'm sure you will get an idea as he gets better." Dave could always be so logical.

Jenna and Todd and their oldest daughter came up that evening as well as nieces from Alabama. They were careful to be cheery and only visit two at a time. Roger seemed to be glad to see them but was in too much pain and had too many tubes to let anyone know if he wondered why they were there. It hit Leah that Roger might get the idea they had come because he was near death, and that really scared her. It was another awful night of doubts, questions, and no sleep.

After everyone left for the night, Roger seemed restless and more tests were ordered, so Leah was sent to the waiting room. She had taken her pillow and blanket and decided to lie down and rest a little. She felt someone touch her arm and looked up to see the mother of the boy in the coma standing by her. She looked at the clock and saw it was nearly one a.m.

"Sorry to disturb you, but I saw your purse beside the sofa and wanted to warn you to keep it under you or behind you. There have been some things taken before."

"There's not enough to worry us. Now we have to be concerned about thieves. What next?"

"I know, but that's the way the world is today—hit the easy targets. Concerned relatives of patients won't be thinking about being robbed."

"Thanks for telling me. I'll be more careful."

They visited for a while, and then Leah stashed her purse behind her and closed her eyes again. The lights were too bright, so she couldn't sleep even with the blanket over her eyes. She did manage to rest for a while and got back into Roger's room around 4 a.m. She passed the next two hours watching Roger's labored breathing until the morning shift changed and scooted her out. This was her cue to go to the cafeteria for coffee and a biscuit. She picked up a paper, got her breakfast, and sat back to relax a bit. However, the second page had an article about the funeral and stated that the passenger's age was seventy-eight. Roger had aged twelve years! It wasn't important, but it broke the dam, and the tears began to trickle down Leah's cheeks. No one was sitting anywhere near her so she let them fall for a while and then pulled out a tissue and blotted her eyes and sipped her coffee. It would be nice to have his age corrected. Maybe she would have Dave call about it. Maybe she would just forget it. She glanced through the rest of the paper but nothing mattered to her and nothing was of interest just now, so she left it on the table and went upstairs to the restroom to wash her face and try to make herself more presentable.

She waited in Roger's room, hoping to see all the doctors as they came in. She spent most of the time praying that Roger would be able to do the things he enjoyed. He would need both legs and feet. Please let them heal! Please let his lungs heal! Please let his mind be okay! Please keep his diabetes under control and let him get off the insulin! As she ran over the injuries in her mind, they seemed to be overwhelming. How could he overcome this with all his previous health problems?

It was early afternoon when the pulmonary doctor came in with his assistant and informed Leah that Roger's breathing was easier and that he was pleased with her husband's progress. Then the plastic surgeon came and removed the bandage from his face. It looked so much better than Leah had anticipated, so she felt very elated. Soon the nurse came to clean and dress the wounds on his left foot. Leah decided to go to the waiting room as this was a very difficult wound for her to see. The children arrived soon after, and she gave them the happy news.

"We stopped by and visited with the missionary family on the way up. They are such nice people and feel they were placed there to minister to our family. They plan to come up to see Dad this weekend," Dave told her.

"I am so anxious to meet them. I wonder if Dad will remember him."

"They had spent several years on a mission ship in third-world countries and had witnessed and dealt with several types of traumatic injuries. That's how Jake, the man who gave Dad CPR, knew exactly what to do. They have quite an interesting story and will bring up a book about some of their travels."

"Wonderful."

They visited and Leah's aunt and mother arrived soon after, and there was much discussion about the funeral and the flyover, trying to make Leah feel a part of it all. Leah was feeling better than she had the past four days when the cardiologist came to inform them the grafts seemed to be holding and he was pleased with Roger's progress. It had been all good news, and Leah was beaming when his assistant came up to Leah and pulled her aside.

"Your husband's condition is being upgraded from critical to serious and that's good, but I don't want to give you the wrong impression. He has a very long way to go, and there are many, many things that could still go wrong. I want you to be prepared."

"I know we have a long way to go, but we have come a very long way already, and I am confident he is going to make it. I feel it in my heart! I don't believe God would have let him suffer so much if he wanted to take him now. He's in control anyway, so I can only pray and believe."

The assistant gave her a questioning look and then smiled.

"Just so you're aware. I didn't want you to get a wrong impression."

"I appreciate your concern. Thank you, but we'll be fine."

"Mother, I brought my things to spend the night with Dad. I think you should go home and sleep in your own bed tonight and until we go home." Dave was waiting when Leah came back to the group.

"I agree with Dave," Melanie added.

"Absolutely!" Suzan chimed in. "You are pale, and you look so tired. His upgrade is very good news, and Dave will call you if anything changes. Please. What was that lady telling you anyway? You look a little concerned."

"She was just trying to keep me aware of all the problems Dad has yet to face, warning me not to be too optimistic. I'm realistic in that I know many things could yet go wrong, but I firmly believe God is taking care of him and nothing anyone does will change that. I just don't believe he would take him now after all he's been through."

Everyone agreed and gave Leah encouragement but little chance to refuse to go home for the night. All the doctors had been in and Leah did feel confident, so she finally agreed. She would wait until eight or nine o'clock and then go home.

"It's almost six, and I'm hungry. Let's go eat," Dave said.

All agreed, and the little group proceeded to the elevator and down to the cafeteria. Fried chicken was on the menu, so Leah decided to try it. Dave and the girls decided on the same thing. As they went through the line, one of the ladies serving them gave Leah a big smile.

"Finally decide to eat? You been goin' on coffee and nerves, and you needs nourishment." Then she served Leah a whole chicken breast with huge helpings of mashed potatoes, gravy, and mixed vegetables.

As they sat down at the table, Dave surveyed each tray.

"Boy, Mom. You got twice as much as the rest of us."

"I know, and there's no way I can eat it. You take half of mine. I guess that lady thinks I'm wasting away!"

Soon it was nine o'clock, and all insisted she go on home and get a shower and a good night's sleep. It was a beautiful moonlit night with stars sprinkled liberally around as they arrived home. The house looked wonderful to Leah, and she wanted to visit with her girls but was so tired she made it only into the shower and then straight to bed, almost asleep when she laid down.

"Good morning." Melanie was sitting at the center island with the newspaper spread out in front of her and a cup of coffee in her hand. "I made coffee. How 'bout a cup?"

"Sounds wonderful," Leah answered, taking the cup she was offered and sitting between her two daughters. "I want to get back to the hospital soon."

"We will, but there's no need to rush. Relax. I'm sure Dave will call or I'll call him if you want," Suzan answered.

"Good idea! Let's check in with him now. The shift change has been over for an hour, so he should be able to give a report." Leah punched in the number of the ICU nurse's station.

"ICU."

"Is Mr. Kerry's son in his room? I'd like to speak to him please. This is Mrs. Kerry." Leah waited as she heard the nurse summon Dave to the phone.

"Hi, Mom."

"How did it go last night?"

"Pretty uneventful. I slept a little in your recliner and talked with the doctors and nurses as they came in. They all seem to think he's doing much better than any of them expected. No change, really, from last night. How did you sleep?"

"Wonderful. I feel much better. We'll be up as soon as we get dressed. We're just having coffee now. Did you eat? Do you want us to bring you anything?

"I went down during shift change to the cafeteria and had a good breakfast. The food is really good here."

"I think their breakfasts are the best. Well, if you think of anything you want, just call and we'll bring it."

"Okay. See you later and don't hurry. Relax. I'm fine."

Leah, Suzan, and Melanie lingered over their coffee and all decided toast was all they wanted. The phone rang, and Leah jumped to get it. It was Roger's cousin inquiring and offering any help needed.

"Just prayers," Leah answered and then gave a full report on his condition, promising to let them know if any change or anything the family needed.

The phone rang several more times before they were dressed and ready to go. There were three long-distance calls from friends who had heard about the accident and wanted to offer their sympathy and help. Leah learned the news had been carried on CNN the day after for most of the day. Thank goodness Roger hadn't seen it...or had he?

They picked up Roger's mother and got to the hospital at almost noon. Jenna and Todd came to say good-bye as they were heading home. Leah's brother and his wife were there, and a longtime family friend came in from across the state. They all went to lunch at a Mexican restaurant close by and enjoyed an hour or so of laughter and conversation, all reliving past experiences in Alaska.

The afternoon and evening produced a steady stream of visitors and passed very quickly. It was agreed that Melanie would stay that night, and Leah again went home to her own bed. She, Dave and Suzan had a nice visit and talked until almost midnight. Dave wanted particulars on insurance, savings, and such to be sure his parents would be okay financially. Leah wasn't sure of anything but would deal with those things later, promising to let him know if they needed any help. She had no idea what the bills would be and didn't care to think about it just now. There was no way of knowing all the needs Roger would have, but she would arrange it somehow. Her mind was too encumbered with his survival just now.

On Friday, Roger had to have another unit of blood. The nurses kept telling Leah it was just to build him up, and it was not due to any new loss. The stitches came out of his face, and she was really encouraged by how good it looked; hard to believe with the way it had looked just five days ago! Most of the out-of-town family had left, and the in-town family was exhausted, so Leah told them all to take a day at home and rest. Grief and fatigue had been very evident on her mother the day before, so she told her aunt to keep her away from the hospital if she could. Leah didn't want another patient.

That afternoon, a physical therapist arrived and started a program of exercise with Leah's help, showing Leah how it was supposed to be done so she could see that he got two to three sessions per day. The braces were so heavy, it was difficult to lift them, but she managed and then showed Dave and the girls also so someone would be available every day.

Roger wasn't very receptive to the movements due to the pain but was tolerant.

Dave went and brought Roger's mother to the hospital, but Roger was in too much pain to seem to care who was there. She would always pat his hands and arms, trying to comfort him, but causing more discomfort. Leah reminded her several times that he was too sore to touch, but she couldn't seem to remember. She insisted on staying until they went home for the night, so Leah had the children get her out for dinner.

Their preacher had spent part of each day with Leah and was a great source of strength to them all. He was a willing ear to let her vent her frustrations over all of the many concerns she had. He tried to comfort and help with any he could, but he mostly tried to keep her rational. Friends came to be with her, and she was constantly getting messages. One came from the local police telling her not to worry about her home as they would keep watch on it. What wonderful people! The whole town was rallying around them and praying for Roger. She still didn't know who had mowed their lawn.

Blake's son and daughter came up to visit and see Roger that night. They went back to his room for just a few minutes and all saw a tear in Roger's eye as they left. Was it because of Blake? Did they remind him of his buddy and friend? Did he know? Leah was very concerned about his frame of mind.

It was Suzan's turn to spend the night, and she wasn't about to miss doing her part, but it was evident she was scared. She had such a soft heart and could hardly bear her father's pain, but she assured them she would be fine with nurses right outside the door. They stayed until half past nine, assuring her she could call anytime.

Sunday dawned bright and beautiful, and the roses around the front drive were covered in blooms. Melanie told her mother that they would let Dave stay with Roger that night, and she and Suzan would help her trim the dead ones the next morning. Blake had told Leah many times that he didn't care for flowers as so many people left the dead ones on, and they looked awful. Leah felt she must keep them trimmed for him; he had always commented that she was different from most flower gardeners. They made pancakes, bacon, and coffee and had a relaxing breakfast before heading to the hospital. Dave called to tell them Roger had suffered a very restless night, so they decided to get right to the hospital.

"I was awake most of the time, though the doctors and nurses tried to be quiet. One doctor picked up your jar of honey and vinegar, looked closely at it, and then asked the nurse what it was. She answered she didn't know but that you drink it every day."

That gave Leah a chuckle, thinking what it looks like and what the doctor must have thought. She told the girls to hurry as she hung up the phone. She wondered if all the company had caused Roger to have the restless night and knew Dave would need to get some rest. The girls were ready, so they left, all feeling anxious.

They arrived to find machines being removed from Roger's room and two nurses standing over him. Dave looked very tired, so Leah convinced him to go to Roger's mother's apartment and get a nap and bring her back that afternoon. That settled, she turned to one of the nurses and asked what all the machines were about. Roger had pneumonia! It was now in both lungs. Leah was stunned and wondered how long he had been dealing with it.

The nurse told her the doctor had increased the antibiotics and that they were keeping a close watch. She knew they were doing all they could, and she and the girls went to the chapel to pray.

The afternoon arrived with lots of company they kept out of Roger's room, explaining about the pneumonia. However, when the missionary family arrived with their two boys, one of whom had witnessed the crash, Leah hugged each of them, expressing her gratitude, and escorted them all to Roger's room two at a time. He did not recognize them but did remember something because he seemed to understand what Leah was talking about when she explained who they were. They visited a short time, promising to keep in touch as they felt a part of their family now. How blessed they were to have been helped by such wonderful people!

Dave arrived around four o'clock with Roger's mother looking much more rested, and they attempted to explain his condition while trying not to upset her. She was still not happy with Leah for waiting until the next morning to tell her about the accident! Leah insisted on spending that night with Roger and made everyone leave at nine o'clock that evening. She spent a restless night awake every hour to check on her spouse. She thought she slept a little but wasn't actually sure. Anyway, she felt okay when the shift changed, and she was ushered out. She left and washed up and then had her usual coffee before returning to the room.

Dave called, and she told him Roger was resting and seemed to be better so to relax and come to the hospital later in the day. That afternoon, the breathing tube was removed to everyone's surprise and delight. All the children were there when the nurse came to get them. He was now wearing an oxygen mask and that had to mean the pneumonia was better. He managed to get out one or two audible words at a time with the mask but was too weak for much conversation. Dave and Suzan were leaving the next afternoon, so Melanie spent that night. All were becoming somewhat proficient at the daily exercise routine, and Roger didn't seem to flinch as much.

That night, Leah asked Dave to help her write a letter to the editor, thanking the missionary and his family for ministering to Roger. Dave typed it on the computer as they formulated it together. They visited for a short time and then fell into bed.

The next morning, the local newspaper called and asked for a story to print about the accident. Leah relayed all she knew and then asked if they would like a copy of the letter they had written. The reporter was happy to get it and offered to take care of faxing a copy to the newspaper and television station for their community segment. It was agreed, and they dropped a copy of the letter off on their way to the hospital.

Melanie called to say that all was going well and to bring her clean clothes as she wanted to spend the night with Leah's mother and aunt after taking Dave and Suzan to the airport. They were scheduled to leave at half past four, and Leah's mother was only a mile or so from the airport. The day went so fast that it seemed they just had time to say good-bye and were gone. Melanie called from her grandmother's that evening, and Leah told her to keep them at home and visit with them. She would read, watch TV, and be fine. She catnapped some, visited in the waiting room some, and read some through the night and into the next morning. The afternoon brought lots of visitors, relatives, and phone calls. Roger slept a lot when no one was taking blood or X-rays and seemed less restless.

The next afternoon, the tubes were taken out of his lungs, which Leah saw as a great stride forward. Melanie insisted on taking turns staying through the night as she was leaving in less than a week and wanted Leah to get all the rest she could. Leah drove home, mindful of the big moon and bright stars, hoping Roger would soon be accompanying her. She showered and fell into bed, planning to watch television awhile but was asleep soon after.

Friday dawned bright, beautiful, and warm. Leah made coffee and dressed to the sound of a mower in the front yard. She opened the front door to find her neighbor and ran out to thank him.

"This is the first time I've cut it, and I'm not trying to pick up the grass as it's still short. I don't know who cut it before but don't worry about it. We'll keep it mowed for you. You just keep taking care of that husband of yours."

Leah picked up the newspaper and locked up the house as she started for the hospital. Passing the cemetery, she pulled in without really giving it any thought. She parked and walked to the back graves and found Blake's. A feather was laying just beyond the marker, and she stared at it thinking it looked like a hawk's. She gazed all around at the sky, remembering the hawk he had rescued from the middle of the highway and taken to a bird sanctuary, making a large donation and asking them to care for the bird. As soon as it recovered, it had been brought to his shop for him to release, and the local paper had taken pictures. Those pictures had been in the paper with his obituary.

Tears filled Leah's eyes and spilled down her cheeks. Looking down at his grave, she began to talk to him.

"What happened? You were always so careful and watchful. You had flown that river many, many times and knew where all the power lines were. Why was this trip different? Did the setting sun blind you? Why were you flying so low? I need you. Roger needs you. You helped him so much; he needs you to help him through this."

She was sobbing now, all the tears she had been holding back came gushing out, and she fell to her knees and buried her face in her hands. The grave was still covered with flowers, most of them dead now, making her even sadder. Finally, she stood up and took a tissue from her pocket. She brushed the grass from her slacks and slowly returned to the car. Maybe the hawk had been paying his respects to the man who saved it but couldn't save himself.

She arrived at the hospital, having been lost in thought most of the way. She stepped out of the elevator and saw Melanie sitting in the waiting room and reading the paper.

"Your letter is in today's paper entitled 'Inexpressible Gratitude.' It's very nice, Mother." Melanie told her handing the paper to Leah.

Leah sat down and read the unchanged letter she and Dave had composed. Afterward, Melanie informed her that the nurse thought Roger would be moved to acute care that afternoon. Leah wasn't sure what that was, but it had to be better than the ICU, meaning he was getting better. Maybe it meant he was 'out of the woods'.

"Hello, darling, you look more like yourself every day."

Leah put a big smile on her face and slipped her hand into Roger's. He attempted to say something, and she made out the words no choice.

"Of course you have a choice. You always have a choice. I'm not sure what you mean."

"No ... choice ... but ...... survive!"

Leah suddenly realized all the time since the accident he had been telling himself he had to survive this. Through the fear and the awful pain and the surgery and the myriad of tests, he had been making choices to fight. Leah silently thanked God for his strength and strong will and asked that he never give up.

"That's right, sweetheart. You made the right choices, and you're going to be all right."

As they were about to leave, two Christian university students came in, gave Roger a big grin, and told him how happy they were he was doing so well. They had just learned he was being moved today and wanted to keep in touch. They had been wonderful to keep Leah company and give her encouragement through prayer and their wonderful smiles during the entire time. They had found Leah two days after the accident and had come every day to sit with her, pray with her, and offer any assistance she needed. Now they both followed Leah and Melanie back to the waiting room.

As they sat down in a private area, Larry asked Leah if Roger had been told about Blake.

"I've been afraid to approach the subject," Leah replied.

"Well, the decision is yours, but I wonder if it wouldn't be a good idea to tell him before he is moved from ICU. That way if he doesn't take it well, all the emergency equipment will be there. It has been ten days. I've been told it is best to inform the patient as soon as they are out of danger."

"You're probably right. It's just so hard to talk about."

"Tina and I will go with you, if you would like."

"I think Larry is right, Mother, and now is as good a time as any."

Leah agreed reluctantly, not sure she could do it without breaking down, and they all walked soberly down the hall to ICU and Roger's room.

"Dad, we'd like to talk to you about Uncle Blake," Melanie began slowly, holding her mother's hand.

Roger kept his eyes fixed on Leah as she slipped her hand into his.

"He didn't make it, darling. Blake is gone." Leah managed to get it out before her voice gave out due to the tears choking her.

Roger laid there for a minute with his one eye closed, and Leah felt panic rising in her body. He opened his eye again, and she could see a tear in the corner start down his cheek.

"I…suspected." Roger looked very sad but took it all in without any adverse reactions. He must have known Blake had to be in very bad shape, and the avoidance of discussing it had surely clued him in. Larry offered a prayer on everyone's behalf, which Roger thanked him for.

Leah was very glad that was over and all was taken well. She felt wiped out, and Roger looked very tired, so they all said their good-byes and walked backed to the waiting room.

"Thank you both so very much for all you've done through this. Please keep in touch."

"We will," Tina said, hugging her. Then Larry also gave her a hug. They both hugged Melanie and told her to have a safe trip home. They would have a long weekend off and not be back until after she had returned to California. They said their good-byes, promising to write and exchanged addresses.

Leah and Melanie sat quietly for a while and then walked back down the hall to the ICU to check on Roger again. Finding him asleep, they decided to go for lunch.

"Let's go to the Olive Garden for a good lunch today and get out of the hospital. If you stay here tonight, you should get away for a bit."

Leah agreed, and they took the elevator to the main lobby, spotting Leah's mother and aunt coming in as they stepped off.

"Roger's sleeping just now so come join us for lunch."

All had a relaxing lunch with Leah bringing them up to date on Roger and his move to acute care. They lingered over dessert and coffee, arriving back in the ICU just as several nurses and technicians arrived to make the move. There were so many machines and apparatus to be moved, but it was accomplished with as little discomfort to Roger as possible.

Chapter 20

Leah was appalled to find that Roger would be in a semi-private room and requested he get a private one she could stay in. She was informed that none were available. When she asked about the vacant one she had seen, she was told someone was waiting for it, so she would have to get on the waiting list. The room was all beige and cream and not very roomy, with supplies for two patients. Melanie left with her aunt and grandmother late in the evening, and Leah managed to get comfortable with a blanket and pillow on the chair. She didn't like the loud TV the other occupant played; he informed her it would be on all night as he couldn't sleep without it. She went to the waiting room but couldn't sleep with the light, so she flipped through magazines and returned to the room around midnight. She actually managed to doze off at some point even with the noise.

The next morning, Melanie called all excited.

"Mother, the television station called about the letter you had faxed to them, and they want to do an interview. They want to come to the hospital to film Dad tomorrow. Do you think he will mind?"

"I don't know, and I don't know if the hospital will allow it. I'll see what I can find out."

She waited until Melanie arrived later in the morning and then inquired about the pending interview. That afternoon, the hospital sent the proper people to the room with forms to sign, and the interview was approved. A hospital representative would be on hand to see that all went as they required, and Melanie called the station and arranged for the next morning. It would air on the five o'clock news after her plane left for California, but she would be there to help with it.

Leah asked the nurses about her going home with Melanie to help her wash and pack, and they said they would keep a very close watch on Roger. A large male nurse came on duty that evening and assured her he would see to it Roger was taken care of and not bothered by his roommate. It seemed the man was waiting to see if he needed pancreatic surgery due to a not-so-good lifestyle. He rolled his IV around the hospital and out into the parking lot to smoke and visit.

They went home a little after nine o'clock and began the sad chore of getting Melanie ready to return home. Leah wrote thank-you notes to her bosses and put the rest of the package in her purse to start on during the long hours at the hospital. This was the only night she would let Roger stay without her as he was being monitored constantly: she needed to help Melanie.

Sunday morning, they packed all the bags into the car and headed for the hospital. Soon after, the news crew arrived and interviewed them in Roger's room, much to their surprise. They had expected it to be in the waiting room and were concerned about how Roger would react. He did fine, even giving the camera a thumbs up when told how glad everyone was that he was doing so well.

The time for Melanie to leave came much too soon, and Leah's aunt came to take her to the airport. Leah insisted they not come back that night. Her mother looked so tired, and she knew the grief over Blake had drained her. Leah watched a little of the news and evening shows, walking around any time Roger slept.

The roommate asked Leah to buy him some hard candy as it was all he could have and he was hungry. She received an okay from the nurses and went to the gift shop for Life Savers, only to find it had closed. She hurried down to the cafeteria to find it was also closed but vending machines were in the hall, so she purchased the only candy they held—Skittles.

They were received with relish and quickly devoured. Soon afterward, he made a phone call, becoming very loud and profane, shouting at the person on the other end. Suddenly, he laid back, and Leah thought he was having some sort of attack. She called for a nurse, and they revived him after a frightening episode. Leah was so afraid that she had given him the wrong candy and caused the attack. Finally, after all was calm again, she mustered the courage to go out and ask the nurses if the attack had been her fault.

"The candy you gave him had nothing to do with it. It was something he took but not your candy. That's his problem. He has put unfit things into his body for too many years and is now paying the price."

Greatly relieved, Leah went back to the room and snuggled down in the chair under her blanket. Once again, she managed to doze off in spite of the loud TV. Suddenly, she awoke, smelling smoke. She roused enough to determine it must be coming from the bathroom. The roommate must be smoking in the bathroom with Roger on oxygen!

She ran to the nurses' station and informed them. They immediately came and got him out of the bathroom and reprimanded him, demanding he never smoke in the room again and informed him of the dangers with oxygen. Leah was thoroughly shaken and determined to get Roger moved. She spent the rest of the night taking short walks, fearing leaving Roger alone with that man.

As soon as it was nine o'clock, she went to the waiting room and called Roger's doctor, informing him of all they had endured, from the loud TV all night to the smoking. The doctor agreed that the behavior was inappropriate and would definitely get Roger moved. Shortly after she returned to the room, a nurse arrived stating that they would soon have another room for them.

That afternoon, they were moved into a private room with a sofa bed. It was heaven! Leah felt great relief and made a mental list of items to bring next time she went home. She had a private bath and could bathe here and stay with Roger constantly except to eat. She would need to go home occasionally to do laundry and get reinforcements, but the accommodations were so much better. She was feeling quite elated and went down to the cafeteria for dinner. She needed some vegetables and indulged in dessert also. She returned to the room to find the ex-roommate loudly talking to Roger and eyeing the bathroom. Was he planning to try to smoke in here?

She slept some that night but woke several times, thinking she heard someone in the room. It was probably just her imagination, but she was relieved when morning came and the doctors all made the rounds, reassuring her things were going well. Roger was still improving, and that was the important thing. By midmorning, the ex-roommate walked in, telling them they were his only friends here.

She just smiled at him and endured his chatter. He left, stating he was going into the public restroom for a smoke, pulling a cigarette from his sleeve. Leah was afraid to leave for anything to eat and got coffee from the nearby station. Later that morning, she called her mother and aunt and told them what had transpired. They said they would be up that afternoon and bring her some food. Knowing her mother, it would probably be enough to last her for days.

She managed to get washed up and dressed with no more interruptions, grateful she had brought a housedress for a robe. That afternoon brought the ex-roommate for another visit while she and her mother and aunt were visiting in the waiting room so Roger could sleep. She returned to the room to find him between Roger's bed and the bathroom and wondered if she had caused him to abort a smoking trip. She was very upset but said nothing except that Roger needed his sleep and to please not wake him. When he left, she went straight to the nurses' station and explained her concerns. She returned to her family in the waiting room and filled them in on what she had found. They were also concerned and felt the hospital should be able to do something about him. They hurried back to the room to find a "No Visitors" sign on the door with instructions to check with the nurses' station before entering.

That night, Leah fell sound asleep for several hours before Roger woke her, saying he was cold.

"Cold! Cold!" he kept repeating while she put several blankets over him. Suddenly, her eye caught a small wet area behind his right shoulder, and she lifted his arm slightly to find he was lying on a wet bed. Then she saw the feeding tube in his nose had come out and was draining on his pillow. He was lying in the liquid nutrition he was being feed through a tube in his nose! She turned on the call light and quickly began to remove the top part of the wet gown. Two nurses arrived and replaced the feeding tube and then got him into a clean gown. The bed was soaked, but he was on a special air mattress with special sheets, so they attempted to clean it up as best they could with towels and got him settled again.

The next morning, the neurosurgeon wanted a CT scan and said it would be done that afternoon. Leah was just getting ready to go for some dinner when a technician came in informing the nurse that the IV would have to be removed.

"We can't remove it! He's still getting antibiotics and other meds."

"He can't have any metal on him for the MRI."

"What about the metal inside his body?" Leah asked.

"What metal?"

"The rod in his left femur and the mesh and pins on the left side of his face and nose."

"How long have they been there?"

"A little over a week."

"He can't have an MRI. The magnetic pull could dislodge all the metal."

"Who ordered an MRI? He's supposed to have a CT scan."

The technician looked dismayed and began backing the gurney out of the room.

"I'd better check this out," he said as he left the room.

Leah turned to the nurse.

"Please check his chart and call his doctor if necessary. We can't let them take him until we straighten this out."

The nurse assured her she would take care of it as Roger reached for Leah's hand. "Don't ... leave ... me."

Both Leah and the nurse turned to him and reassured him no one was going to take him anywhere without Leah at his side. The nurse patted his hand and then gave Leah's shoulder a pat as she left the room.

Leah wondered what was next. All the trauma of the past two weeks had her nerves really frayed. Family came that evening, and Leah unloaded all her problems to them. Her brother told her they would be up on Sunday to take her out to dinner and away from the hospital. They would get her mother as her aunt was going home the next day, and they would try to make it a relaxing day for all. Leah felt she should be able to get away a bit by then.

Saturday brought lots of visitors as well as several acquaintances they had not seen for years and didn't know they were back in the area but had seen the interview on television. Roger seemed to know them but didn't try to speak much. He did smile a little at some of the stories of the jobs they had been on.

Sunday morning was quiet until Ralph, Sue, and their mother came to take Leah to lunch. As the elevator opened, a lady looked at Leah's mother and exclaimed, "I know you! What's your name?"

She was shocked and taken aback so blurted out "Naomi!"

"That's right! We met at the group at the hospital after your husband died!"

They all left, laughing at the episode and had a lovely Asian lunch and lots of light conversation. It was really nice to get away even though it was only for a couple hours. Leah had felt good about leaving as the male nurse on duty was one of the most personable and competent they had had, and he assured her he would take good care of Roger.

The next week went by quickly with physical therapy twice a day. Roger was taken off the feeding tube in his nose and put on liquids by mouth. Leah checked over the tray to find lots of sugar. She complained, and the dietician was sent in.

"I don't understand why his diabetic status wasn't transferred with him."

She was assured that the dietician had not been informed and would work out a diabetic diet for him. Roger was fitted for a back brace so that he could sit up some, but still all the exercises remained in a lying down position. He needed a CT scan before allowing him to dangle his legs from the side of the bed.

The director of rehab came to explain the procedure as well as the rules and regulations, offering to give Leah a tour. Roger should be able to go to a rehabilitation facility within a week or so. She agreed and was impressed but discussed it with Roger before deciding. They agreed all his doctors were here and it would probably be best to stay with them, so it was set up for him to move to rehab the next week. They had now spent ten days in the ICU, and it would be eleven in acute care. Would they ever have a normal life again? Leah was very depressed as the time to move again drew near. What would they encounter this time?

The CT scan was done that afternoon without a problem with Leah at Roger's side all the way to the X-ray room. It showed the vertebrae seemed to be healing and Roger's pain upon sitting up would determine if anything further needed to be done. Leah prayed his back would heal itself with no more surgery.

The move was made with as little discomfort to Roger as possible since they moved him in his bed. The move took place on Tuesday afternoon, which was explained to Leah as his 'bath day', so they both looked forward to it that evening. Leah had been shown a gurney that could be rolled into the large shower so that Roger would not have to stand to get a full shower. He had been given only sponge baths for three weeks, which left a lot to be desired. The nurses had done the best they could, but sand still worked its way out of his hair. Leah hadn't been able to see all of his back.

Chapter 21

The new room was comfortable with cream walls, beige vinyl floors, and beige and blue blankets. The large window looked out over the front parking lot, with trees, grass, and flowers visible. Leah had Roger placed near the window, and he seemed pleased with the view. Acute care had offered only a view of the concrete parking garage with little green showing. The evening came and went with only aides in and out and no shower. Late that night, she inquired about when he would get his shower and was told they had all been done and that there was not enough staff at night to get him one now. Leah was upset but held her temper until the doctor came in next morning. Then she informed him about how Roger had not had a bath in nearly a month, explaining how he had been found, how he had gone through all the surgeries and tests with only sponge baths, and how he had looked forward to a full shower. The doctor apologized and told her he would get one that day.

However, when evening came and she asked the aide about it, she was informed he was in a Tuesday/Thursday/Saturday room and would get one the next evening. The next morning, she reported it to the doctor who again apologized. He changed Roger to a soft diet, stating he needed more calories to gain his strength back. When the tray came he, again, had lots of sugar. Again, Leah complained, and the dietician came and again said the diabetes had been left off the order. That evening, he finally got a thorough sponge bath as no one to help the aide get him on the gurney. Roger was grateful as it was much better than what he had been given before and slept fairly well that night.

Leah had been sleeping in the vacant bed in the semi-private room, though she had been informed she couldn't continue if enough patients came in to rehab. In the wee hours of the morning, she awoke to hear rain and wind, thunder and lightning. As she roused, she marveled at how hard it must be raining as it sounded as if it were in the room. Becoming fully awake, she realized the water was coming in the room through a hole in the ceiling, and Roger's bed was standing with all its electrical cords in a small lake. She jumped out of bed and turned on the call light as she gathered all blankets and towels and threw them down into the water.

Soon, two aides came in and gave stunned reports to the night nurse. Several came into the room with more blankets and began unplugging the bed, informing her they would have to move him down the hall. It turned out to be a blessing as the new room was a private one with a sofa bed, so there was no fear of having another roommate. They settled into the new room that day, and all the therapists were late finding his room; anywhere from ten to twenty minutes late with a thirty minute period allotted to him. Getting him into the wheelchair took the balance of the time, and one after another would leave, saying they had to get to another appointment. The only therapy he got that day was recreational, answering some questions, and playing a game of dominoes. That therapist was very sweet and compassionate but could do nothing about the rest of his therapy.

That evening, Leah inquired right after dinner about his shower; she was going to get him in early. However, she was informed that he was now in a Monday/Wednesday/Friday room and would have to wait as no one had put him on the schedule, and there was no time left. The next morning Leah, complained again and again he got a sponge bath. The only therapy was a wheelchair class on Saturday, so that entire week, he had only received two full therapy sessions, and they had learned to get him into the chair by themselves. Leah had called for help to get him onto a bedpan once, but after waiting fifteen minutes, somehow managed to do it herself. Now she took care of all his hygiene, receiving little help from the staff, but she couldn't even get him a lousy shower! She grew angrier as time went by and realized he would never get well if things continued this way.

Sunday dawned beautiful and bright, and Roger seemed in good spirits. Leah helped him shave, wash up, and put on clean pajamas. After lunch, they had several visitors, and the day passed rapidly. Monday therapy started the same as it had the previous week with the therapists arriving ten or more minutes late, but Leah got him into the wheelchair and ready to go, so he got about fifteen minutes of two or three of the daily therapies. He was supposed to get three hours a day, and Leah decided to take him where he could. He would be in here for months if she didn't do something.

After lunch, she drove over to her mother's and called another rehabilitation facility. One of the local men had been treated there and couldn't say enough good things about it. It had to be better than what they were getting! She gave them all the information and found out what she needed to do and scheduled a tour for 3:00 p.m. that afternoon. She stopped back by the hospital and then kept the appointment. They had less equipment, but Roger hadn't been using much anyway, and the atmosphere was so much better, so she made all the arrangements, leaving the date open. They were less crowded and smaller, so patients received more attention, and the schedules were more flexible.

Returning to the room, she filled Roger in on all the details. Due to the size of the rooms, she wouldn't be able to stay the night but could drive up each morning and stay until bedtime. Roger agreed, and they were deciding when the door opened and a gentleman they hadn't seen before walked in.

"I'm Dr. Daniels," he said and extended his hand to Leah.

"Okay," she replied, shaking his hand with a puzzled look on her face. They had many doctors, but this was an entirely new one. "And what is your specialty?"

"I'm the family counselor, here to offer any assistance you need and keep things going smoothly for you."

"Oh, well. You needn't even start with us as we are leaving. Our stay has been anything but smooth!"

"Tell me about it."

"It's a waste of time as I made arrangements to move him to another facility."

"Why?"

"Because he hasn't been getting the therapy he's supposed to. He can't even get a lousy shower, and we were promised three a week. He has been here a week today and still gets sponge baths. I take care of all his personal hygiene, and I'm not on the payroll nor am I a nurse. We are going where he can get well enough to go home!" Leah really unloaded once she started. Tears filled her eyes, and she glared at the doctor. "I've suffered a great loss and been under a lot of stress, and these conditions make it unbearable. I can't deal with it all, so we're leaving."

Dr. Daniels excused himself as she finished speaking, saying he would be back shortly. He returned soon after with the director, the head of physical therapy, and the head of the nursing staff.

"Please repeat what you told me if you don't mind."

"I don't mind as they need to know," Leah began and went through all the trials they had suffered.

All four in the room apologized and promised to straighten it out and solicited an agreement to give them a few more days. That night, Roger got his first shower in the gurney, and he loved it. The next morning, all therapy was on time, and the first therapist in the morning even dressed him. Everyone seemed to be endeavoring to give him what he had come there for. It lasted one day, and then the slacking off returned. He had little therapy on Thursday, so Leah called the other rehab hospital and informed all they would be picked up and to have everything ready to sign him out the next morning. This time she would listen to no arguments and made it obvious, so it was agreed.

By noon, they were settled in his room in the new facility, and therapy had already been scheduled. He got more in that afternoon than a whole day previously. The room was small but painted in a soft blue and carpeted in a medium blue; the halls were also carpeted, which cut down on noise. That afternoon and evening, he had a very nice diabetic lunch and dinner and then a whirlpool bath to help heal his wounds on the left ankle. They looked so much better. Leah felt very relieved, and Roger was very content. He showed no anxiety and insisted she go home at eight o'clock before it got really dark and sleep in her own bed. This place seemed like heaven after all they had been through.

Leah drove home in high spirits, so happy Roger was now getting good care and therapy. She headed for the post office to collect all the mail that must be overloading the box but stopped abruptly in front of Blake's business. The sign in front read "Good-bye, Old Friend,"; it took her by surprise, and the tears began to fall. Soon, she was seeing him at his desk and sobbing. How many times they had engaged in long conversations at that desk and how many problems he had helped her work through. She missed him so and needed to talk to him. She was sobbing so hard she pulled into the parking lot until she could regain composure. She was still shaking when she emptied the mail box and headed home.

The yard was in great shape as Leah pulled into the drive. She had to find out who was doing it so she could express her gratitude. The roses needed trimming again and the garden needed weeding badly, but it would just have to wait. She looked around the house, noticing it needed dusting but little else so she showered, dressed for bed, and looked through the mail. There was nothing pressing, so she went to bed planning to watch some TV but fell asleep immediately after the news.

That weekend, they had lots of company, and Roger talked at length, trying to make her understand how happy he was they had made the move. Leah was spending each night at home, getting up early, trimming roses, or weeding for an hour or so before showering and going to the hospital. She made a point of getting there before lunch, which always pleased Roger. He hated to eat alone. He didn't care for doing much alone and was anxious for her to watch his therapy sessions! He was improving and soon could walk with a walker. He couldn't get far, but both ankles were working and getting stronger. New growth had nearly filled the wounds on the left ankle and looked really good. He would always have scars, but he had both feet. God is so good! She could tell he had pain, but he was so strong-willed he wouldn't admit it; he just pushed harder. His speech was getting better, but he seemed to have regressed a great deal from after the stroke and had trouble getting the right words out. Leah was often unsure if he could remember things or get his thoughts together.

Blake's birthday was two days away, so she stopped at a shop near the hospital and found bunches of artificial forget-me-nots and some peach blossoms to make an arrangement for his grave. She also found a small eagle. She had purchased his birthday present and card just weeks before his death and promised herself she would never again buy gifts in advance. She spent the day with Roger, showing him her purchases, and then spent the evening at home making the arrangement. She placed the eagle on a long stick, signed the card, and stuck it just below the eagle sealing it and placing it in the middle of the arrangement. It was his card, she had picked it out special for him and he would have it! Tears streamed down her face the whole time she worked on it, and she ached inside. The morning of his birthday, she went early to his grave and stuck the vase firmly in the ground, telling him she missed him so much and always would, but she and Roger were going to be alright.

They had been in the new facility almost a week when a psychologist came into Roger's room and began conversing with him at length. He told him he wanted to give him a test of sorts to determine his comprehension ability. He then took Leah out to the waiting area and explained there was some brain damage due to the blow to the head, and the tests would help determine how much and the need for counseling. He wanted Leah to attend some of the sessions as he felt she needed the counseling also because she was also a victim. She was almost afraid to get the results of the tests but agreed to cooperate fully.

That night, she went home very tired and just fell into bed to watch some TV early. The show was about a couple who wanted children badly but had suffered several miscarriages. The wife was pregnant and farther along than ever before. Suddenly, she began to have pain, and the scene changed to a hospital emergency room. Leah was suddenly back in the emergency room the night of the accident and could hardly breath. She became pale, began shaking all over, and cried hysterically. She felt all the fear, anguish, and shock all over again and broke out in a cold sweat. It seemed like time was repeating, and she sat rocking back and forth on the bed for several minutes. Finally, she began to come out of it and ran to the bathroom, throwing cold water on her face. She was still shaking and crying as she got into bed and turned off the TV. She lay there for some time before she fell asleep, trying to keep her mind on other things but having little luck. Blake kept coming back to her, and she finally cried herself to sleep.

The next day, Leah dressed as the coffee brewed. She actually felt pretty good this morning, so she decided she should visit Blake's grave again and try to accept the fact he was gone. Her mind knew it, but her heart kept talking to him and seeing him every time she saw a hawk or anything peach, his favorite, or the coconut he hated, or so many other things. She drove to the cemetery and spent some time remembering and crying. Then she noticed her card had been opened, so she took it off the arrangement, wondering who would do that. It was a personal card and note to Blake and for him only. As she started to leave, she spied another hawk's feather and surveyed the sky, wondering.

The psychologist came in just after lunch and went over the tests with Roger. Leah went down to the gift shop, thinking she might distract him. Browsing, she found some trinkets she thought would make nice gifts and spied a sale table with several kinds of preserves. She picked up several and started to the cashier when her eye caught sight of some helicopter ornaments. She picked one up thinking it would be nice to add to Blake's collection. A knifelike pain shot through her as she remembered Blake was dead and would not be collecting any more aircraft ornaments for his Christmas tree. Tears filled her eyes and the shortness of breath returned. She returned the ornament to its box and silently paid for her purchases and then went to sit in the waiting area. Her eyes were still brimming with tears when the psychologist came out and sat beside her.

"I would like to visit with you some if you feel like it."

"That's fine. How did Roger do?"

"Well, it will take a few days for me to evaluate everything, but the damage appears to be minimal."

"I've observed that he seems to have regressed to the problems he had not long after the stroke."

"Well, I would like to talk about you. How are you doing?"

"I'm fine."

"How about your brother? He was the pilot?"

"Yes. He...he...I can't talk about him," Leah finished, her voice breaking, and tears again filling her eyes.

"You have to. You aren't dealing with your loss, and you must face it to go on."

"I just can't right now. Every time I think of him, it hurts so much that I just cry, can't breathe, and can't talk."

"I'll be in tomorrow, and we'll try then."

Leah sat there for some time before she went to Roger's room. He told her a little about the tests and said everyone wanted to know how much he remembered.

"Really! What do you remember? Do you know why Blake was flying so low...or so slowly? Do you know what...caused the accident?"

"We... hit power...lines... crashing on me."

"What happened just before?"

"Blake...saw.....orange...towers....bridge...said...weren't going... deal... power lines.... turning around... never..saw..line..hit."

Roger's eyes filled with tears, so Leah changed the subject. She showed Roger her purchases, and soon it was time for therapy.

Leah was so encouraged by the way Roger could now take hold of the bars and pull himself up out of his wheelchair by himself and walk between the bars. The therapist said he would try him next week on the walker, and once he mastered that, he could go home and change to outpatient therapy. That meant he might be going home in another week! Leah was ecstatic! The therapist informed her they would provide her with a commode riser, wheelchair, walker, and shower hose. She made an appointment for the therapist to visit their home and determine what needed to be done to make it accessible to Roger. They would then bring Roger down in a van to see if he could manage. It was all very exciting!

The following week all went as planned; the house passed inspection with just a few minor changes, and Roger was scheduled to go home the next week. That evening, Leah received a call from Melanie that she was coming to help them adjust, which was more good news. Leah spent the next few mornings cleaning and getting everything ready for Roger's return. He had been reluctant to leave the day he had come in the van to see if he could make it around in his home, and Leah had wanted to keep him. His leg braces would make showers difficult as he couldn't stand without them. Leah would just have to remove them after he sat down on the shower seat. It was so good that they had installed handicap showers; they had thought it was for the mothers. The wide halls and doors allowed the wheelchair to pass easily from room to room; again, they had been put in for the mothers. How could they have known?

Melanie arrived the day before Roger was scheduled to go home, and she and Leah shopped for groceries and then went to get him. He was now able to maneuver himself into the front seat of the car. They took him, wheelchair and all, to have lunch before going home. He ate little but enjoyed the outing immensely. He was very tired and went right to bed after they got him home. Leah was so glad to have Melanie there to help. She wasn't really sure she could have managed by herself.

Many things were difficult, but the three of them figured them out together and managed to find a way. The wheelchair fit under the center island in the kitchen for eating, and the wheelchair and walker got Roger to the shower seat, and then the braces were removed until he finished his shower. Leah would dry his lower half and replace the braces before he stepped out. She found she needed at least six towels per shower for him. She quickly learned to shower with him as she was soaked regardless.

A week later, Melanie flew home, and they were alone. The family all came to visit and offer any help they could. Leah and Roger slowly managed to do everything just fine alone. On one Saturday afternoon when her mother and brothers and their wives were visiting, she casually mentioned finding the hawk's feathers on Blake's grave. Ralph put his arm around her shoulders as he said, "Sis, the next time you see a feather, pick it up and bring it home. The mind can play some pretty mean tricks on you, and it can seem very real when it isn't. You've been through an awful lot, and I'm worried about you."

Leah couldn't believe they thought she was imagining the feathers. She sure wasn't going to tell them about silently talking to hawks flying over the house, wondering if they were actually Blake. Maybe she was losing it! Maybe she was imagining things! Every time she looked out her window at the spot in the field they had taken off from that awful night, she still saw the helicopter sitting there as Blake made his check. Then she would see it rising and choke back tears. She felt a little faint and queasy each time.

That night as she was relaxing and watching TV in bed beside Roger, she suddenly saw herself walking toward the downtown street corner, and Blake was there with his back to her. He was in jeans and the blue-and-white checked shirt he wore so often and turned just as she came near, and the look on his face told her he was trying to tell her something important, but she couldn't hear it. Then he was gone. She sat very still, hoping he would come back and then realized it had all been just a vision or something. She was seeing things again! When would it stop? When would the pain go away? Was she really okay? Tears filled her eyes, and she silently cried herself to sleep.

The next morning she awoke early to find Roger still snoring. She hurriedly dressed and put on the coffee and then drove the two miles to the cemetery. She walked through the damp grass to Blake's grave, and there it was—a hawk feather inches away from the back of the marker. She blew a kiss up at the sky and smiled as she thought of Blake looking down at her and chuckling at her coming to collect a feather. She picked it up and walked back to the car, clutching it in her hand. It was real!

She arrived home and placed the feather inside the birthday card she had picked out for Blake just weeks before the accident. She heard Roger stirring and went in to help him get washed up and ready for coffee. She got him into his braces and the wheelchair and into the kitchen and then poured them both a cup of coffee and sat down near him. Roger reached over and picked up the card and feather and looked up at Leah.

"What..these?"

"Proof I'm not going crazy!" she said, laughing. Roger reached for her hand and gave it a squeeze with a reassuring kiss on her cheek.

She took the card and feather from him and placed them in the drawer with all the other things she planned to put into an album about Blake. She was okay, and Roger was okay, and they would be fine! Thank you, Father!

Life got easier with each day, and the routine they set up worked, so they decided they could attend church after a few weeks. Many of the members had come by, bringing food and offering help, so they were anxious to let all know how much they loved and appreciated their concern.

Leah parked at the back entrance and helped Roger out with his walker and then pulled the car over and parked, hurrying to help him in. As they entered from the front of the auditorium, the entire congregation began clapping and singing "God Answers Prayers"! It moved Leah to tears, and many wanted to talk to them after the service. When people mentioned their condolences for Blake, Leah found she couldn't talk, and tears filled her eyes. She just shook her head, and they hurried out as fast as possible.

She found she couldn't deal with people in town expressing their feelings about Blake and the accident, so she shopped while on their visits to doctors forty miles away. She went for the mail at night after Roger was in bed, hoping to see no one. This went on for six months, with Blake visiting periodically, always in the same clothes and on the same corner trying desperately to tell her something. If only she knew what it was! She saw a hawk on a tree from the kitchen window and actually thought it might be Blake. She was really afraid she was losing her mind!

So many trips to doctors were made, each requiring a forty-mile drive each way, it seemed that was all they did. Leah would usually do what shopping she needed while in the city, so they always killed a day. They had to have additional surgery on Roger's eye to adjust muscles and stop the double vision. He had three eye doctors, a plastic surgeon, an orthopedic surgeon, and his internist. He attended a support group for head injuries but didn't like it, so their doctor canceled it.

Her brother and sister-in-law had been pressing her to file a lawsuit but she and Roger had never been the sue-happy types. They had worked hard for everything they had and figured they always would. However, one Wednesday evening in church, she saw Blake standing in front of her, looking very insistent. The next morning, she went to his grave, hoping to get some idea of what to do. She was so deep in thought she saw nothing until she pulled inside the cemetery gate and looked up. The first headstone she saw said, "Goforth!" Thinking this could not be an accident but a sign, she made a decision to see an attorney. It had been twenty months since the accident, and Roger was stronger, so she got a recommendation from her neighbor and scheduled an appointment. Blake never returned after that!

Leah's mother never stopped grieving for Blake and developed cancer, dying three years later. She had made Leah executrix of her estate and, though small, necessitated several trips to court, selling house, and dealing with the siblings. It was exhaustive and the stress of dealing with it all was taking a toll.

Chapter 22

Leah was just learning to cope with it all when, seven months later, she found Roger in the bathroom floor, having suffered another stroke. She immediately called 911, only to learn they didn't have that service in their small town, so she called their pastor, who got the paramedics. She had, at first, panicked but quickly regained control as trauma seemed to be the way of life for her. This stroke left him with little feeling on the right side of his face and no use of his right arm or leg. This necessitated two months in the hospital and more rehab, and he lost much of the speech he had regained.

Again, Leah decorated the hospital room with orange—candles, room spray, flowers, and fabric. Nurses remarked that he seemed to improve and work harder after the orange decor and the dietician arranged for oranges and orange Jell-O often. She spent many hours there during the next two months and became amazed at all the serious health problems and the adjustments the families made. It made her very grateful that she still had Roger no matter what his condition.

The stroke also necessitated a scooter that enabled him to accompany her on trips and enjoy some of the activities she and Jessie took part in. Jessie adored him and spent much time helping Roger relearn his colors and work on his speech. He responded so much better to her than to Leah and never got impatient.

A year later, Roger became sick to his stomach after eating and spent the day in bed. He began vomiting blood late that night but insisted he would be okay until morning. Leah stayed awake all night, anxious to get him to a doctor. She called and was told to take him straight to the hospital. It turned out to be a perforated ulcer, and immediate surgery was necessary. He did fine and was sent to Progressive Care the second week when Leah got a phone call that his mother was having difficulty breathing.

She was ninety-four, so Leah called an ambulance, and Roger's mother was rushed to the hospital—the same one Roger was in, just two floors up in the cardiac ICU as she was anemic and had survived heart surgery two years before. Sometimes Leah forgot which floor she was going to, trying to take care of both of them. Roger was released on Friday, so Leah took him home and got him settled in and then went in on Saturday to check on his mother. She was scheduled for several tests on Monday to determine the cause of the loss of blood but kept saying she didn't want them. She stated several times that she wished she could just go to sleep and not wake up as most of her family and friends were already gone, and Roger could hardly speak, so she was ready to go to the next life. This was the last thing she said to Leah as she left at eight o'clock that night.

Leah slept on the sofa to be able to hear and see Roger, afraid she might bump him. At 1:00 a.m., the phone rang, and she almost fell onto the floor. It was the hospital telling her to get there as quickly as possible. She drove as fast as she could as there was no traffic at that hour. However, she needn't have hurried as Roger's mother was already gone soon after she had been called. The doctor assured her everything possible had been done, but her heart just slowed then stopped. She had indeed gone to sleep never to wake again!

Melanie convinced Leah that she needed to get a dog to keep Roger company when she had to leave him alone. They settled on a poochon, mainly poodle, and she immediately bonded with Roger, jumping up in his lap at the first chance. She would sit in his recliner with him and watch television. When he attempted to pet her with his left hand, she pushed it away with her nose and nosed under the right one, trying to force use of the paralyzed arm. She was named Cookie because Roger had problems with the k sound, so it would make him practice. If he couldn't get it out, he said "Muffin" and she responded to that too.

The next spring, Leah decided to take him on a trip to the Pacific Northwest, which he loved. They spent a week in Idaho, a week in Washington and then went up to Birch Bay. There they had a condo right on the ocean and could dip their feet in warm water as the sand absorbed the sun while the tide was out and warmed the water as it came in. They discovered many berry farms and a cheese factory and made a trip into Canada, touring Vancouver. They were gone almost a month, and he loved it even though Leah had to do all the driving. He didn't like that but was resigned and loved his scooter and seemed to feel a freedom with it. They loved Birch Bay and planned to spend much more time there, even looking into buying a condo. Little did they imagine it was the last time they would be there together!

One morning in August, Leah was heading out to weed before the sun heated, but Cookie didn't seem to want her to go. She ran to Roger's door then back to the garage door several times, trying to delay her.

After nearly an hour in the heat, Leah glanced at her watch to see it was almost half past eight, so she headed in to get Roger's breakfast. He usually woke at nine o'clock, so she was shocked to see Cookie standing in the hall barking at her. As she entered the kitchen, she saw Roger lying in the floor. He had fallen from the bar stool and couldn't get up, and she knew she couldn't lift him by herself. Realizing he was hurt, she called for an ambulance, and they headed to the hospital again. Sure enough, his hip was broken, and he needed surgery to put in a metal plate and pin. The doctor told them it was a fragility fracture due to all the medication he was taking, and he would need more therapy.

This time, he was reluctant to do it again as he was tired of the hospital and working so hard to regain strength and abilities. He balked until Leah told him he was making her as handicapped as he was, so he agreed to try it one more time. However, he didn't try very hard, and the speech therapist asked him if he was bored as he needed to work with her.

"Why?"

"Don't you want to work to get better?"

"Why?"

"You seem to be giving up. Would you like to talk to a counselor about your feelings?"

"Why?"

Leah took him out to lunch and then home for a nap, having made an appointment with his doctor and counselor the next day. Roger refused to go, so she spoke to both on the telephone.

"I'm afraid he's giving up."

"Well, I suppose it's understandable as he has been through a great deal."

"I don't know what to do."

"Not much you can do. He is still very independent and wants to control his own life. Give him some time, and maybe he will decide to try later. If not, we'll deal with it later."

The doctor was very fond of Roger and seemed to understand him, but Leah felt whipped. She just wasn't prepared for him to give up but felt helpless and knew nothing to do about it.

Chapter 23

The weather cooled and then became cold as winter blew in. Roger was definitely in pain due to all the metal in his body, and Christmas was a chore for him as he was spending more time in bed, which concerned Leah. She and Melanie decided to find a warmer climate for him and searched the Internet, finding a condo in San Jose del Cabo, Mexico. Leah rented it for the months of February and March and made arrangements for a flight, packing all his meds and obtaining a note from his doctor in case she was questioned by security. They had to leave the scooter but took the wheelchair and an insulated bag with enough food for Roger for the first couple days. His diabetes required regular meals; she wasn't sure what she would have available.

They arrived in Mexico, not knowing what lay before them. Fortunately, vans were available to shuttle tourists to their hotels, and Leah quickly obtained one that would accommodate them and their luggage. The trip took nearly an hour as their reservations were in San Jose Del Cabo, nearly twenty miles from the airport. The condo was across from Plaza Costa Azul, her landmark, and overlooked the ocean and beach. The driver observed the downward slope of the parking lot and offered to help Leah with Roger. Thank goodness! She knew she couldn't control the wheelchair since Roger was seventy pounds heavier than she was. She could just imagine the wheelchair taking off with him and knew they would be obliged to stay on the premises with an elevator to get them to their rooms.

The condo was very nice, with a terrace and a great ocean view. The only problem was that the shower had no seat for Roger, so Leah had to hold him while he cleaned up that evening. There also was no market on the premises. Leah had packed enough food to keep them for a day or two, and she needed to keep him on his diet. She mentally kicked herself for not thinking about that. The next day, they went down to the pool area and met several tenants and then found the restaurant next to the complex. It had a varied menu, and Leah bought lunch for them to eat at the tables provided around the pool. She overheard two men talking about exchanging travelers' checks and grocery stores and introduced herself explaining she would be grateful if they would direct her. They kindly offered to allow her to join them that afternoon on their excursion downtown and to the grocery store.

She got Roger settled for a nap after lunch and informed the manager he would be there alone napping for a couple hours. She exchanged some checks and then made many food purchases, enough for at least a week, and learned a bus would pick her up just outside the condo, taking her right to the grocery. Wonderful! She expressed her gratitude to Matt, the neighbor, who offered any help they needed. Jeff also offered help; he was spending the month of February there.

They did fine, but Leah needed a better way to give Roger a shower, so she caught the bus next day and went to the grocery store, which had a department store section with summer clothing and beach supplies. She bought a folding camp chair she could easily carry back. The produce department had papayas, mangos, and fruits she had never seen before, so she bought some of those too. That night was much easier with Roger in the chair, though it was still a chore making sure he didn't tip over.

"I'm sorry, honey. There are a few things I didn't prepare for, but I will next time."

Roger just smiled his knowing smile as usual. He never complained, and she could see his gratitude for each and every thing she did. He seemed to feel much better in Mexico in the warmth. Each day after breakfast, they would go down to the beach, and Leah would get him situated in a lounge chair and slathered with sunscreen and then take a walk on the beach while he snoozed. She would frequently order lunch, take Roger up the room and then go back and pick up their order. After lunch, he was ready for a nap and spent most of the afternoon in bed. He went to bed shortly after dinner, so she would read if there was nothing on TV.

Their routine varied little. Sometimes Matt would help Roger into the pool and hot tub. Other visitors would often offer help, so everything was going well. One morning when they went down, two of the German ladies visiting said they had been talking about Leah.

"Oh?"

"We think you are very brave to bring a husband in a wheelchair here alone."

"Not brave. Stupid! I didn't really think it through and have had some real challenges, but all of you have been so helpful. It's been great to get to know all of you."

"Well, we still think you are brave."

A month later, Dave and his youngest joined them for a week. They spent her spring break in Mexico and had a great time. They walked the beach and collected beach glass and golf balls washed over from the other resorts. They accompanied Leah on the bus to the grocery store and department store. They were all loaded with sacks of goods when they returned. Leah took them downtown by taxi to visit some of the shops. Afterward, they ate at Dante's on the beach. All in all, it was a great time; it just ended much too soon. Roger seemed to perk up when Dave was around, so Leah really hated it when time came for them to leave.

Two weeks later was Jessie's spring break, and Leah took a cab to the airport to get her learning the Spanish word for granddaughter before leaving. It was a good thing she had thought of it as Jessie had been left at a different terminal than she had been told. She panicked and was looking everywhere. Finally, they brought Jessie to her, and they took a taxi back to the resort. Jessie loved walking the beach and collecting shells while letting the waves wash over her. An occasional jellyfish would wash up, and a fisherman would quickly kick sand on it. She went home brown and full of stories to share with her classmates. Roger really enjoyed her tales about the ocean and the whales and dolphins she had seen.

Their two months were almost up, and they were ready. Roger began having some dizziness when getting up two days before their flight was scheduled, so Leah called home and arranged for a doctor's appointment the day after they returned.

When they saw him, the doctor gave Roger a thorough exam and then told him his heart valve had calcified and he needed more tests. He would actually need surgery, but the doctor wasn't sure he could find a surgeon willing to operate a third time. Roger stood up and looked at Leah as he said, "No!"

Both Leah and the doctor were shocked. The doctor asked,

"Why?"

Roger just looked from one to the other but said nothing. He was expressionless as the doctor continued to ask and finally Roger answered, saying, "I tired."

The doctor looked somewhat resigned as he said, "It sounds like you are ready for hospice. Is that what you want?"

Leah couldn't believe what she was hearing, and then Roger answered yes.

"No. You can't mean that! That's giving up!"

She dropped to her knees almost hysterical, pleading with him to change his mind, but he just looked at her. She looked at him with tear-filled eyes a moment longer and then got up as the doctor began writing on the chart.

"I think his mind is made up, and you need to try to accept it. Hospice is on the fourth floor, so I will write the orders and call them to let them know that you are coming down."

Leah felt like her world had just ended. She just couldn't wrap her mind around what was happening. She felt hollow, as if her insides were gone. She wanted to scream and didn't want to go down to the fourth floor, but she moved along with Roger like a robot.

They were met by a lady who situated them at a desk and began to tell them what to expect. Leah hoped she had some written info as she wasn't absorbing what was said; it seemed like a bad dream, and she was praying to wake up and find that it had been. She signed papers, picked up the instructions, and they left. The doctor had told Roger that he could not go to bed and just wait to die; he needed to work with Leah if she was to take care of him or he could go to a nursing home. Leah wasn't about to let him do that; she was sure if she tried hard enough, she could convince him to change his mind. They picked up the prescriptions and then started the long drive back home. It was only thirty miles, but it seemed to take so much longer than any time before. They talked very little as Leah was lost in thought, feeling very alone already. How would she manage without Roger? For almost forty-six years, he had been the focus of her life. She couldn't imagine living without him. He was her best friend, emotional support, and lover; he was her everything. Her brother, mother, uncle, and mother-in-law were all gone. Now she was losing Roger. She didn't think she could survive another loss and really didn't care whether she did.

When they arrived home, Roger went into the bedroom and, though it was only three o'clock, put on his pajamas and laid down. Leah supposed the day had exhausted him as it had her, so she set about getting things ready for dinner. She wanted to yell or scream or just sit down, bury her face, and cry. Knowing it would gain nothing, she just tried to keep busy and not think about it, which was impossible! Her mind would not stop replaying the scene in the doctor's office, and the emotions came flooding back, causing silent cries again. She had taken care of their children until they were out on their own and then Roger when he retired, and she had no idea what she would do after he was gone. Blake and both mothers were gone. She was just plain scared!

Dinner was eaten, and then they watched TV with little conversation. Roger went back to bed early, so Leah read the Bible and then started a new novel, not able to keep her mind focused on either one. She finally gave up and took her allergy medicine, which also helped her sleep.

The next few weeks were pretty monotonous with the routine of Leah trimming and weeding before Roger awoke, coming in with just time to read her Bible and pray for the strength to get through that day. He was eating so little that cooking was unnecessary. The local senior center sent his favorites weekly.

Chapter 24

The hospice nurse and counselor she had met during the months before her mother died had kept in touch and came to have lunch with her. While they were eating, they heard Roger fall while returning to bed from the bathroom. God had again taken care of things by having them there, and they immediately got Roger into bed and called for a hospital bed and help for Leah. They heard Roger laughing and talking to someone who wasn't there, and the nurse told Leah it would be advisable to call the children and tell them what was happening. Roger could be having transitional illusions that could signal the end was nearing.

"There's no need to frighten them or get upset yourself as it could still be awhile, but you should let them know, and they can decide what they want to do."

After everything settled down that evening, Leah called the children and conveyed the events of the day. They all wanted to come see him while he could enjoy them, so they all arrived the following week. It was the week of Mother's Day, and Leah was in a drama at church playing a lady with dementia with just one word in her part. Dave went with Leah to the first service, and the girls stayed with Roger until the sitter came, and then they went for second service. When they asked Dave how the drama had been, he told them jokingly, "Girls, it was so embarrassing! Mom forgot her lines and only remembered one word!"

After the service, they went home and had a great dinner, with Roger eating a little as they gathered around his bed. He seemed to be much better while they were there, but they had to leave at the end of the week, and he seemed to lose some of his stamina after they were gone.

Hospice sent a nurse out to check on them, and she would help Leah cope. One day, the nurse informed Leah it was going to take a long time as Leah hadn't given Roger permission to go.

"But I did! I told him I knew he was uncomfortable and ready, so he could go."

"You told him with your lips but not your heart."

"How can I do that? I don't want to give him up, but I don't want him to suffer because of me."

It bothered Leah to think Roger would hang on and suffer just because she wasn't strong enough to make him believe she was ready. This brought her much grief in the following days as she didn't know how to convince him, much less herself. She couldn't get it out of her head that a miracle might happen and he would get better with his speech and energy returning to some degree. She just couldn't believe he was leaving her permanently.

The following week as she and the aide were bathing Roger, he grabbed his right side, and Leah found a circle of tiny blisters. She put cortisone cream on the area after cleaning it well. The next morning, the blisters had congregated into larger blisters, and Roger indicated that it hurt. When the nurse came that afternoon, Leah called attention to the now red and blistery circle.

"It's a shingle! He may get more, but he might not. I'll call for some ointment to treat it. Is he eating anything?"

"He seems to have some problem chewing and swallowing, so I am giving him soft foods and smoothies. He sometimes purses his lips and refuses to take his medicine."

"Leah, you must get his pain meds down him regularly because you have to keep control of it. If you ever lose that control, you will not be able to get it back."

"I've been able to crush the pills and empty the capsules, and then I add them to the smoothies or cream of wheat. That's unless he decides not to eat and won't open his mouth."

They went back to his bedroom, and the nurse examined him and remarked that he had lost more weight.

"I know. He is so thin you can see where the injuries have had pins and other things put in."

"Roger, why won't you eat for Leah? She is trying to help you be more comfortable."

"Die… no good" came out faintly.

"Do you think she is trying to keep you alive with all the meds?"

Roger nodded his head yes.

"She is not. She is trying to keep you out of pain, and you must work with her. If you lose control, you won't get it back, so please cooperate. She is just trying to make you as comfortable as she can, and you need to help her."

Roger smiled and closed his eyes, so they walked back into the kitchen. It was obvious he would do as he pleased. He was in control and did not intend to relinquish it.

"I'm going to leave you some laxative suppositories and some empty ones, so if he won't open his mouth, you can put the meds in them and insert them rectally."

"That should go over well!"

"Remember what I said: if you lose control of his pain, you won't get it back, so do whatever works."

The following week, a friend came to visit Roger, and Leah left them alone. After about fifteen minutes, the friend came into the kitchen with tears streaming down his cheeks.

"He's dying, and he's trying to cheer me up!"

"He seems quite at peace with his decision to not go through any more treatments. He knows they would just postpone the inevitable as he can't get well without a miracle, and that doesn't seem to be happening. I've finally accepted it."

Several men came to see him, but none stayed very long as he tired so quickly and tried too hard to get out a word or two. Many of the neighbors called to see if there was anything they could do, but there was nothing. He seemed to enjoy Leah reading to him, and she usually read the Bible to him in the morning and a chapter from The Purpose-Driven Life in the afternoon. She was never sure if he was asleep as his eyes closed shortly after she would start reading, but she would continue.

Leah nearly collapsed the first time she found a break in his skin. He was so thin, though; she made smoothies with egg whites for the protein. His ankles were the first site, and then she found the skin on his ear split and bleeding. She took a soft knit pillowcase and sewed a circle for his ear, stuffing the rest with soft filler so there would be no pressure on his ear. He had soft moon boots for his wounds on his ankles, but the problems kept coming. Then he decided he would not eat or take any more meds, pursing his lips so tight she couldn't convince him to open it. She became very frustrated and finally told him, "It's okay if you don't want to open your mouth. The nurse left me some rectal capsules, so I can put all your meds in one and just stick it up your butt!"

Roger's eyes popped open and stared at her for a minute, and then he opened his mouth. As she feed him the smoothie, he kept starring at her with his big brown eyes as if to say he believed she would do it. She had no problem getting him to open his mouth after that. That afternoon he even indicated he wanted a kiss which felt like a farewell kiss to Leah so she pulled back. Roger gave her a questioning look which would haunt her for years to come.

Some days, he would seem so much better, but it would only last a day or two, and then he would go down again. The up days were becoming shorter, and the down ones longer. He seemed to be on a roller coaster that was losing ground with each round. Hospice had called to say they had a lady who would come sit with Roger if Leah needed to get out for errands, so Leah scheduled an appointment with a doctor doing a research study on fibromyalgia medicine. The sitter came at 9:00 a.m. and Leah went in for the initial appointment to get the new medicine. She was home by noon, and Roger was having difficulty breathing. It was very labored and frightened her. The nurse came that afternoon, checked him over, and informed Leah that the end would probably be within a week.

"I don't think I can take his struggling like this to breathe for a week."

"I know it's difficult, but there is nothing more to do except keep him comfortable."

She left around 4:00 p.m., and Melanie called to see how things were and to tell Leah she had to make a trip to another town before she came home, putting them home by half past six.

"That's okay. He's really struggling to breathe, but there is nothing to do."

Leah thought Roger relaxed when she read to him, and it might help his breathing, so she took out her Bible and asked if he would like her to read to him. He nodded, so she began with the twenty-third psalm and continued until she couldn't see the print as tears were streaming down her cheeks, listening to him struggle to breathe. She closed the Bible and took his hand.

"Darling, I want to pray. You have fought so hard to come back from every surgery and stroke, and it's time for you to get some rest and your reward."

She thanked God for all his help and intervention and asked Him to send his angels to carry Roger to Paradise and to make it a safe and painless trip with no fear. As she finished, Roger gasped twice more and stopped breathing.

Leah sat there in the silent room for some time after she kissed Roger good-bye and let it sink into her consciousness that her spouse was gone. She felt more alone than she could ever remember. Everyone she loved was leaving her. Finally, she called Melanie and told her Roger was gone, and then she called hospice and told them. She just sat beside him holding his lifeless hand and waited silently thanking God for carrying them through.

Printed in the United States
By Bookmasters